• TROFEOS •

Intervención

Guía del maestro

Grado 2

Harcourt

Orlando Boston Dallas Chicago San Diego

Visite *The Learning Site*
www.harcourtschool.com

Printed in the United States of America

ISBN 0-15-326482-9

1 2 3 4 5 6 7 8 9 10 048 10 09 08 07 06 05 04 03 02 01

Contenido

What are Intervention Strategies?

Intervention strategies are designed to facilitate learning for those students who may experience some difficulty no matter how well we have planned our curriculum. These strategies offer support and guidance to the student who is struggling. The strategies themselves are no mystery. They are based on the same time-honored techniques that effective teachers have used for years—teaching students on their instructional reading level; modeling previewing and predicting; directed and giving direct instruction in strategic-reading, vocabulary, phonics, fluency, and writing.

Intervention works best in conjunction with a strong core program. For an intervention program to be effective, instruction should focus on specific needs of students, as determined by systematic monitoring of progress.

Components of the Intervention Program

The goal of the *Trofeos* Intervention Program is to provide the scaffolding, extra support, and extra reading practice that below-level readers need to succeed in the mainstream reading program. The program includes the following components:

- ***Skill Cards*** to preteach and reteach the Focus Skill for each lesson
- ***Intervention Practice Book*** with the following practice pages for each lesson:

  Fluency Page with word lists and phrase-cued sentences that parallel the reading level of the *Intervention Reader* selection

  Phonics Practice Page that reinforces prerequisite phonics/decoding skills and can be used as a teacher-directed or independent activity

  Comprehension Practice Page that gives students an opportunity to respond to the *Intervention Reader* selection and show that they have understood it

  Focus Skill Review Page that provides an additional opportunity to practice and apply the focus skill for that lesson
- ***Intervention Reader*** to provide reading material at students' instructional reading level
- ***Vocabulary Game Boards*** and related materials to provide additional practice and application of vocabulary skills
- ***Intervention Assessment Book*** opportunities to monitor progress and ensure success

Using the *Intervention Teacher's Guides* with *Trofeos*

The *Intervention Teacher's Guide* gives support for below-level readers in key instructional strands of *Trofeos*, plus prerequisite phonics skills and oral-reading fluency. Each *Intervention Teacher's Guide* lesson includes the following resources:

- The **Phonics/Decoding Lesson** reviews prerequisite phonics and word analysis skills. Each skill is systematically applied in the corresponding *Intervention Reader* selection.
- **Preteach/Reteach Vocabulary** activities to teach key vocabulary that appears in both the *Intervention Reader* selection and the corresponding *Trofeos Pupil Edition* selection.
- **Fluency Builders** reinforce important vocabulary while providing reading practice to promote oral reading fluency. You may also wish to use the *Oral Reading Fluency Assessment* periodically to measure student progress.
- **Preteach/Reteach Focus Skill** activities reinforce the objective of *Trofeos* Focus Skills, ensuring that below-level readers get the in-depth instruction they need to reach grade skill-level standards.
- **Preview and Summarize** provide support for comprehension of each main selection in *Trofeos Pupil Editions*.
- **Directed Reading Lesson** for the *Intervention Reader* selection that reinforces basic comprehension skills, using questions and teacher modeling.
- **Writing Support** for writing lessons in *Trofeos* provides interactive writing experiences for the key aspects of the corresponding writing forms and skills.
- **Weekly Review** provides additional support as students review phonics, vocabulary, and focus skills and prepare for testing.

The *Intervention Teacher's Guide* lessons clearly identify the most appropriate times during the *Trofeos* lesson plan to provide supplemental instruction. Look for the BEFORE or AFTER tag that appears next to each of the key instructional strands, along with page numbers from the core pogram. For example:

BEFORE
Skills/Strategies
pages 305I–305J

This tag alerts you that *before* you teach the Skill and Strategy lessons that appear in *Trofeos* on pages 305I–305J, intervention strategies may be useful. Appropriate preteach activities are provided. Reteaching activities are indicated by the AFTER tag.

Depending on your individual classroom and school schedules, you can tailor the "before" and "after" instruction to suit your needs. The following pages show two options for pacing the instruction in this guide.

Suggested Lesson Planners

Option 1:

DAY 1

BEFORE — Building Background and Vocabulary

Review Phonics
- Identify the sound
- Associate letters to sound
- Word blending
- Apply the skill

Introduce Vocabulary
- Preteach lesson vocabulary

AFTER — Building Background and Vocabulary

Apply Vocabulary Strategies
- Use decoding strategies
- Reteach lesson vocabulary

Fluency Builder
- Use *Intervention Practice Book*

DAY 2

BEFORE — Reading the *Trofeos* Selection

Focus Skill
- Preteach the skill
- Use Skill Card Side A

Prepare to Read the *Trofeos* selection
- Preview the selection
- Set purpose

AFTER — Reading the *Trofeos* Selection

Reread and Summarize

Fluency Builder
- Use *Intervention Practice Book*

Option 2:

DAY 1

AFTER — Weekly Assessments

Self-Selected Reading
- Choosing books
- Conduct student-teacher conferences

Fluency Performance
- Use passage from *Intervention Reader* selection

BEFORE — Building Background and Vocabulary

Review Phonics
- Identify the sound
- Associate letters to sound
- Word blending
- Apply the skill

Introduce Vocabulary
- Preteach lesson vocabulary

DAY 2

AFTER — Building Background and Vocabulary

Apply Vocabulary Strategies
- Use decoding strategies
- Reteach lesson vocabulary

Fluency Builder
- Use *Intervention Practice Book*

BEFORE — Reading the *Trofeos* Selection

Focus Skill
- Preteach the skill
- Use Skill Card Side A

Prepare to Read the *Trofeos* selection
- Preview the selection
- Set purpose

DAY 3	DAY 4	DAY 5
BEFORE **Making Connections** **Directed Reading of *Intervention Reader* selection** ■ Read the selection ■ Summarize the selection ■ Answer *Think About It* Questions	**BEFORE** **Writing Lesson** **Writing Support** ■ Build on prior knowledge ■ Construct the text ■ Revisit the text ■ On Your Own	**BEFORE** **Weekly Assessments** **Review Vocabulary** ■ Vocabulary activity **Review Focus Skill** ■ Use *Intervention Practice Book* **Review Test Prep** ■ Use the core *Pupil Edition*
AFTER **Skill Review** **Focus Skill** ■ Reteach the skill ■ Use Skill Card Side B **Fluency Builder** ■ Use *Intervention Practice Book*	**AFTER** **Spelling Lesson** **Connect Spelling and Phonics** ■ Reteach phonics ■ Build and read longer words **Fluency Builder** ■ Use passage from *Intervention Reader* selection	**AFTER** **Weekly Assessments** **Self-Selected Reading** ■ Choosing books ■ Conduct student-teacher conferences **Fluency Performance** ■ Use passage from *Intervention Reader* selection

DAY 3	DAY 4	DAY 5
AFTER **Reading the *Trofeos* Selection** **Reread and Summarize** **Fluency Builder** ■ Use *Intervention Practice Book*	**AFTER** **Skill Review** **Focus Skill** ■ Reteach the skill ■ Use Skill Card Side B **Fluency Builder** ■ Use *Intervention Practice Book*	**AFTER** **Spelling Lesson** **Connect Spelling and Phonics** ■ Reteach phonics ■ Build and read longer words **Fluency Builder** ■ Use passage from *Intervention Reader* selection
BEFORE **Making Connections** **Directed Reading of *Intervention Reader* selection** ■ Read the selection ■ Summarize the selection ■ Answer *Think About It* Questions	**BEFORE** **Writing Lesson** **Writing Support** ■ Build on prior knowledge ■ Construct the text ■ Revisit the text ■ On Your Own	**BEFORE** **Weekly Assessments** **Review Vocabulary** ■ Vocabulary activity **Review Focus Skill** ■ Use *Intervention Practice Book* **Review Test Prep** ■ Use the core *Pupil Edition*

Fluency

*"**So that students will understand why rereading is done, we have involved them in a discussion of how athletes develop skill at their sports. This discussion brings out the fact that athletes spend considerable time practicing basic skills until they develop speed and smoothness at their activity. Repeated readings uses this same type of practice.**"*

S. Jay Samuels
The Reading Teacher, February 1997
(originally published January 1979)

In the years since S. Jay Samuels pioneered the technique of repeated reading to improve fluency, continuing research has confirmed and expanded upon his observations. Ideally, oral reading mirrors the pacing, smoothness, and rhythms of normal speech. Fluency in reading can be defined as a combination of these key elements.

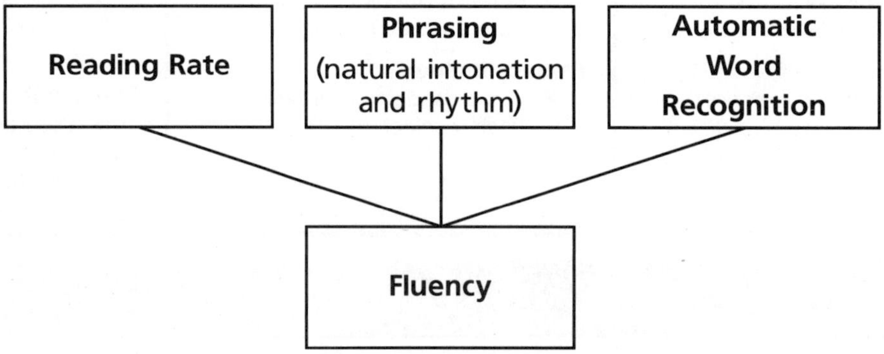

How Do Students Become More Fluent Readers?

Research and the experiences of classroom teachers make it clear that certain practices can and do lead to significant improvements in reading fluency. Techniques that have been shown to be successful include

- **Teacher modeling**
- **Repeated reading of short passages**
- **Daily monitoring of progress**

A program that incorporates these three elements will help struggling readers gain fluency and improve their comprehension.

Using Fluency Builders in the *Intervention Teacher's Guide*

The plan for each lesson in the *Intervention Teacher's Guide* includes daily fluency practice that incorporates the elements of teacher modeling, repeated reading, and self-monitoring.

The fluency portion of the lesson is designed to be completed in five or ten minutes, although you may adjust the time according to students' needs and as your schedule allows.

About the *Intervention Practice Book* Fluency Page

The *Intervention Practice Book* Fluency page is designed to correlate with the phonics elements taught in the *Intervention Teacher's Guide*, as well as with key vocabulary from the *Trofeos* and *Intervention Reader* selections. A total of twenty words that fall into these three categories are listed at the top of the Fluency Page for each lesson.

On the bottom half of the page, you will find a set of numbered sentences that incorporate the words from the lists. Slashes are used to divide each sentence into phrases. To help students improve natural phrasing, model reading each phrase smoothly, as a unit, and encourage students to follow the same procedure in their repeated-reading practice.

This chart gives an overview of the fluency portion of the Intervention Program.

Day	Materials	Explanation
1	*Intervention Practice Book* Fluency Page	Teacher models reading aloud word lists. Students then practice reading aloud the word lists with partners.
2	*Intervention Practice Book* Fluency Page	Teacher models reading aloud the phrased fluency sentences. Students then practice repeated rereadings of the sentences with partners.
3	*Intervention Practice Book* Fluency Page	Students read the fluency sentences on tape, assess their own progress, and then reread the sentences on tape to improve pacing and tone.
4	*Intervention Reader* selection	Students read aloud a selected short passage from the *Intervention Reader* selection three times, monitoring their progress after each reading.
5	*Intervention Reader* selection	Students read the same passage aloud to the teacher. Both teacher and student assess the student's progress.

Rhyming Activities

Rhyme-a-Day

Start each day by teaching students a short rhyme. Periodically throughout the day, repeat the rhyme with them. Say the rhyme together, have them say it alone, pause and leave out words for them to insert, or ask volunteers to say each line. Students will develop a repertoire of favorite rhymes that can serve as a storehouse for creating their own rhymes.

Rhyme Sort

Place on a tabletop pictures of items that rhyme. Have students sort the pictures into groups, according to names that rhyme. You may also want to try an "open sort" by having students create categories of their own to sort the picture cards

Rhyme Pairs

To assess students' ability to recognize pairs of words that rhyme, say a list of twenty or more pairs of words. Half of the word pairs should rhyme. Students tell which word pairs rhyme and which do not. Have students indicate *yes* with a card marked *Y* or another symbol.

If working with **one child** (or small group), have students use one of the Game Boards. From each correct response, the player can move a marker ahead one space. Provide word pairs until the player has completed the game.

What Word Rhymes?

Use theme-related words from across the curriculum to focus on words that rhyme. For example, if you are studying animals, ask: *What rhymes with oso? lobo? zorro? venado? sapo? gallo? chivo? pez? ballena?* If a special holiday is approaching, ask: *What rhymes with bandera, año,* or *corazón?* Use these word groups for sound-matching, sound-blending, or sound-segmenting activities.

Sound-Matching Activities

Odd Word Out

Form a group of four students. Say a different word for each group member to repeat. The student with the word that does not begin (or end) like the other words must step out of the group. For example, say *rana, regla, puerta, rico*. The student whose word is *puerta* steps from the group. The odd-word-out player then chooses three students to form a new group and the procedure continues.

Souvenir Sound-Off

Have students imagine that a friend has traveled to a special place and has brought them a gift. Recite the following verse, and ask a volunteer to complete it. The names of the traveler, the place, and the gift must begin with the same letter and sound.

- Mi amiga [persona]
  Mi amiga María
- quien fue a [lugar]
  quien fue a México
- me trajo [cosa]
  me trajo mazapán.

After repeating this activity a few times, ask **partners** to recite the missing words. As an alternative, you can focus on words with initial blends and digraphs. Students can focus on social studies and phonics skills by using a world map or globe to find names of places.

Match My Word

Have students match beginning or ending sounds in words. Seat students in pairs, sitting back-to-back. One student in each pair will say a word. His or her partner will repeat the word and say another word that begins with the same sound. Repeat the activity, reversing the roles of partners and focusing on ending sounds.

Sound Isolation Activities

What's Your Name N-N-N-Name?

Invite students to say their names by repeating the initial phoneme in the name, such as *Mi-Mi-Mi-Miguel.* Have students say the names of others, such as friends or family members.

Singling Out the Syllables

Form groups of three students. Students can decide who will name the beginning, the middle, and the ending syllables in three-syllable picture names. Given a set of pictures, the group identifies a picture name, and then each group member isolates and says the syllable he or she is responsible for. Group members can check one another.

Chain Reaction

Have students form a circle. The student who begins will say a word such as *sapo*. The next child must isolate the ending syllable in the word, *po*, and say a word that begins with that syllable, such as *pomo*. If the word is correct, the two students link arms, and the procedure continues with the next child isolating the final syllable in *pomo* and giving a word that begins with *mo.* You will want all students to be able to link arms and complete the chain, so provide help when needed.

Syllable Addition, Deletion, or Substitution Activities

Add-a-Syllable

Explain that the beginning sound is missing in each of the words you will say. Students must add the missing sound and say the new word. Some examples follow.

Add:

pa to *lo* (palo)	*va* to *le* (vale)
pi to *el* (piel)	*ma* to *yo* (mayo)
si to *no* (sino)	*co* to *se* (cose)
sal to *ir* (salir)	*gra* to *ve* (grave)
sa to *la* (sala)	*po* to *ni* (poni)
to to *me* (tome)	*bu* to *que* (buque)

Remove-a-Syllable

Reinforce rhyme while focusing on the deletion of initial syllables in words to form new words. Ask students to say:

- *mono* without *mo* (no)
- *bate* without *ba* (te)
- *clase* without *cla* (se)
- *pala* without *pa* (la)
- *come* without *co* (me)
- *maya* without *ma* (ya)
- *sale* without *sa* (le)

Continue with other words in the same manner.

Mixed-Up Tongue Twisters

Think of a simple tongue twister such as *tres tristes tigres*. Say the tongue twister for students, but replace the initial letter in each word with another letter, such a *p*, to create nonsense words: *pres pristes pigres*. Explain to students that you need their help to make sense of the tongue twister by having them replace /p/ with /t/ and say the new tongue twister. Use the same procedure for other tongue twisters.

- nueve nidos nuevos
- seis sillas suaves
- preciosos perros peludos
- raras ranas rubias

Then ask partners to do this activity together.

The Name Game

Occasionally when a new sound is introduced, students might enjoy substituting the first sound of their names for the name of a classmate. Students will have to stop and think when they call one another by name, including the teacher. For example, Paul would call Ms. Vega, Ms. Pega; Carmen becomes Parmen; Jason becomes Pason; and Kiyo becomes Piyo. Just make certain beforehand that all names will be agreeable.

Count the Syllables

Tell students that you are going to say a word. Have them listen and count the number of syllables they hear in that word. For example, say the word *tomate*. Have children repeat the word and tell how many syllables they hear. Students should reply *tres*.

lupa (2)	tesoro (3)
galleta (3)	baloncesto (4)
sábado (3)	motocicleta (5)
biblioteca (5)	cumpleaños (4)
museo (3)	ferrocarril (4)
inolvidable (5)	periódico (5)

Vocabulary Games

Vocabulary Game Boards

To give students additional vocabulary practice, use the Vocabulary Game Boards and copying masters provided in the Intervention Kit. Two different games can be played on each game board. Directions for each game are printed on the back of the board on which the game is played. There are a total of five game boards, which students can use to play ten different games. For best results, use the games to review vocabulary at the end of each theme, so that there are more words to play with.

Copying Masters

The copying masters that accompany the game boards provide some other materials that students will need to play the games. These include:

- spinners
- game pieces
- game cards

Illustrated directions on the copying masters show students how to create the game materials. They may need scissors, crayons or colored markers, and glue. Pencils and paper clips are used to construct spinners. When game markers are called for, provide students with buttons, counters, or some other small item.

Additional Materials

When the directions for a game call for **word cards**, use the vocabulary word cards from *Trofeos*. In addition, some games require the use of a vocabulary list, definition cards that students can create, a dictionary, and commonly available items such as a paper bag.

Use the following charts to plan for and organize the vocabulary games.

Game Board 1: La rayuela

Games	Skills Practiced	Players	Additional Materials
Wordscotch	definitions	2	Wordscotch Copying Master *Trofeos* word cards dictionary game markers
Syllable Hop-Along	number of syllables	2	Syllable Hop-Along Copying Master *Trofeos* word cards dictionary game markers

Game Board 2: Tres en raya

Games	Skills Practiced	Players	Additional Materials
Tic-Tac-Know	creating sentences	2	word cards with meaning on back (to be made by students) game markers
Riddle Me	definitions and number of syllables	4	word cards with meaning on back (to be made by students) paper bag vocabulary list game markers

Game Board 3: ¿Te acuerdas?

Games	Skills Practiced	Players	Additional Materials
Match a Pair	definitions	2	word cards with meaning on back (to be made by students) *Trofeos* word cards
Syllable Match	number of syllables	2	*Trofeos* word cards dictionary

Game Board 4: Safari

Games	Skills Practiced	Players	Additional Materials
Safari Spin	number of syllables	2	Safari Spin Copying Master *Trofeos* word cards dictionary
Safari Wordwatch	definitions	2–4	Safari Wordwatch Copying Masters vocabulary list dictionary

Game Board 5: Castillo de palabras

Games	Skills Practiced	Players	Additional Materials
Castle Construction	definitions	2	Castle Construction Copying Master *Trofeos* word cards dictionary
Knight's Syllablle Spin	number of syllables	2	Knight's Syllable Spin Copying Masters *Trofeos* word cards dictionary

Vocabulary Activities

The six activities on the following pages provide additional opportunities for vocabulary practice and application. Two activities are offered for individual students, two for pairs of students, and two for small groups of three or four students. All require a minimum of preparation and call for materials that are readily available in the classroom.

Word Book

INDIVIDUAL ACTIVITY

MATERIALS
- paper
- markers
- stapler
- simple binding materials

As students progress through a theme, encourage them to identify new vocabulary that they find interesting or that they think will be useful to them. Have students create a page for each of the special words they choose. Encourage them to check the spelling of the word and to include the definition and other information they might find helpful, such as how the word is divided into syllables, how it is pronounced, whether it has a prefix or a suffix, synonyms and antonyms, and how the word may be related to other words they know. Students can also draw pictures and include captions and labels.

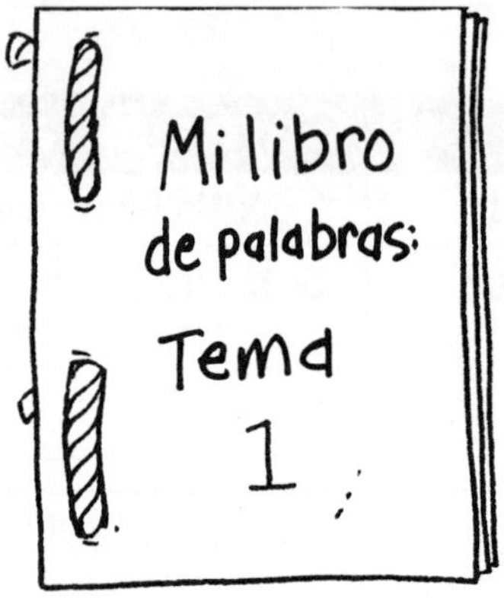

Upon completion of the theme, have students make a cover for the book. Staple the pages together or help students use simple materials to bind them. Encourage them to share their word books with classmates and to use them as a resource for their writing.

Draw a Smile

PARTNER ACTIVITY

MATERIALS
- list of vocabulary words from a complete theme
- two sheets of paper and markers or chalk and chalkboard
- dictionary

Pairs of students can play this game on paper or on the board. Players should be designated Player 1 and Player 2. Player 1 begins by choosing a vocabulary word from the list for Player 2 to define. If Player 2 defines the word correctly, he or she gets to draw one part of a smiling face. If Player 2 cannot define the word correctly, he or she cannot draw on that turn. Players take turns choosing words for each other to define and adding parts to their drawings each time they define a word correctly. Encourage students to use a dictionary to check definitions as necessary.

A completed drawing has five parts, to be drawn in this order: (1) head, (2) one eye, (3) the other eye, (4) nose, (5) smile. The first player to draw a complete smiling face wins the game.

Make a Word Garden

SMALL GROUP ACTIVITY

MATERIALS
- bulletin board
- colored construction paper
- markers
- scissors
- masking tape
- pencil
- paper

Students can create a word garden by drawing and cutting out large flowers from construction paper. Encourage them to use their imaginations to create flowers in a variety of shapes and colors. Have students use markers to write a vocabulary word on each flower and then arrange the flowers to make a garden on the bulletin board.

Then have students create a key on a separate sheet of paper by making a small drawing of each of the large flowers and writing the definition of the word that appears on the matching large flower. Students should display the key on the bulletin board with their garden.

What's the Score?

INDIVIDUAL ACTIVITY

MATERIALS
- list of vocabulary words from a theme or several lessons within a theme
- pencil and paper
- dictionary

Make a list of six to eight vocabulary words that may have given students some difficulty. Have students copy the words from the list and write a definition for each word from memory. Then have them use a dictionary to check their definitions. Tell them to keep score by writing down the number of words they defined correctly.

Then have students copy the words from the list in reverse order, beginning at the bottom. Have them again write a definition for each word from memory, check the definitions in a dictionary, and count the words they defined correctly. Tell students to compare this score to their first score to see how much they improved.

Finger Puppets

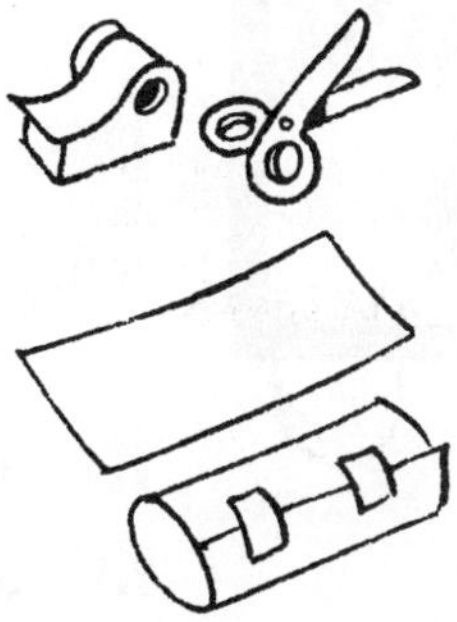

SMALL GROUP ACTIVITY

MATERIALS
- finger puppet pattern
- construction paper
- markers
- scissors
- tape
- list of vocabulary words from a theme

Give students a simple pattern that they can trace to make finger puppets. Have students use construction paper and markers to create puppets that represent favorite characters from a particular theme.

Have students work together to make up simple dramatizations using the finger puppets. Challenge students to use as many words as possible from the vocabulary list. They can keep track of the words they use by checking them off the list.

Guess My Word

PARTNER ACTIVITY

MATERIALS
- list of vocabulary words from a theme
- scrap paper
- pencils

Display the list of vocabulary words where both players can see it. Students take turns choosing a word from the list for each other to guess. The student who is guessing may ask questions about the meaning of the word, how it is spelled, the number of syllables, or any other information they think may help them, as long as the questions can be answered with *yes* or *no*. Encourage students to jot down information that they find out about the word that can help narrow down the list. You may want to give examples of questions that players might ask and explain how they can use the information they obtain.

QUESTION: Does the word begin with a consonant?

INFORMATION: If the answer is *yes*, you can look at the words that begin with consonants and ask more questions to figure out which of those is the correct word. If the answer is *no*, you can rule out the words that begin with consonants and focus on those that begin with vowels.

LESSON 1

BEFORE

Building Background and Vocabulary

INTERVENTION PRACTICE BOOK

page 4

Use with "El camaleón confundido"

Review Phonics: Diptongos *ie, io*

Identify the sound. Read aloud the following sentence: *Veo siete gatos graciosos con diez dedos en cada pie.* Ask children to repeat the sentence three times, identifying the words that have the /ie/ and /io/ sounds. (siete, graciosos, diez, pie)

Associate letters to sound. Write the sentence *"Veo siete gatos graciosos con diez dedos en cada pie"* on the board, and have a volunteer underline the words that contain the letters *ie* or *io*. Tell children that in these words, the letters *ie* or *io* stand for the dipthongs *ie* and *io.*

Word blending. Model how to blend and read the word *siete.* Slide your hand under the word as you elongate the sounds /seeehtay/. Then say the word naturally—*siete.* Follow a similar procedure for the words *graciosos, diez,* and *pie.*

Apply the skill. *Substitution* Write the following words on the board, and have children read each aloud. Make the changes necessary to form the words in parentheses. Have volunteers read aloud each new word.

vio (dio)	**curioso** (gracioso)	**piel** (miel)
pie (piel)	**cielo** (hielo)	

Introduce Vocabulary

PRETEACH lesson vocabulary. Tell children that they are going to learn seven new words that they will see again when they read a story called *El camaleón confundido.* Teach every vocabulary word using the following process.

Write the word.

Say the word.

Track the word and have students repeat it.

Give the meaning or context.

Use the following suggestions or similar ideas to give the meaning or context.

descolorido	Show a shirt or piece of paper that has been discolored by sun, water or use.
emocionante	Related words: *emoción, emocionar.*
bellos	Relate to *hermosos* or *lindos.*
atrapar	Related words: *cazar, coger.*
mezcolanza	Relate to the small word part *mezcla* and demonstrate mixing.

brillante	Relate to glitter or another bright object in the classroom.
pegajosa	Demonstrate attaching something to the board as you say the word and children repeat.

For vocabulary activities, see Vocabulary Games on pages 2–3.

Vocabulary Words

atrapar cazar, coger

bellos bonitos, agradables

brillante con mucho color, luminoso

descolorido con poco color

emocionante lleno de emoción

mezcolanza algo muy mezclado

pegajosa que se pega

AFTER

Building Background and Vocabulary

Apply Vocabulary Strategies

Use synonyms/antonyms. Write the word *atrapar* on chart paper and ask children for some synonyms of the word (*cazar, coger*). Tell children that they can figure out the meaning of the word if they know synonyms or antonyms.

MODEL **Cuando veo la palabra *atrapar,* me ayuda a recordar su definición pensar en sus sinónimos como *cazar* y *coger.* Los sinónimos me ayudan a hacer una imagen mental y recordar mejor la definición de la palabra.**

Guide children in using a similar procedure to decode the words *bellos* and *brillante.*

RETEACH **lesson vocabulary.** Have children listen to each of the following questions. Tell them to hold up the word card that answers each question. Reread the questions aloud with the correct answers. Then discuss how children made their choices.

1. ¿Qué palabra podría describir una vuelta en la montaña rusa? (*emocionante*)
2. ¿Qué palabra significa bonitos, agradables? (*bellos*)
3. ¿Qué palabra es otra manera de decir muy *mezclado*? (*mezcolanza*)
4. ¿Qué palabra significa lo opuesto de colorido? (*descolorido*)
5. ¿Qué palabra describe algo que se pega con facilidad? (*pegajosa*)

FLUENCY BUILDER Using *Intervention Practice Book* page 3, read each word in the first column aloud and have children repeat it. Then have children work in pairs to read the words in the first column aloud to each other. Follow the same procedure with each of the remaining columns. After partners have practiced reading aloud the words in each column separately, have them practice the entire list. Save *Intervention Practice Book* page 3 for use on pages 11 and 13.

BEFORE

Reading ***El camaleón confundido pages 16–45***

Focus Skill Main Idea

PRETEACH the skill. Point out to children that the main idea of a story is the most important idea. Explain that often the first sentence states the main idea, but sometimes they have to read the whole piece to figure out which idea is the most important. Discuss why it helps readers to know which idea in a story is the most important one.

USE SKILL CARD 1A

Have children look at **side A of Skill Card 1: Main Idea**. Read the definition of main idea and supporting details. Next read the paragraph and then have children reread it with you.

Now call attention to the chart and have volunteers take turns reading the sentences aloud. Ask:

- **¿Cómo podemos saber cuál es la idea principal?** (*Possible response: Todas las claves muestran la idea principal.*)
- **¿Por qué es importante que haya una idea principal?** (*Possible response: Para que los lectores puedan entender de qué trata el cuento.*)

Prepare to Read: *El camaleón confundido*

Preview. Tell children that they are going to read a selection entitled *El camaleón confundido.* Explain that this is a fantasy selection. Tell children that *El camaleón confundido* tells about a make-believe chameleon. Then preview the selection.

Para ti pages 16–45

- **Pages 16–17:** Veo el título, *El camaleón confundido,* y el nombre del autor en la página 17. Veo un dibujo de un camaleón en las páginas 16–17 y pienso que ese debe ser el camaleón confundido.
- **Pages 18–19:** En estas páginas, veo dibujos del camaleón. Parece diferente en cada dibujo. Creo que esta sección va a contar como cambia el camaleón.
- **Pages 20–21:** Veo un dibujo del camaleón comiendo una mosca. Esta parte debe tratar de su vida cotidiana, su comida, etc.
- **Pages 22–23:** Hay muchos animales diferentes en estas páginas. Son muy diferentes al camaleón. Quizás él mira a los animales y también sus diferencias.

Set Purpose. Model setting a purpose for reading *El camaleón confundido.*

MODEL **Por lo que he visto en estas páginas, pienso que voy a descubrir qué ocurre para que el camaleón cambie y deje de estar confundido. Voy a leer para ver si al final del cuento él sigue siendo un camaleón.**

AFTER

Reading *El camaleón confundido* pages 16–45

Reread and Summarize

Have children reread and summarize *El camaleón confundido* in sections, as described below.

Pages 19–23
Leamos las páginas 19–23 para recordar cómo es el camaleón y cómo fue su vida cotidiana.

Summary: El camaleón es pequeño y verde y puede cambiar de colores. No tiene una vida muy emocionante hasta que conoce a los animales del zoológico.

Pages 24–41
Leamos las páginas 24–41 para recordar cómo se confundió el camaleón.

Summary: El camaleón quería ser como todos los animales del zoológico. Cada vez que deseaba cambiar, cambiaba, hasta que tuvo un pedazo de cada animal. Pero ya no fue más aquel pequeño y verde camaleón.

Pages 42–43
Leamos las páginas 42–43 para recordar por qué el camaleón no pudo cazar a la mosca.

Como tenía un pedazo de cada animal, no parecía a sí mismo, y no pudo cazar a la mosca.

Pages 44–45
Volvamos a leer las páginas 44–45 para recordar quéle pasó al camaleón confundido al final.

Summary: Esperaba volver a ser él de nuevo, y su sueño se realizó. entonces, pudo cazar a la mosca.

FLUENCY BUILDER Use *Intervention Practice Book* page. 3. Call attention to the sentences on the bottom half of the page. The slashes break the sentences into phrases to allow you to work on natural phrasing. Tell children that their goal is to read each phrase or sentence smoothly. Model appropriate pace, expression and phrasing as you read each sentence and have children read it after you. Then have children practice by reading the sentences aloud three times to a partner.

BEFORE

Making Connections
pages 50–51

Directed Reading of *El sueño de Mac se hace realidad*

Sonidos alegres
pp. 6–13

Ask a volunteer to read aloud the title. Help children to see that the character Mac is a turtle. Read pages 6–7 while children listen to find out what Mac is feeling.

Ask: **¿Cómo se siente Mac sobre su vida?** (*Possible response: Está aburrido de sus amigos y no le gusta su apariencia.*) **INTERPRET STORY EVENTS**

Ask: **¿Cuál es la idea principal?** (*Possible response: Mac no está satisfecho con su vida.*) Focus Skill **MAIN IDEA**

Pages 8–9

Have children read pages 8–9 to find out what happens when Mac's wishes come true. Ask: **Mac cada vez que sus deseos se convierten en realidad?** (*Possible response: Parece diferente y puede hacer cosas nuevas.*) **IMPORTANT DETAILS**

Pages 10–11

Focus Strategy **Use Decoding/Phonics.** Discuss the strategies children use to help them figure out how to pronounce unfamiliar words. Have a volunteer read aloud page 11. Ask: **¿Cómo sabías la pronunciación de *bellos*?** (*Possible response: Miré a las letras y leí cada sonido por su letra.*)

DECODING/PHONICS Read aloud page 10 to children. Model using the Decoding/Phonics strategy by writing the word hambrientos on the board. Slide your hand slowly underneath the letters elongating, or stretching, each sound.

MODEL Cuándo leo esta página, veo que algunas palabras son nuevas para mí. Miro las vocales y las consonantes para ayudarme leer las palabras nuevas. También trato de unir los sonidos. Miro a la palabra ***hambrientos*** en la página 7 y pienso en los sonidos de cada letra. Digo la palabra lentamente (ham...bri...en...tos). Luego la digo rápidamente ***haammbbriieenntoos.*** Focus Strategy **USE DECODING/PHONICS**

Page 12

Have children read page 12 to find out what Mac learned in the end of the story. Ask: **¿Qué aprendió Mac después de que se cumplió su último deseo?** (*Possible response: Ser uno mismo y tener sus amigos no es tan malo después de todo.*) **DRAW CONCLUSIONS**

Summarize the selection Ask children to think about why people sometimes wish to be like someone else.

INTERVENTION PRACTICE BOOK page 5

Answers to *Piénsalo* Questions

1. Porque sus sueños se hicieron realidad y tenía una forma de animal. **CAUSE AND EFFECT**
2. Mac descubrió que podría ser un animal hermoso pero no tendría amigos y se sentiría muy solo. **NOTE DETAILS**
3. Las respuestas pueden variar. **TASK**

AFTER

Skill Review *page 5I*

USE SKILL CARD IB

Focus Skill Review Main Idea

RETEACH the skill. Have children look at **side B** of **Skill Card I: Main Idea**. Read the skill reminder with them, and have a volunteer read the paragraph aloud.

Read aloud the set of directions. Explain that children will work with partners to create their own charts. Remind them to remember the difference between a clue and the main idea.

After children have completed their main idea charts, have them display and explain their work. Point out that the selection *El sueño de Mac se hace realidad* has a main idea and clues that tell about the main idea. Ask volunteers to name the main idea and some clues from the selection.

Focus Skill Review the Phonics Skill from *El camaleón confundido*

RETEACH diptongos *ie, io.* Read aloud the following sentence: *Pienso que vió la miel en el mercado.* Have children listen for the *ie* and *io* sounds. Then read this list aloud and have children raise their hands when they hear the *ie* and *io* sounds: *triste, patio, grande, curioso, pierna, estadio, sueño, viernes.*

FLUENCY BUILDER Use *Intervention Practice Book* page 3. Explain that today children will practice the sentences on the bottom half of the page by reading them aloud on tape. Assign new partners. Have children take turns reading the sentences aloud to each other and then reading them on tape.

INTERVENTION PRACTICE BOOK page 3

BEFORE

Drafting a Journal Entry
page 53C

Developing Ideas and Topics: Journal Entry

Build on prior knowledge Tell children that they are going to talk and write about things they might write in a journal. Discuss that they can write about many different things in a journal. Guide children to see that a person writes a journal for him- or herself, but parts of it may be shared with others. Explain that a topic is a main idea. Display and read aloud the following list:

> **Tema del diario: Mi perro Miel**
> **Idea l: Miel es un cachorro.**
> **Idea 2: A Miel le gusta jugar con la pelota.**
> **Idea 3: Miel sabe cómo correr hacia atrás.**

Construct the text Guide them in writing a journal entry based on the topic *Mi perro, Miel* and the list of ideas. For example:

Mi perro se llama Miel. Miel es un cachorro. A Miel le gusta jugar con la pelota. Miel sabe como correr hacia atrás.

Revisit the text Go back and read the journal entry. Ask: **¿Si no tuviera una idea principal, que pasaría con mis ideas?** (*Possible response: No hablarían sobre la misma cosa.*)

- Guide children to combine ideas and use connecting words, such as *y,* to make the ideas flow more smoothly. For example: Mi perro Miel es un cachorro. A Miel le gusta jugar con la pelota y sabe como correr hacia atras.
- Ask: **¿Qué pronombre podemos usar en lugar de Miel en la segunda frase?** (*él*) Make appropriate change.
- Have children read the completed journal entry aloud and then copy it on their papers.

On Your Own

Have children brainstorm a list of journal topics. Ask them to choose one and write a list of ideas for it. Then have children write a three-sentence journal entry about their topic.

AFTER

Spelling Lesson
page 47H

Connect Spelling and Phonics

RETEACH **diptongos *ie, io.*** Tell children to number their papers 1–8. Dictate the following words, and have children write them. After each word is written, write it on the board so children can proofread their work. They should draw a line through a misspelled word and write the correct spelling below it.

1. emocionante*	**2. vio***	**3. hambrientos***	**4. hiciera***
5. quién*	**6. viera***	**7. descubrió***	**8. cielo***

*** Word appears in *El sueño de Mac se hace realidad.***

Dictate the following sentence and have children write it: *Vio que los animales estuvieron emocionantes y hambrientos.*

Build and Read Longer Words

Remind children that they have learned how to decode words with dipthongs *ie, io.* Explain that now they will use what they have learned to help them read some longer words.

Write the word *hambrientos* on the board. Tell children that they can sometimes figure out long words by looking for smaller words. Cover *ientos* and have a volunteer read *hambr.* Then cover hambr and have a volunteer read *ientos.* Point out that *hambr* is almost the smaller word *hambre.* Have children blend the word parts to read the longer word *hambrientos.* Follow a similar procedure with these words: *gracioso, miedoso,* and *curiosidad.* Encourage children to build other long words like these. Suggest that they use a dictionary to look up words they are not sure about.

FLUENCY BUILDER Have children choose a passage from *El sueño de Mac* se hace realidad to read aloud to a partner. You may have children choose passages that they found particularly interesting, or have them choose one of the following options:

- Read pages 6–8. (From *Mac se sentó. . .* through. . . *vio correr an un animal.* Total: 105 words.)
- Read pages 9–11. (From *¡Caramba!. . .* through. . . *Me gustaría volver a ser yo mismo.* Total: 94 words.)

Children should read the selected passage aloud to their partners three times. Have the child rate each reading on a scale from 1 to 4.

SCALE	
1	Not so good
2	Pretty good
3	Good
4	Great!

BEFORE

Weekly Assessments

Review Vocabulary

To revisit vocabulary words prior to the weekly assessment, use these clues. Have volunteers take turns reading aloud the clues and choices. Children identify the correct choice and explain why that choice makes sense in the sentence.

1. Si un gato va a agarrar un ratón, lo va a
   a. atrapar
   b. descolorido

2. Algo que ha perdido su color está
   a. atrapar
   b. descolorido

3. Algo que es excitante es
   a. emocionante
   b. brillante

4. Si tus ojos son hermosos son.
   a. bellos
   b. mezcolanza

5. Cuando mamá pone varios ingredientes para una receta, en una cacerola y los bate, hace una
   a. mezcolanza
   b. brillante

6. Si no te bañas después de jugar todo el día, tu piel estará
   a. bellos
   b. pegajosa

Correct responses: 1a, 2b, 3a, 4a, 5a, 6b.

You may want to display the vocabulary words and definitions on page 00 and have children copy them to use when they study for the vocabulary test.

INTERVENTION PRACTICE BOOK
page 6

Focus Skill Review Main Idea

To review Main Idea before the weekly assessment, distribute Intervention Practice Book page 6. Have volunteers read aloud the first direction line and the paragraph. Guide children to think about the most important thing that they read.

Review Test Prep

Para ti
page 53

Ask children to turn to page 53 of the *Pupil Edition.* Call attention to the Tips for answering the test questions. Tell children that paying attention to these tips can help them answer not only the test questions but also other test questions like these.

INTERVENTION ASSESSMENT BOOK

Have children follow along as you read each test question and the tip that goes with it. Discuss how each sentence in question 1 relates to the other sentences in the paragraph. Then have children reread the paragraph four times, each time omitting a sentence from question 2 in order to help them make their decision.

AFTER

Weekly Assessments

Self-Selected Reading

Have children select their own books to read independently. They might choose books from the classroom library shelf, or you may wish to offer a group of appropriate books from which children can choose.

- *Las ardillas hacen cosas de ardillas* See page 530 of the *Teacher's Edition* for plan.
- *Elmer* por David McKee, Altea, 1990.
- *Irene, la valiente* por William Steig. Farrar, Straus & Giroux, 1991.

After children have chosen their books, give each child a copy of "Mi diario de lectura," which can be found on page R35 in the back of the *Teacher's Edition.* Have children fill in the information at the top of the form. Then have them use the log to keep track of their reading and to record their responses to the literature.

Conduct student-teacher conferences. Arrange time for each child to conference with you individually about his or her self-selected reading. Have children bring their Reading Logs to share with you at the conference. Children might also like to choose a favorite passage to read aloud to you. Ask questions about the book designed to stimulate discussion. For example, you might ask what information the child learned from a nonfiction text, or how the animals in the story compare to a turtle.

FLUENCY PERFORMANCE Have children read aloud to you the passage from *El sueño de Mac se hace realidad* that they selected and practiced with their partners. Keep track of the number of words the child reads correctly. Ask the child to rate his or her own performance on the 1–4 scale. If children are not happy with their oral reading, give them an opportunity to continue practicing and then to reread the passage to you again.

See *Oral Reading Fluency Assessment* for monitoring progress.

LESSON 2

BEFORE

Building Background and Vocabulary

Use with

"¡Levántate y anda!"

Phonics/Vocabulary
Review Phonics: The silent *h*

Identify the sound. Read aloud the following sentence: *Hicimos el postre de huevos, harina e higos y le pusimos helado encima.* Ask children to repeat the sentence three times, identifying the words that have the silent *h* sound.

Associate letters to sound. Write the sentence *Hicimos el postre de huevos, harina e higos y le pusimos helado encima* on the board, and underline the silent *h*'s. Point to the letter *h* telling the children that this letter is not pronounced, it is silent. Explain that the letter *h* takes the sound of the vowel which follows it as in the word *higo.*

Word blending. Model how to blend and read the word *hicimos*. Slide your hand under the word as you elongate the sounds /iisiimos/. Then say the word naturally—*hicimos*. Follow a similar procedure for the words *huevos, harina, higos* and *helado*.

INTERVENTION PRACTICE BOOK page 8

Apply the skill. *Syllabication* Pronounce the word *ha-cha* syllable by syllable clapping once as each is read. Ask children to clap along with you and afterwards ask how many syllables they heard. Repeat this procedure with the rest of the words. Remind children that each syllable includes a vowel sound. Circle the letter *h* and say the word again. Repeat the process with the rest of the words. Ask children to copy the words and circle the syllable with the letter *h*. Afterwards, encourage children to read the words aloud.

hormiga	**hilo**	**hambre**	**hipopótamo**	**hijo**
hija	**halcón**	**hiena**	**hospital**	**héroe**

Introduce Vocabulary

PRETEACH lesson vocabulary. Tell children that they will learn five new words that will help them when they read a story called *¡Levántate y anda!* Teach every vocabulary word using the following process.

Write the word.
Say the word.
Track the word and have children repeat it.
Give the meaning or context.

Use the following suggestions or similar ideas to give the meaning or context.

siempre	Suggest synonyms such as *todos los días, cada día, con mucha frecuencia*
tarea	Demonstrate the word with a volunteer's homework assignment.
minutos	Point out the minutes on an analog clock.

AFTER

Building Background and Vocabulary

acurrucar	Demonstrate by making two dolls or stuffed animals hug and cuddle.
premio	Point out the small word *eat*. Explain that sometimes a treat can be eaten.

For vocabulary activities, see Vocabulary Games on pages 2–7.

Vocabulary Words

siempre todo el tiempo

tarea el trabajo de la escuela que se hace en casa

minutos unidades de tiempo; sesenta minutos representa una hora

acurrucar abrazar y encoger

premio recompensa

Apply Vocabulary Strategies

Use synonyms/antonyms. Write the word *premio* on chart paper and ask children to give synonyms for the word (*regalo, recompensa*). Tell children that they can sometimes figure out the meaning of the word by looking for synonyms that they know.

> MODEL **Cuando pienso en los sinónimos de la palabra *premio* me hace entender la palabra mejor. Sé que es un *regalo* o *recompensa* y eso me ayuda recordar qué es un premio.**

Guide children in using a similar procedure to decode the word *minutos*.

RETEACH **lesson vocabulary.** Have children listen to each of the following groups of words. Tell them to hold up the word card that matches each group. Reread the group aloud with the correct answer. Then discuss how children made their choices.

1. trofeo regalo especial *(premio)*
2. libro papel casa *(tarea)*
3. reloj hora tiempo *(minutos)*
4. cada día todas las veces muchas veces *(siempre)*
5. cómodo tocar juntos *(acurrucar)*

FLUENCY BUILDER Using *Intervention Practice Book* page 7, read each word in the first column aloud and have children repeat it. Then have partners to read the words in the first column aloud to each other. Tell children to follow the same procedure with each of the remaining columns. After partners have practiced reading aloud the words in each column, have them practice the entire list.

BEFORE

Reading *¡Levántate y anda!* *pages 56–76*

Focus Skill Author's Purpose

PRETEACH the skill. Point out to children that the author's purpose is the reason why the author wrote the story. Explain that there are many purposes or reasons why authors write stories. Give examples of author's purposes, such as *to entertain* and *to tell facts*. Discuss why it helps an author to have a purpose before she or he begins to write.

USE SKILL CARD 2A

Have children look at **side A** of ***Tarjeta de destreza 2: Propósito del autor*** **Skill Card 2: Author's Purpose**. Read the definition of author's purpose. Next read the story, and then have children reread it with you. Then have volunteers take turns reading the information in the chart aloud. Ask:

- **¿Cómo sería el cuento si el propósito del autor fuera enseñar sobre las hormigas?** *(Possible responses: El cuento no hubiera sido sobre una niña; sino sobre una hormiguita graciosa.)*
- **¿Cómo te ayudan las pistas para entender el propósito del autor?** *(Possible response: Apoyan la razón del autor para escribir.)*

Prepare to Read: *¡Levántate y anda!*

Para ti pages 56–76

Preview. Tell children that they are going to read an informational story called *¡Levántate y anda!* Explain that this is a story about how much time it takes a girl to get ready for school. Then preview the selection.

- **Pages 56–57:** Veo el título, *¡Levántate y anda!* y el nombre del autor y del ilustrador. También veo un dibujo de una niña durmiendo con su osito de juguete. Pienso que el cuento debe tratar sobre esta niña y qué ocurre cuando se levanta.
- **Pages 58–59:** Veo un dibujo de un perro con una niña. El texto me da a entender que alguien está hablando con la niña. Pienso que el perro habla con ella, diciendo que ella tiene que fijarse en el tiempo para no llegar tarde.
- **Pages 60–6 l:** Las palabras muestran que el perro trata de contar los minutos que pasan mientras que la niña se arregla. Las líneas representan los minutos.

Set purpose. Model setting a purpose for reading *¡Levántate y anda!*

MODEL **Por lo que he visto en estas páginas, creo que voy a descubrir cuánto tiempo pasa mientras que la niña se arregla. Voy a leer para descubrir si llega a tiempo o tarde.**

AFTER

Reading
¡Levántate y anda!
pages 56–76

Reread and Summarize

Have children reread and summarize *¡Levántate y anda!* in sections, as described below.

Pages 58–65
Volvamos a leer las páginas 58–65 para averiguar quién cuenta los minutos y por qué.

Resumen: El perro cuenta los minutos para asegurar que la niña no llega tarde.

Pages 66–69
Volvamos a leer las páginas 66–69 para averiguar qué hizo la niña y por cuánto tiempo.

Resumen: Cepilló sus dientes y su pelo por 6 minutos y se vistió en 7 minutos. Son 13 minutos en total.

Pages 70–73
Volvamos a leer las páginas 70–73 para saber qué más hizo la niña y por cuánto tiempo.

Resumen: Empacó en 4 minutos y abrazó al perrodurantel minuto. Son 5 minutos en total.

Pages 74–76
Volvamos a leer las páginas 74–76 para recordar todo lo que hizo la niña y por cuánto tiempo en total.

Resumen: Le tomó 5 minutos para acurrucarse, 3 minutos para lavarse, 8 minutos para comer, 2 minutos para dar el bocadillo al perro, 6 minutos para cepillarse los dientes y el pelo, 7 minutos para vestirse, 4 minutos para empacar y 1 minuto para abrazar al perro. Son 36 minutos en total.

FLUENCY BUILDER Use *Intervention Practice Book* page 7. Call attention to the sentences on the bottom half of the page. The slashes break the sentences into phrases to allow you to work on natural phrasing. Tell children that their goal is to read each phrase or sentence smoothly. Model appropriate pace, expression, and phrasing as you read each sentence, and have children read it after you. Then have children practice by reading the sentences aloud three times to a partner.

BEFORE

Making Connections
pages 78–79

Directed Reading: *¡Ya llegan los invitados!* pp. 14–20

Sonidos alegres
pp. 14–20

Ask a volunteer to read aloud the title. Help children to see that the family's house is messy. Read pages 14–15 while children listen to find out what the family is doing. Ask: **¿Cuál es el problema?** *(Possible response: Ya llegan los invitados y no están listos.)* **INTERPRET STORY EVENTS**

Ask: **¿Cuál es el propósito del autor?** *(Possible response: Para divertir o enseñar cómo decir la hora.)* Focus Skill **AUTHOR'S PURPOSE**

Pages 16–17

Have children read pages 16–-17 to find out who else isn't ready and what they are doing. Ask: **¿Qué hace la familia?** *(Possible response: Cass se acurruca con Alf y Stan está tendido sobre el felpudo.)* **IMPORTANT DETAILS**

Pages 18–19

Focus Strategy **Read Aloud.** Discuss how reading aloud might help children better understand an author's purpose. Have a volunteer read aloud page 19. Ask: **¿Cómo te ayudó leer en voz alta?** *(Possible response: Me reí cuándo toda la familia estaba lista menos el papá. Entendí que el propósito del autor fue divertirme.)* **READ ALOUD**

Read aloud page 18 to children. Model using the Read Aloud strategy to point out details in the picture that accompany the text.

> MODEL **Algunas veces cuándo leo en silencio, no entiendo todo del cuento. Pero si leo en voz alta es más fácil recordar los detalles. Puedo también aprender más del propósito del autor.**

Page 20

Have children read page 20 to find out what happened to Dad at the end of the story. Ask: **¿Estaba lista toda la familia cuándo llegaron las visitas?** *(Possible response: Todos estaban listos menos el papá.)* **DRAW CONCLUSIONS**

Summarize the selection. Ask children to think about why people want their houses to be neat when company comes to visit. Then, have them complete *Intervention Practice Book*, page 9.

INTERVENTION PRACTICE BOOK
page 9

Answers to *Think About It* Questions

1. Que casi no tienen tiempo y hay muchas cosas por terminar de hacer en la casa. **NOTE DETAILS**
2. Papá es un buen padre porque está pendiente de cada uno de los niños y del tiempo que tienen para terminar de hacer sus cosas. **PERSONAL OPINION**
3. Las respuestas pueden variar. **DRAW CONCLUSIONS**

AFTER

Skill Review
pages 81C–81D

USE SKILL CARD 2B

Focus Skill Author's Purpose

RETEACH the skill. Have children look at **side B** of ***Tarjeta de destreza 2: Propósito del autor*** **Skill Card 2: Author's Purpose**. Read the skill reminder with them, and have a volunteer read the paragraph aloud.

Read aloud the directions. Explain that children will work with partners to create their own charts. Remind them to think about the difference between the author's purpose and the clues to the purpose.

After children have completed their author's purpose charts, have them display and explain their work. Point out that the the author of the selection *"¡Ya llegan los invitados!"* had a purpose in writing it. Ask volunteers to tell what they think the author's purpose is and some clues to that purpose that are found in the selection.

Review Phonics Skill: The silent *h*

RETEACH the silent *h*. Read the following sentence aloud and have children repeat it three times: *La hormiga y el halcón llevaron al hipopótamo al hospital.* Ask volunteers to write the words on the board that have a silent *h*.

FLUENCY BUILDER Use *Intervention Practice Book* page 7. Explain that children will practice the sentences on the bottom half of the page by reading them aloud on tape. Assign new partners. Have children take turns reading the sentences aloud to each other and then reading them on tape.

BEFORE

Drafting Detail Sentences
page 81G

Writer's Craft: Adding Details

Build on prior knowledge. Tell children that they are going to talk and write about adding details so their writing can be clearer and more interesting to readers. Guide children to see that details give readers more information and help answer questions that they may have about what they read. Display and read aloud the following information:

montar en bicicleta
ir al parque
ver a un hombre
ver a unas flores
tener un picnic

Construct the text. "Share the pen" with children. Guide them in writing sentences based on the information. For example:

> Monté en bicicleta en el parque. Vi a un hombre con unas flores. Luego, tuve un picnic.

Revisit the text. Go back and read the sentences. Ask: **¿Qué podemos hacer para crear frases más interesantes?** *(añadir más detalles para dar a los lectores más información)*

- Guide children to add details to make the sentences more interesting. For example: *Monté mi bicicleta nueva en el parque cerca de mi casa. Vi a un hombre cortando unas flores azules.*
- Ask: **¿Qué detalles podemos usar para describir el almuerzo?** *(rico; delicioso)* Make appropriate changes.
- Have children read the completed detail sentences aloud and then copy them onto their papers.

On Your Own

Have children write detail sentences describing what they see in the classroom. Encourage them to include words that tell about size, shape, and color.

AFTER

Spelling
page 81A

Connect Spelling and Phonics

RETEACH the silent *h*. Tell children to number their papers 1–8. Dictate the following words, and have children write them. After children write each word, write it on the board so that they can proofread their work. They should draw a line through a misspelled word and write the correct spelling beside it.

1. haciendo*	**2. ha***	**3. hace***	**4. ahora***
5. hipopótamo*	**6. héroe***	**7. hormiga**	**8. huracán***

**** Word appears in ¡Ya llegan los invitados!***

Dictate the following sentence and have children write it: *Ahora hace calor, ésto hará que se aleje el huracán.*

Build and Read Longer Words

Remind children that they have learned how to decode words with the silent *h*. Explain that now they will use what they have learned to help them read some longer words.

Write the word *hacer* on the board. Tell children that they can sometimes figure out long words by looking for syllables. Cover *ha* and have a volunteer read *cer*. Then cover *cer* and have a volunteer read *ha*. Point out that *ha* has the silent *h*. Have children blend the word parts to read the longer word *haciendo*. Follow a similar procedure with these words: *hallar-hallando, helar-helando,* and *hinchar-hinchando*. Encourage children to build other long words like these. Suggest that they use a dictionary to look up words they are not sure about.

FLUENCY BUILDER Have children choose a passage from *¡Ya llegan los invitados!* to read aloud to a partner. You may have children choose passages that they found particularly interesting, or have them choose one of the following options:

- Read pages 14–15. (Total: 78 words.)
- Read pages 16–17. (Total: 83 words.)

Children should read the selected passage aloud to their partners three times. Have children rate each of their own reading on a scale from 1 to 4.

SCALE	
1	Not so good
2	Pretty good
3	Good
4	Great!

BEFORE
Weekly Assessments

Review Vocabulary

To review the Vocabulary Words prior to the weekly assessment, use these sentences. Have volunteers take turns reading aloud the sentence stems and choices. Children identify the correct choice and explain why that choice makes sense.

1. Si **siempre** haces algo, lo haces
   a. de vez en cuando.
   b. todo los días.

2. Debes hacer tu **tarea**
   a. en casa.
   b. durante una prueba.

3. Si algo dura por seis **minutos**, dura menos de
   a. seis horas.
   b. seis segundos.

4. Cuándo **acurrucas** a una mascota, te sientes
   a. bien.
   b. horrible.

5. Si alguien te da un **premio**, debes
   a. tirarlo.
   b. agradecerle.

Correct responses: 1.b, 2.a, 3.a, 4.a, 5.b.

You may want to display the Vocabulary Words and definitions from page 19, and have children copy them to use when they study for the vocabulary test.

Focus Skill Review Author's Purpose

INTERVENTION PRACTICE BOOK
page 10

Para ti
pages 56–76

To review Author's Purpose before the weekly assessment, distribute *Intervention Practice Book* page 10. Have volunteers read aloud the first direction line and the paragraph. Guide children to think about the reason the author wanted to write the paragraph.

Review Test Prep

INTERVENTION ASSESSMENT BOOK

Ask children to turn to page 81 of the *Pupil Edition*. Call attention to the Tips for answering the test questions. Tell children that paying attention to these tips can help them answer not only the questions on this page but also other test questions like them.

Have children follow along as you read each test question and the tip that goes with it. Discuss how to find clues that help readers understand an author's purpose. Remind children to check their answers when they finish taking the test.

AFTER

Weekly Assessments

Self-Selected Reading

Have children select their own books to read independently. They might choose books from the classroom library, or you may wish to offer appropriate books from which children can choose, such as these:

- *¿Qué hora es?* por Judy Nayer. INDEPENDENT READER.
- *Y Domingo, siete* por Robert Baden. Albert Whitman, 1990.
- *Clifford el perro bombero* por Norman Bridwell. Scholastic, 1994.

After children have chosen their books, give them a copy of *Mi diario de lectura*, which can be found on page 35R in the back of the *Teacher's Edition*. Have children fill in the information at the top of the form. Then have them use the log to keep track of their reading and to record their responses to the literature.

Conduct student-teacher conferences. Arrange time for each child to conference with you individually about his or her self-selected reading. Have children bring their Reading Logs to share with you at the conference. Children might also like to choose a favorite passage to read aloud to you. Ask questions about the book designed to stimulate discussion. For example, ask what information the children learned, why they chose the book, and whether the book was what they expected.

FLUENCY PERFORMANCE Have children read aloud to you the passage from *¡Ya llegan los invitados!* that they practiced. Observe children's pronunciation, intonation, phrasing, and the amount of words, in general, that they read correctly. Have children use the 1–4 scale to rate their performance. Give them a second chance to read if they are not satisfied with their performance. See ***Evaluación de la fluidez oral de la lectura.*** If children are not happy with their oral reading, give them an opportunity to continue practicing and then to reread the passage to you again.

LESSON 3

BEFORE

Building Background and Vocabulary

Use with

"¡Qué sorpresa de cumpleaños!"

Review Phonics: Words Stressed on the Third-to-Last Syllable

Identify the sound. Ask children to repeat the following rhyme aloud three times: *Rómulo y Rémulo son gemelos idénticos; Rómulo es fotógrafo; Rémulo es matemático*. Have children identify the words that are accented on the third to last syllable. (*Rómulo, Rémulo, idénticos, fotógrafo, matemático*)

Associate letters to sound. Write *Rómulo y Rémulo son gemelos idénticos; Rómulo es fotógrafo; Rémulo es matemático.* On the board. Ask a volunteer to underline the words that have accents on the third to last syllable. Tell children that in these words, the accented syllable is stressed. Have children read the underlined words with you.

Word blending. Model how to blend and read the word *párpado*. Slide your hand under the word as you exaggerate the stress /pár–pado/. Then say the word naturally *párpado*. Follow a similar procedure for the words *pájaro* and *música*.

Apply the skill. Write the word *América* on the board. Pronounce this word syllable by syllable clapping once as each is read. Ask children to clap along with you and afterwards ask how many syllables they heard. Repeat this procedure with the following words. Remind children that each syllable includes a vowel sound. Circle the accented syllable and say the word again. Ask children to copy the words and circle the syllable with the accented syllable. Afterwards, encourage children to read the words aloud.

sílaba **sábanas** **máquina** **película** **mágica** **título**

Guide children to see that when a vowel is accented in the third to last syllable that syllable is stressed.

INTERVENTION PRACTICE BOOK

page 12

Introduce Vocabulary

PRETEACH lesson vocabulary. Tell children that they are going to learn five new words that they will see again when they read a story called *¡Qué sorpresa de cumpleaños!* Teach the vocabulary words using the following process.

Write the word.

Say the word.

Track the word and have children repeat it.

Give the meaning or context.

Use the following suggestions or similar ideas to give the meaning or context.

adolescente Discuss the age of adolescence and how many years children have until they reach it.

elegante	Encourage children to name things (clothing, places, etc.) and people that they consider *elegante*.
increíble	Point out the word part *creíble* and relate it to *creer*.
mandados	Encourage children to tell of some *mandados* they have done for someone in school or at home
reunión	Have children consider words in the same family (reunir, unir, etc.)

For vocabulary activities, see Vocabulary Games.

Vocabulary Words

adolescente muy joven; no adulto todavía

elegante gracioso, distinguido

increíble que no se puede creer

mandados recados

reunión conjunto de personas

AFTER

Building Background and Vocabulary

Apply Vocabulary Strategies

Use prefixes and suffixes. Write the word *increíble* on chart paper and underline the letters *in*. Tell children that they can sometimes figure out the meaning of the word by looking for prefixes that they know.

MODEL **Sé que este prefijo puede significar el opuesto de lo que sigue. Sé que *creíble* significa "que se puede creer" por lo que *increíble* debe significar "difícil de creer, no creíble".**

Guide children in using a similar procedure to decode the words reunion, inconveniente e indestructible.

RETEACH **lesson vocabulary.** Have children listen to each of the following descriptions. Tell them to hold up the word card that is the opposite of each description. Reread the descriptions aloud with the correct answer. Then discuss how children made their choices.

1. Una persona con gracia y buenas maneras es (*elegante*)
2. Otra manera de decir *recados* es (*mandados*)
3. El opuesto de *creíble* es (*increíble*)
4. Un conjunto de personas es una (*reunión*)
5. Un niño de diez y seis años es un (*adolescente*)

FLUENCY BUILDER Using *Intervention Practice Book* page 11, read aloud each word in the first column and have children repeat it. Then have children work in pairs to read the words in the first column aloud to each other. Follow the same procedure with each of the remaining columns. After partners have practiced reading aloud the words in each column, have them practice the entire list.

BEFORE

Reading *¡Qué sorpresa de cumpleaños! pages 84–95*

USE SKILL CARD 3A

Focus Skill Narrative Elements (Setting)

PRETEACH the skill. Point out to children that every story has a setting. Explain that the setting of a story is the time and place in which it happens. Give examples of story settings, such as the woods or the city. Discuss how readers can tell what the setting of a story is by looking for words that describe a place.

Have children look at **side A** of ***Tarjeta de destreza 3: Elementos Narrativos (Escenario)*/Skill Card 3: Narrative Elements (Setting)**. Read the definition of setting. Next read the story and then have children reread it with you.

Now call attention to the chart and have volunteers take turns reading the information in the boxes aloud. Ask:

- **¿Cómo cambiaría la escena si el autor escribe de un mar especial que se llama el Parque de peces?** (*Possible response: La escena sería un mar especial.*)
- **¿Cómo te ayudan los pistas?** (*Possible response: Me muestran detalles sobre el lugar y el tiempo.*)

Prepare to Read: *¡Qué sorpresa de cumpleaños!*

Preview. Tell children that they are going to read a selection entitled *¡Qué sorpresa de cumpleaños!* Explain that this is a realistic fiction story about a girl and her sister's birthday party. Then preview the selection.

Para ti
pages 84–95

- **Pages 84–85:** Veo el título, *¡Qué sorpresa de cumpleaños!* y los nombres del autor y ilustrador. Veo unos regalos y una foto de una familia (padre, madre y dos hijas). El texto describe las dos hermanas, Cuqui la mayor y Lori, la menor. El cuento debe tratar de un cumpleaños de una de las hermanas.
- **Pages 86–87:** En estas páginas, veo a Lori y a sus padres. El texto me dice algo del cumpleaños de Cuqui. El texto dice que Lori quiere comprar un regalo especial para Cuqui. Creo que Lori va a tratar de comprar un regalo con su mamá.
- **Pages 88–89:** En estas páginas, leo sobre la visita a la casa de tía Sabina y al mercado de México. El texto describe todas las cosas que considera Lori para el regalo de Cuqui. Parece que Lori no consiguió nada para su hermana.
- **Pages 90–94:** En estas páginas veo que algo cambió. Cuqui dio su celebración a Lori. Lori recibe los regalos que le gustaban a ella el día anterior.

Set Purpose. Model setting a purpose for reading *¡Qué sorpresa de cumpleaños!*

MODEL De lo que he visto en estas páginas, creo que voy a leer sobre el cumpleaños de las dos hermanas. Voy a ver cómo comparten sus cumpleaños y por qué.

AFTER

Reading ***¡Qué sorpresa de cumpleaños! pages 84–95***

Reread and Summarize

Have children reread and summarize *¡Qué sorpresa de cumpleaños!* in sections, as described below.

Pages 85–87

Leamos las páginas 85–87 para recordar de quién es el cumpleaños y qué quiere hacer la hermana menor.

Summary: El cumpleaños es de Cuqui. La hermana menor, Lori, quiere comprar un regalo para ella.

Pages 88–90

Leamos las páginas 88–90 para ver qué considera Lori para su regalo.

Summary: Lori considera un perrito, unas muñecas y una piñata pero nada le parece bien para Cuqui.

Page 91

Leamos la página 91 para ver cómo se viste y cómo se siente Lori en el día del cumpleaños de Cuqui.

Summary: Lori se viste en un vestido nuevo y aunque no tiene regalo para Cuqui, se siente contenta por estar tan elegante.

Pages 92–95

Leamos las páginas 92–93 para recordar cómo cambiaron sus cumpleaños las dos hermanas.

Summary: Cuqui sentía que no necesitaba una fiesta tan grande, así que decidió regalar su fiesta a Lori. Entonces, Lori recibió todos los regalos, la comida y la atención.

FLUENCY BUILDER Be sure children have copies of *Intervention Practice Book* page 11. Call attention to the sentences on the bottom half of the page. Model appropriate pace, expression and phrasing as you read each sentence and have children read it after you. Then have children practice by reading the sentences aloud three times to a partner.

INTERVENTION PRACTICE BOOK

page 11

BEFORE

Making Connections
pages 96–97

Directed Reading: *Un paseo por el bosque,* pp. 22–27

Sonidos alegres
pp. 22–27

Have a volunteer read the title aloud. Then ask children to describe the characters and setting. Ask: **¿Cuál es la escena del cuento?** (*Accept reasonable responses*) Focus Skill **NARRATIVE ELEMENTS (SETTING)**

Ask: **¿Qué le gusta a la chica del paseo por el bosque?** (*Possible response: Le gusta caminar y mirar a las hojas.*) **NOTE DETAILS**

Ask: **¿Qué le gusta al perro?** (*Possible response: Le gusta oler las hojas.*) **NOTE DETAILS**

Pages 24–25

Have children read pages 24–25 to compare Linda and Caramelo's experience in the woods. Ask: **¿Cuáles son las similitudes y las diferencias entre lo que hace Linda y lo que hace Caramelo en el bosque?** (*A los dos les gusta el bosque en el otoño. Linda recoge manzanas y Caramelo busca a las ardilla.*) **COMPARE AND CONTRAST**

Page 25

Ask children to predict whether Linda and Caramelo will follow the chipmunk. Have them read page 25 to find out. Ask: **¿Van a seguir a la ardilla?** (*Possible response: sí*) **MAKE PREDICTIONS** Ask: **¿Cómo lo sabes?** (*Possible response: porque Linda pregunta —¿Puedes encontrar su árbol?*) **DRAW CONCLUSIONS**

Page 26

Have children describe what has happened in the illustration on page 26. Then have them read the page to find out what the chipmunk will do. Ask: **¿Piensas que va a bajar del árbol la ardilla?** (*Possible response: no*) **NOTE DETAILS**

Ask: **¿Por qué no baja?** (*Possible response: Tiene miedo de Caramelo.*) **CAUSE AND EFFECT**

Page 27

Read aloud page 27 to children. Model using the Self-Correct strategy so children can help themselves when they notice that a word they read does not make sense with the other words in the sentence.

> MODEL **Cuándo leo la página 27, leo las palabra *listada* como *lista.* Sé que esto no tiene sentido, así que vuelvo a leer la palabra lentamente para corregir mi error y descubro qué significa la frase.**
> Focus Strategy **SELF-CORRECT**

INTERVENTION PRACTICE BOOK
page 13

Summarize the selection. Ask children to work in small groups and summarize the story by acting it out. They might use crumpled balls of paper for apples. One child can play Linda talking to Caramelo, and another can describe the walk in the woods.

Answers to *Think About It* Questions

1. Porque a los dos les gustaba el otoño. A Linda le encantaba caminar entre las hojas del otoño y los manzanos del sur del bosque. A Carmelo le gustaba oler las hojas del otoño y las ardillas listadas. **SUMMARY**
2. Las respuestas pueden variar: Porque seguramente tenía miedo. **INTERPRETATION**
3. Las respuestas pueden variar. **TASK**

AFTER

Skill Review
page 99C

USE SKILL CARD 3B

Focus Skill Narrative Elements: Setting

RETEACH the skill. Have children look at **side B** of ***Tarjeta de destrezas 3: Elementos Narrativos*/Skill Card 3: Narrative Elements (Setting)**. Read the skill reminder with them, and have a volunteer read the paragraph aloud.

Read aloud the set of directions. Explain that children will work with partners to complete their own charts. Remind them to think about the difference between clues that tell when and clues that tell where.

After children have completed their setting charts, have them display and explain their work. Point out that the selection *Un paseo por el bosque* has a setting, and clues that tell when and where. Ask volunteers to name the setting and some clues that tell about when and where.

Focus Skill Review Phonics Skill from *Qué sorpresa de cumpleaños*

RETEACH the skill. Read the following sentence aloud and have children repeat it three times: *La música de los pájaros suena como mágica.* Ask volunteers to write the words on the board that have an accent on the third to last syllable.

FLUENCY BUILDER Be sure that children have copies of *Intervention Practice Book* page 11. Explain that today children will practice the sentences on the bottom half of the page by reading them aloud on tape. Assign new partners. Have children take turns reading the sentences aloud to each other and then reading them on tape.

INTERVENTION PRACTICE BOOK
page 11

BEFORE

Drafting a Paragraph
page 97A

Writing Process: Paragraph

Build on prior knowledge. Tell children that they are going to talk and write about paragraphs. Lead children to see that paragraphs are made up of sentences that are put in order to tell about the same topic. Display and read aloud the following sentences:

> **Pimienta es amarillo con manchas negras.**
> **A Pimienta le encanta jugar.**
> **Tengo un perro que se llama Mochito.**
> **Pimienta es la mejor mascota del mundo.**
> **Hoy, compré una gatita. Se llama Pimienta.**

Construct the text. "Share the pen" with children. Guide them in organizing the sentences into a paragraph. Help them see that not all the sentences can be used. For example:

- Hoy, compré una gatita. Se llama Pimienta. Pimienta es amarilla con manchas negras. A Pimienta le encanta jugar. Pimienta es la mejor mascota del mundo.

Revisit the text. Go back and read the sentences. Ask: **¿Qué palabra podemos usar para reemplazar a Pimienta?** (*ella*) Make the appropriate changes.

- Guide children to think of another sentence that they could add to the paragraph after the sentence A Pimienta le encanta jugar. For example: Le encanta correr y saltar.
- Ask: **¿Por qué no usamos la frase sobre Shep?** (*no tiene la misma idea principal*)
- Have children read the completed paragraph aloud and then copy it on their papers.

On Your Own

Have children write a paragraph that begins with the sentence *Tengo un perro que se llama Mochito.* Have them write three or more sentences that tell what Shep likes to do.

AFTER

Spelling Lesson
page 95H

Connect Spelling and Phonics

RETEACH **phonics: Palabras esdrújulas** Tell children to number their papers 1–8. Dictate the following words, and have children write them. After children write each word, write it on the board so children can proofread their work. They should draw a line through a misspelled word and write the correct spelling below it.

1. mágica	**2. título**	**3. sentémonos***	**4. imagínate**
5. árboles*	**6. México**	**7. caminábamos**	**8. festejábamos**

*** Word appears in *Un paseo por el bosque*.**

Dictate the following sentence and have children write it: *En África usábamos la lámpara para ver los árboles por la noche.*

Build and Read Longer Words

Remind children that they have learned how to decode words with short vowel /i/. Explain that now they will use what they have learned to help them read some longer words.

Write the word *imagínate* on the board. Tell children that they can sometimes figure out long words by looking for word parts. Cover *te* and have a volunteer read *imagina*. Then cover *imagina* and have a volunteer read *te*. Point out that together the word parts make the accented word *imagínate* Have children blend the word parts to read the longer word *imagínate*. Follow a similar procedure with these words: *festejábamos* and *sentémonos*. Encourage children to build other long words like these. Suggest that they use a dictionary to look up words they are not sure about.

FLUENCY BUILDER Have children choose a passage from *Un paseo en el bosque* to read aloud to a partner. Tell children they may select an interesting passage, or have them choose one of the following options:

- Read pages 22–24. (From *A Linda y a Caramelo*... through ...*Le encantaba buscar ardillas listadas.* Total: 57 words.)
- Read pages 25–26. (From *Mira allí*... through ...*pero ella no bajó.* Total: 67 words.)

Children should read the selected passage aloud to their partners three times. Have children rate each of their own readings on a scale from 1 to 4.

SCALE	
1	Not so good
2	Pretty good
3	Good
4	Great!

BEFORE

Weekly Assessments

Review Vocabulary

To revisit Vocabulary words prior to the weekly assessment, use these sentence frames. Have volunteers take turns reading aloud the sentence stems and choices. Children identify the correct choice and explain why that choice makes sense.

1. **adolescente**
   a. no adulto todavía
   b. bebé
2. **elegante**
   a. largo
   b. distinguido
3. **increíble**
   a. que no se puede creer
   b. dulce
4. **mandados**
   a. recados
   b. sobres
5. **reunión**
   a. ejército
   b. conjunto de personas

Correct responses: 1.a, 2.b, 3.a, 4.a, 5.b.

You may want to display the vocabulary words and definitions on page 29 and have children copy them to use when they study for the vocabulary test.

INTERVENTION PRACTICE BOOK
page 13

Focus Skill Narrative Elements (Setting)

To review Narrative Elements (Setting) before the weekly assessment, distribute *Intervention Practice Book* p. 14. Have volunteers read aloud the first direction line and the paragraph. Guide children to think about the setting of the paragraph.

INTERVENTION ASSESSMENT BOOK

Review Test Prep

Ask children to turn to page 99 of the *Pupil Edition*. Call attention to the Tips for answering the test questions. Tell children that paying attention to these tips can help them answer not only the test questions but also other test questions like these.

Para ti
pages 84–95

Have children follow along as you read each test question and the tip that goes with it. Remind children to think about the reasons for their answers.

AFTER
Weekly Assessments

Self-Selected Reading

Have children select their own books to read independently. They might choose books from the classroom library shelf, or you may wish to offer a group of appropriate books from which children can choose.

- *Fiesta de manzanas.* See page 99S of the *Teacher's Edition* for an Independent Reading Plan.
- *Hermanas* por David McPhail. Espasa-Calpe, 1989.
- *Una torta de cumpleaños para Osito* por Max Velthuijs. Ediciones Norte-Sur, 1996.

After children have chosen their books, give each child a copy of *Mi diario de lectura,* which can be found on page R35 in the back of the Teacher's Edition. Have children fill in the information at the top of the form. Then have them use the log to keep track of their reading and to record their responses to the literature.

Conduct student-teacher conferences. Arrange time for each child to meet with you individually to discuss his or her self-selected reading. Have children bring their *Diarios de lectura* to share with you at the conference. Children might also like to choose a favorite passage to read aloud to you. Ask questions designed to stimulate discussion of the book. For example, you might ask what information the child learned about things that friends do together, or what people do when they go to the woods.

FLUENCY PERFORMANCE Have children read aloud to you the passage from *Un paseo en el bosque* that they selected and practiced with their partners. Keep track of the number of words the child reads correctly. Ask the child to rate his or her own performance on the 1–4 scale. If children are not happy with their oral reading, give them an opportunity to continue practicing and then to reread the passage to you again.

See *Evaluación de la fluidez oral de la lectura* for monitoring progress.

LESSON 4

BEFORE

Building Background and Vocabulary

Use with

"Días con Sapo y Sepo"

Introduce Diphthong *ui:*

Identify the sound. Ask children to repeat the following sentence aloud several times: *Yo fui a mirar al ruiseñor por mi ventana*. Have children identify the words that have the diphthong *ui*. (*fui* and *ruiseñor*)

Associate letters to sound. On the board, write: *Yo fui a mirar al ruiseñor por mi ventana*. Ask a volunteer to underline the letters *ui* in each word. Tell children that in these words, the letters *ui* stand for the diphthong *ui*.

Word blending. Model how to blend and read the word *ruina*. Slide your hand under the letters as you slowly elongate the sounds /ruuuiiina/. Then read the word naturally *ruina*. Follow a similar procedure for *substituir*, *ruido*, and *cuidado*.

INTERVENTION PRACTICE BOOK page 16

Apply the skill. After blending the syllables, have children blend the syllables to read the word. Repeat this procedure with the rest of the words. Point out words at random and ask volunteers to read them.

arruinado **juicio** **huir** **destruir** **juicioso**

Introduce Vocabulary

PRETEACH lesson vocabulary. Tell children that they are going to learn six new words that they will see again when they read a story called *Días con Sapo y Sepo.*

Teach each Vocabulary Word using the following process.

Write the word.
Say the word.
Track the word and have students repeat it.
Give the meaning or context.

Use the following suggestions or similar ideas to give the meaning or context.

solo	Relate by grouping children singularly and in small groups.
animar	Relate by role-playing the act of cheering up a sad person.
bonito	Related words: good, nice, beautiful.
pradera	Relate by showing pictures of meadows, describing a large area of grass and flowers.
razón	Relate to cause and effect. Demonstrate a simple cause and effect in the classroom.

arruinado Relate by showing a whole, clean piece of paper and a dirty, torn piece of paper.

For vocabulary activities, see Vocabulary Games on pages 2–7 (*Intervention Teacher's Guide*).

AFTER

Building Background and Vocabulary

Vocabulary Words

animar dar ánimo

arruinado dañado

bonito bello

pradera terreno donde crece hierba

razón causa

solo sin compañía

Apply Vocabulary Strategies

Use familiar patterns. Write the word *arruinado* on chart paper and underline the letters *rr*. Tell children that they can sometimes figure out the meaning of the word by looking for letter patterns that they know.

MODEL **Reconozco la letra *rr*. La he visto en palabras como *perro* y *ferrocarril*. Cuándo leo esta letra en combinación con el diptongo *ui* puedo pronunciar la palabra *arruinado*.**

Guide children in using a similar procedure to decode the words *pradera* and *razón.*

RETEACH **lesson vocabulary.** Have children listen to each of the following groups of words. Tell them to hold up the word card that matches each group. Reread the group aloud with the correct answer. Then discuss how children made their choices.

1. dañado roto sucio (*arruinado*)
2. uno singular soltero (*solo*)
3. hierba flores afuera (*pradera*)
4. contento feliz gracioso (*animado*)
5. bello lindo hermoso (*bonito*)
6. causa motivo justificación (*razón*)

FLUENCY BUILDER Using *Intervention Practice Book* page 15, read aloud each word in the first column and have children repeat it. Then have children work in pairs to read the words in the first column aloud to each other. Follow the same procedure with each of the remaining columns. After partners have practiced reading aloud the words in each separate column, have them align the entire list.

(Save *Intervention Practice Book* page 15 to use on pages 41 and 43.)

BEFORE

Reading *Días con Sapo y Sepo* pages 102–116

USE SKILL CARD 4A

Focus Skill Compare and Contrast

PRETEACH the skill. Point out to children that they can compare things that happen with what they already know. For example, they can compare new people they meet to people they already know, or contrast new places with familiar ones. Discuss how readers can compare and contrast characters in stories.

Have children look at **side A** of ***Tarjeta de destreza 4: Compara y contrastar*/Skill Card 4: Compare and Contrast**. Read the definition of compare and contrast. Next read the stories and have children read them with you.

Now call attention to the diagram and have volunteers take turns reading the information aloud. Ask:

- **¿Por qué hacemos una comparación entre personajes?** (*Possible response: para entender lo que leemos*)

Prepare to Read: *Días con Sapo y Sepo*

Preview. Tell children that they are going to read a selection titled *Días con Sapo y Sepo.* Explain that this is a story. Tell children that *Días con Sapo y Sepo* tells about a make-believe pair of friends. Then preview the selection.

Para ti
pages
102–117

- **Pages 102–103:** Veo el título *Días con Sapo y Sepo* y el nombre del autor en las páginas 102–103. Veo un dibujo de una rana y una rana. Creo que ellos deben ser los amigos en el cuento.
- **Pages 104–105:** En la página 104, leo la nota que dejó Sapo para Sepo. En la página 105, veo un dibujo de Sepo leyendo la nota. Creo que el cuento tratará sobre la razón por la que Sapo quiere estar solo.
- **Pages 106–107:** En la página 106, leo sobre todos los lugares dónde busca Sepo a Sapo. En la página 107, hay un dibujo de Sapo sentado en una isla. Leo que Sepo piensa que Sapo está triste. Creo que esta selección va a tratar sobre cómo se siente Sapo por estar solo.
- **Pages 108–116:** En estas páginas, veo las cosas que Sapo hace para hacer feliz a Sepo. En la página 16, veo a los amigos juntos.

Set Purpose. Remind children to think about how the characters are alike and different as they read the story.

MODEL **Por lo he visto, creo que voy a leer sobre la razón por la que quiere estar solo Sapo y sobre si Sapo y Sepo tienen un picnic. Voy a leer para ver si a Sapo le gusta estar solo o prefiere estar con Sepo.**

AFTER

Reading *Días con Sapo y Sepo* pages 102–116

Reread and Summarize

Have children reread and summarize *Días con Sapo y Sepo* in sections, as described below.

Pages 102–106

Leamos las páginas 102–106 para recordar qué pasa cuando Sapo escribe una nota para Sepo.

Summary: Sapo escribe una nota para Sepo diciendo que quiere estar solo. Sepo no entiende por qué Sapo quiere estar solo y va a buscarlo.

Pages 107–109

Leamos las páginas 107–109 para averiguar dónde está Sapo y qué hace Sepo cuando encuentra a Sapo.

Summary: Sapo está sentado en una isla. Sepo va a su casa prepara una comida campestrre y vuelve rápidamente a Sapo.

Pages 110–112

Leamos las páginas 110–112 para recordar qué hace Sepo después de que Sapo no le escucha ni quiere verlo.

Summary: Sepo se monta en una tortuga y va a la isla dónde está sentado Sapo. Mientras Sepo le habla a Sapo se resbala y cae en el río.

Pages 113–116

Leamos las páginas 113–116 para recordar qué les pasó a Sapo y Sepo.

Summary: Sapo ayudó a Sepo a llegar a la isla. Los bocadillos estaban mojados y no había té con hielo. Sapo le dijo a Sepo que estaba contento de estar vivo y tener un amigo como Sepo. Disfrutaron de su picnic juntos.

FLUENCY BUILDER Be sure children have copies of *Intervention Practice Book* page 15, which you used for yesterday's Fluency Builder activity. Call attention to the sentences on the bottom half of the page. The slashes break the sentences into phrases to allow you to work on natural phrasing. Tell children that their goal is to read each phrase or sentence smoothly. Model appropriate pace, expression and phrasing as you read each sentence and have children read it after you. Then have children practice by reading the sentences aloud three times to a partner.

BEFORE
Making Connections
pages 120–121

Directed Reading of *Una noche inolvidable pp. 30–36*

Sonidos alegres
pages 30–36

Ask a volunteer to read aloud the title. Help children to see that Tito is an owl who is sitting at home alone. Read pages 30–31 while children listen to find out how Tito is feeling. Ask: **¿Cómo se siente Tito?** (*Possible response: Se siente triste.*) **NOTE DETAILS**

Ask: **¿Qué similitudes y qué diferencias hay entre Tito y Rudi?** (*Possible response: Tito y Rudi son animales y los dos están en casa. Tito está triste y Rudi está tomando su siesta.*) Focus Skill **COMPARE AND CONTRAST**

Pages 32–33

Have children read pages 32–33 to find out what Tito will do next. Ask: **¿Qué hace Tito en seguida? ¿y qué hace después?** (*Possible response: Llama a Sami; Luego, llama a Gil.*) **SEQUENCE OF EVENTS**

Pages 34–35

Read aloud pages 34–35 to children. Model using the Create Mental Images strategy in order for children to picture how Tito is feeling and what he is doing.

> MODEL **En estas páginas, los amigos hablan de Tito. No veo a Tito pero los amigos dicen que Tito está triste y no quiere estar solo. En mi mente creo una imagen de Tito y de cómo se sentirá por estar solo. Recuerdo cómo me siento cuándo estoy solo y triste y me ayuda entender mejor el cuento.** Focus Strategy **CREATE MENTAL IMAGES**

Pages 36–37

Have children look at the picture on page 36 and read page 37 to find out what happened to Hal in the end of the story. Ask: **¿Por qué le gusta estar solo a alguna gente?** (*Possible response: No todos les gusta estar solo.*) **DRAW CONCLUSIONS**

INTERVENTION PRACTICE BOOK
page 17

Summarize the selection. Ask children to think about why people might feel sad being home all alone. Then have them complete *Intervention Practice Book* page 17.

Answers to *Think About It* Questions

1. Porque estar con amigos es bueno para todos. **SUMMARY**
2. Porque estar solo lo ponía triste. **INTERPRETATION**
3. Las respuestas pueden variar. **TASK**

AFTER

Skill Review
page 121I

USE SKILL CARD 4B

Focus Skill Compare and Contrast

RETEACH the skill. Have children look at **side B** of ***Tarjeta de destrezas 4: Comparar y contrastar*/Skill Card 4: Compare and Contrast.** Read the skill reminder with them, and have a volunteer read the story aloud.

Read aloud the set of directions. Explain that children will work with partners to create their own diagrams. Remind them to look for all the ways in which the characters are alike and different.

After children have completed their compare and contrast diagrams, have them display and explain their work. Point out that the selection *Una noche inolvidable* has characters that are alike and different from each other. Ask volunteers to name some of the ways these characters are alike and different.

Review Phonics Skill from *Días con Sapo y Sepo*

RETEACH diphthong *ui*. Read aloud the following sentence: *Luis y yo fuimos con cuidado cuando escuchamos un ruido raro.* Have children listen for the *ui* sound. Then read this list aloud and have children raise their hands when they hear the *ui* sound: *cuidar, manzana, construido, arruinado, mesa, hombre, destruir.*

FLUENCY BUILDER Be sure that children have copies of *Intervention Practice Book* page 15. Explain that today children will practice the sentences on the bottom half of the page by reading them aloud on tape. Assign new partners. Have children take turns reading the sentences aloud to each other and then reading them on tape.

INTERVENTION PRACTICE BOOK
page 15

BEFORE

Drafting a Friendly Letter
page 121A

Writing Process: Friendly Letter

Build on prior knowledge. Tell children that they are going to talk and write about information they might share in a friendly letter. Explain that a friendly letter is a message that may be written from someone to a friend or relative. Guide children to see that friendly letters may tell about all sorts of things.

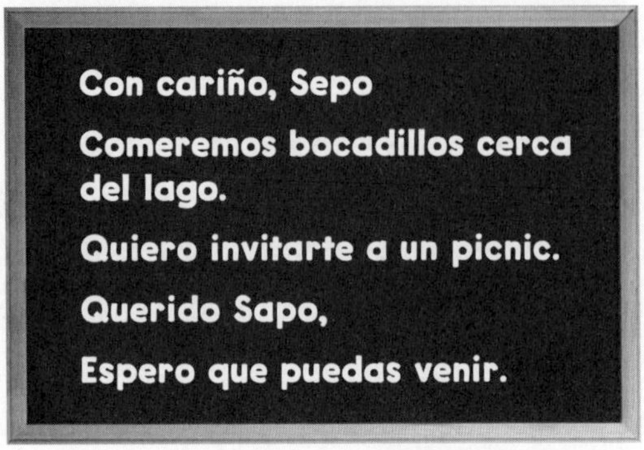

Construct the text. "Share the pen" with children. Help them organize the list above into a friendly letter. For example:

Querido Sapo,

Quiero invitarte a una comida campestre. Comeremos bocadillos cerca del lago. Espero que puedas venir.

Con cariño,

Sepo

Revisit the text. Go back and read the letter together. Ask: **¿Falta información en la nota de Sepo?** (*sí, el día y tiempo del picnic*) Make the appropriate change.

- Guide children to see the different parts of the friendly letter. Ask: **¿Cómo sabemos para quién es la nota?** (*Es para Sapo. Lo sabemos porque dice "Querido Sapo".*)
- Ask: **¿Cómo sabemos de quién es la nota?** (*Es de Sepo. Lo sabemos porque dice "Con cariño, Sepo".*)
- Have children read the completed friendly letter aloud and then copy it on their papers.

On Your Own

Have children write a list of topics for friendly letters they would like to write. Encourage them to write who each letter is for.

AFTER

Spelling Lesson
page 117H

Connect Spelling and Phonics

RETEACH **phonics: diphthong *ui*.** Tell children to number their papers 1–7. Write *juicio* on the board and tell children that all the words you will say will have the same diphthong *ui*. Dictate the following words, and have children write them. After each word is written, write it on the board so children can proofread their work. They should draw a line through a misspelled word and write the correct spelling below it.

1. arruinado* **2. cuidado** **3. descuidado** **4. huir**
5. ruido **6. Luis** **7. destruir**

*** Word appears in *Una noche inolvidable*.**

Dictate the following sentence and have children write it: *Cuidado, Luis vas a destruir mi proyecto.*

Build and Read Longer Words

INTERVENTION ASSESSMENT BOOK ✓

Remind children that they have learned how to decode words with the diphthong *ui*. Explain that now they will use what they have learned to help them read some longer words.

Pronounce the word *descuidado,* syllable by syllable, clapping once as each is read. Ask children to clap along with you and afterwards ask how many syllables they heard. Repeat this procedure with other words. Remind children that each syllable includes a vowel sound. Circle the diphthong and say the word again. Ask children to copy the words and circle the syllable with the diphthong. Afterwards, encourage children to read the words aloud.

FLUENCY BUILDER Have children choose a passage from *Una noche inolvidable* to read aloud to a partner. You may have children choose passages that they found particularly interesting, or have them choose one of the following options:

- Read pages 30–32. (From *Tito estaba sentado...* through *...no esté cavando.* Total: 114 words.)
- Read pages 33–34. (From *Tito estaba sentado...* through *...¡Qué bueno es tener amigos!* Total: 93 words.)

Children should read the selected passage aloud to their partners three times. Have children rate each of their own readings on a scale from 1 to 4.

SCALE	
1	Not so good
2	Pretty good
3	Good
4	Great!

BEFORE
Weekly Assessments

Review Vocabulary

To revisit vocabulary words prior to the weekly assessment, use these questions. Have volunteers take turns reading aloud the questions. Then have children identify the answer and explain why that choice makes sense.

1. Cuando estás **solo**, no estás
   a. acorralado.
   b. acompañado.
2. Algo **bonito** es algo
   a. bello.
   b. feo.
3. En la **pradera** la vaca puede
   a. pastar.
   b. comprar.
4. Si tiene una **razon**, tienes una
   a. molestes.
   b. causa.
5. Algo que te puede **animar**, te puede
   a. entristecer.
   b. estimular.
6. Una cosa **arruidada** está
   a. destruida.
   b. en buen estado.

You may want to display the vocabulary words and definitions on page 39 and have children copy them to use when they study for the vocabulary test.

INTERVENTION PRACTICE BOOK
page 18

Focus Skill Review Compare and Contrast

To review compare and contrast before the weekly assessment, distribute *Intervention Practice Book* page 18. Have volunteers read aloud the first direction line and the sentences. Guide children to think about the ways in which characters are alike and different.

Para ti
pages 102–116

INTERVENTION ASSESSMENT BOOK

Review Test Prep

Ask children to turn to page 123 of the *Pupil Edition*. Call attention to the Tip for answering the test questions. Tell children that paying attention to these tips can help them answer not only the test questions on this page but also other test questions.

Have children follow along as you read each test question and the tip that goes with it. Discuss how it is important to reread each question to make sure you understand what is being asked.

Self-Selected Reading

Have children select their own books to read independently. They might choose books from the classroom library shelf, or you may wish to offer a group of appropriate books from which children can choose.

- *A veces solo, a veces con amigos.* See page 123M of the *Teacher's Edition* for an Independent Reading Plan.
- *Amigos* por Alma Flor Ada. Santillana USA, 1996.
- *Sapo en invierno* por Max Velthuijs. Ekaré-Banco del Libro, 1994.

After children have chosen their books, give each child a copy of *Mi diario,* which can be found on page R35 in the back of the *Teacher's Edition*. Have children fill in the information at the top of the form. Then have them use the log to keep track of their reading and to record their responses to the literature.

Conduct student-teacher conferences. Arrange time for each child to conference with you individually about his or her self-selected reading. Have children bring their *Diarios de lectura* to share with you at the conference. Children might also like to choose a favorite passage to read aloud to you. Ask questions about the book designed to stimulate discussion. For example, you might ask what children like to do when they are alone and how their activities might differ if they are with friends.

FLUENCY PERFORMANCE Have children read aloud to you the passage from *Una noche inolvidable* that they selected and practiced with their partners. Keep track of the number of words the child reads correctly. Ask the child to rate his or her own performance on the 1–4 scale. If children are not happy with their oral reading, give them an opportunity to continue practicing and then to read the passage to you again.

See *Evaluación de la fluidez oral de la lectura* for monitoring progress.

LESSON

5

Use with "Un gran rugido"

BEFORE

Building Background and Vocabulary

Review Phonics: Hard and soft *r*

Identify the sound. Ask children to repeat the following sentence aloud several times: *La mariposa rosa está en la rama*. Have children identify the words that have the hard and soft *r* sound. (*soft-mariposa, rosa hard-rama*) Ask children to raise their hands each time they hear a word with the hard or soft *r* sound. Then say, *burro, salto, tarro, fila, loro, cuándo, cara.*

Associate letter to sound. On the board, write: *La mariposa rosa está en la rama*. Ask a volunteer to underline the words with the hard and soft *r* sound. Tell children that in these words, the letter *r* has either a soft or hard sound.

INTERVENTION PRACTICE BOOK

page 20

Word blending. Model how to blend and read the word *mariposa*. Slide your hand under the letters as you slowly elongate the sounds /maa-rii-posa/. Then read the word naturally—*mariposa*. Follow a similar procedure for *rosa* and *rama.*

Apply the skill. Write the following words on the board, one at a time, and have children read them aloud. Then have children decide whether the *r* sound is soft or hard.

miro **fuera** **valero** **regalo** **rubí** **faro**

Introduce Vocabulary

PRETEACH lesson vocabulary. Tell children that they are going to learn five new words that they will see again when they read a story called *Un gran rugido.*

Teach each Vocabulary Word using the process shown in the box below.

Write the word.

Say the word.

Track the word and have children repeat it.

Give the meaning or context.

Use the following suggestions or similar ideas to give the meaning or context.

sorprendente Relate by role-playing facial expressions and gestures that people experience when seeing something amazing.

equipos Relate by grouping children to do some task.

juntos Relate by gathering classroom objects into a bag.

AFTER

Building Background and Vocabulary

rugido	Have children practice big roars.
monstruoso	Point out the word *monstruo* within the larger word.

For vocabulary activities, see Vocabulary Games on pages 2–7.

Apply Vocabulary Strategies

Use synonyms/antonyms. Write the word *rugido* on chart paper and ask children to give synonyms for the word (grito, ruido...). Tell children that they can sometimes figure out the meaning of the word by looking for synonyms that they know.

Vocabulary Words

sorprendente que causa sorpresa

juntos unidos

rugido grito fuerte

equipos grupos de personas con propósito similar

monstruoso enorme, horroroso

MODEL **Cuando pienso en los sinónimos de la palabra *rugido* me hace entender la palabra mejor. Sé que es un grito o ruido y eso me ayuda recordar qué es un rugido.**

Guide children in using a similar procedure to decode the words *equipos* and *sorprendente.*

RETEACH **lesson vocabulary.** Have children listen to each of the following riddles. Tell them to hold up the word card that answers each riddle. Reread the riddle aloud with the correct answer. Then discuss how children made their choices.

1. describe a los niños gritando fuerte (*rugido*)
2. describe a gente trabajando junta (*equipo*)
3. describe a objetos o personas que están muy cerca unos de otros (*juntos*)
4. significa que algo causa sorpresa (*sorprendente*)
5. significa que algo es enorme, horroroso (*monstruoso*)

FLUENCY BUILDER Use *Intervention Practice Book* page 19. Read each word in the first column aloud and have children repeat it. Then have children work in pairs to read the words in the first column aloud to each other. Follow the same procedure with each of the remaining columns. After partners have practiced reading aloud the words in each column separately, have them practice the entire list.

(Save *Intervention Practice Book* page 19 to use with pages 51 and 53.)

BEFORE

Reading
Un gran rugido
pages 126–145

Focus Skill Narrative Elements: Character

PRETEACH the skill. Tell children that characters are the people or animals in a story. Point out how they can tell what a character is like by paying attention to what a character says, his or her words, and what a character does, his or her actions. Discuss how readers can also use their own personal experience to understand why characters talk and act the way they do.

USE SKILL CARD 5A

Have children look at **side A** of ***Tarjeta de destreza 5: Elementos narrativos (personaje)*/Skill Card 5: Narrative Elements (Character).** Read the definition of *personaje.* Next read the story and have children read it with you.

Now call attention to the chart and have volunteers take turns reading the information aloud. Ask:

- **¿Qué pasaría si Martín estuviera llorando?** (*Possible response: El cuadro cambiaría*)
- **¿Por qué es importante prestar atención a lo que hacen y dicen los personajes?** (*Possible response: para entender como son los personajes*)

Prepare to Read: *Un gran rugido*

Preview. Tell children that they are going to read a selection entitled *Un gran rugido.* Explain that this is a story that could really happen. Explain to children that *Un gran rugido* tells about a boy who does everything alone. Then preview the selection.

Para ti
pages
126–145

- **Pages 126–127:** Veo el título, *Un gran rugido,* y el nombre del autor. Veo un dibujo de niños jugando y un niño sentado solo. Pienso que el cuento va a hablar del niño solo.
- **Pages 128–129:** En estas páginas veo niños juntando sus mesas. Wilson está sentado solo. Wilson no está contento de estar solo. Pienso que esta sección debe tratar de la tristeza de Wilson por estar tan solo.
- **Pages 130–131:** En estos dibujos, veo a los niños sentados juntos en la cafetería, menos Wilson que está sentado solo. Pienso que algo va a pasar con Wilson.
- **Pages 132–133:** En estas páginas, veo que todos los niños juegan juntos, menos Wilson. Me gustaría saber si Wilson finalmente juegua con ellos.

Set Purpose. Model setting a purpose for reading *Un gran rugido.*

MODEL **Por lo que he visto, pienso que voy a descubrir cómo se siente Wilson por estar solo. Voy a leer para ver si Wilson puede jugar con los otros niños.**

AFTER
Reading
Un gran rugido
pages 124–145

Reread and Summarize

Have children reread and summarize *Un gran rugido* in sections, as described below.

Pages 128–131
Leamos las páginas 128–131 para recordar qué hacen los niños y Wilson en la escuela.

Summary: Los niños estudian y comen juntos, pero Wilson se sienta solo en la clase y en la cafetería.

Pages 132–135
Leamos las páginas 132–135 para recordar qué más hacen los niños y Wilson y cómo se siente Wilson.

Summary: Juntos, los niños juegan, leen y hacen muñecos de nieve, pero Wilson juega, lee y camina solo. Él no se ríe. Me parece que se siente triste.

Pages 136–139
Leamos las páginas 136–139 para recordar qué pasa cuando viene la niña Sara.

Summary: Cuando viene Sara, se sonríe todo el tiempo. Se sienta, come, lee y juega sola por un día. Luego, se junta con los niños y hace todo con ellos. Wilson la mira y cuándo ella se da cuenta, le hace un rugido grande.

Pages 140–144
Leamos las páginas 140–144 para recordar qué le pasa a Wilson al final del cuento.

Summary: Wilson le devuelve el rugido a Sara, y desde este momento él empieza hacer todo con el grupo también. Nunca más estuvo solo.

FLUENCY BUILDER Be sure children have copies of *Intervention Practice Book* page 19. Call attention to the sentences on the bottom half of the page. Tell children that their goal is to read each phrase or sentence smoothly. Model appropriate pace, expression, and phrasing as you read each sentence and have children read it after you. Then have children practice by reading the sentences aloud three times to a partner.

BEFORE

Making Connections
pages 146–147

Directed Reading of *Solos tú y yo*

Sonidos alegres
pages 38–43

Ask a volunteer to read aloud the title. Help children to see that the boy is alone and the other children are together. Read pages 38–39 while children listen to find out what the boy does when his parents tell him to make a friend. Ask: **¿Qué quieren decir los padres cuándo le dicen al niño que "haga un amigo"?** (*Possible response: que juegue con otro amigo.*) **INTERPRETATION**

Ask: **¿Cómo muestran su personalidad las acciones del niño?** (*Possible response: Se sienta solo y parece triste.*)
Focus Skill **NARRATIVE ELEMENT (CHARACTER)**

Page 40

Have children read page 40 to find out what the boy does with his snow friend. Ask: **¿Cómo juegan el niño y su amigo de nieve? ¿Juegan juntos?** (*Possible response: El niño corre y salta, pero Bob sólo mira; en realidad, no juegan juntos.*) **DRAW CONCLUSIONS**

Page 41

Have children read page 41 to find out how Bob brings the other children over. Ask: **¿Por qué quieren acercarse a Bob los otros niños?** (*Possible response: Es un muñeco de nieve sorprendente.*) **NOTE DETAILS**

Pages 42–43

Read aloud pages 42–43 to children. Model using the Make and Confirm Predictions strategy to help children learn how to be active readers.

> MODEL **Cuando leí que hizo un muñeco de nieve, adiviné que a los otros niños les gustaría acercarse y mirar a Bob. Luego, adiviné que entonces, ellos querrían jugar con el niño porque hizo un muñeco de nieve sorprendente. Ahora, leo para ver si mis predicciones son correctas y veo que ¡tengo razón!** Focus Strategy **MAKE AND CONFIRM PREDICTIONS**

Ask: What happens after the other children ask about Bob? **NOTE DETAILS** (*Possible response: They ask the boy to play with them.*)

INTERVENTION PRACTICE BOOK
page 21

Summarize the selection. Have children summarize the selection by telling what happened at the beginning, middle, and end of the story in three or four sentences.

Answers to *Think About It* Questions

1. Haciendo primero un muñeco de nieve al que llamó Bob. **SUMMARY**
2. Porque en el calor, la nieve se derrite. **INTERPRETATION**
3. Las respuestas pueden variar. **TASK**

AFTER

Skill Review
pages 147

USE SKILL CARD 5B

Focus Skill Narrative Elements: Character

RETEACH the skill. Have children look at **side B** of ***Tarjeta de destreza 5: Elementos narrativos (personaje)*/Skill Card 5: Narrative Elements (Character).** Read the skill reminder with them, and have a volunteer read the story aloud.

Read aloud the set of directions. Explain that children will work with partners to create their own charts. Guide them to picture the story in their mind as they think about what the characters say and do.

After children have completed their character charts, have them display and explain their work. Point out that the selection *Solos tú y yo* has characters that say and do many things. Ask volunteers to name some of the things these characters say and do.

Focus Skill Review Phonics Skill from *Un gran rugido*

RETEACH the skill. Read aloud the following sentence: *El loro regaló la rama al burro*. Have children listen for the hard and soft *r* sounds. Then read this list aloud and have children raise their hands when they hear the hard or soft *r* sound: *rugido, amigo, pirata, cafetería, escuela, cara, perro, niños.*

FLUENCY BUILDER Be sure children have copies of *Intervention Practice Book* page 19. Explain that today children will practice the sentences on the bottom half of the page by reading them aloud on tape. Assign new partners. Have children take turns reading the sentences aloud to each other and then reading them on tape.

BEFORE

Drafting a Thank-You Note
pages 147A

Writing: Thank-You Note

Build on prior knowledge. Tell children that they are going to talk and write about information they might share in a thank-you note. Explain that a thank-you note is similar to a friendly letter, but it includes a message thanking someone for something they did or gave. Guide children to see that thank-you notes may be written to all sorts of people.

Con cariño, Wilson

Gracias por jugar conmigo.

Gracias por ser una buena amiga.

Querida Sara:

Espero que seamos amigos por siempre.

Construct the text. "Share the pen" with children. Help them to organize the list into a thank-you note. For example:

> Querida Sara:
>
> Gracias por ser una buena amiga. Gracias por jugar conmigo. Espero que seamos amigos por siempre.
>
> Con cariño,
> Wilson

Revisit the text. Read the thank-you note together. Guide children to see the different parts of the friendly letter. Ask: **¿Cómo sabes para quién es la carta?** (*Es para Sara porque dice: "Querida Sara".*)

Ask: **¿Cómo sabes quién escribió la carta?** (*Wilson escribió la carta porque dice: "Con cariño, Wilson".*)

- Ask: **¿Cómo podemos combinar las primeras líneas para que la nota de agradecimiento sea más fluida?** (*Gracias por ser buena amiga y por jugar conmigo.*) Make the appropriate change.
- Have children read the completed thank-you note aloud and then copy it on their papers.

On Your Own

Have children write a list of topics for thank-you notes they would like to write. Encourage them to write who each thank-you note is for.

AFTER

Spelling Lesson
page 145H

Connect Spelling and Phonics

RETEACH phonics. Tell children to number their papers 1–7. Dictate the following words, and have children write them. After each word is written, write it on the board so children can proofread their work. On their papers, they should draw a line through a misspelled word and write the correct spelling below it.

1. sorprendente*	**2. pero***	**3. corrían***	**4. era***
5. sombrero*	**6. miraba***	**7. reunían***	

*** Word appears in *Solos tú y yo.***

Dictate the following sentence and have children write it: *Se reunían y miraban al burro grande.*

Build and Read Longer Words

Remind children that they have learned how to decode words with the hard and soft *r* sound. Explain that now they will use what they have learned to help them read some longer words.

INTERVENTION ASSESSMENT BOOK

Write the following words on the board: *corriendo, reuniendo*, and *mirando*.

Remind children that they should look for words they know in longer words. Point to *corriendo* and read it aloud. Ask children which part of the word says *corri* and which part says *endo*. Ask children what *corri* and *endo* together say. Have children blend the word parts to form the longer word *corriendo*. Repeat this procedure with each word on the board.

FLUENCY BUILDER Have children choose a passage from *Solos tú y yo* to read aloud to a partner. You may have children choose passages that they found particularly interesting, or have them choose one of the following options:

- Read pages 38–39. (From *Yo no tenía...* through *...puse un trapeador*. Total: 82 words.)
- Read pages 40–41. (From *Bob, mi amigo...* through *...decían.* Total: 74 words.)

Children should read the selected passage aloud to their partners three times. Have the child rate each reading on a scale from 1 to 4.

SCALE
1 Not so good
2 Pretty good
3 Good
4 Great!

BEFORE
Weekly Assessments

Review Vocabulary

To revisit Vocabulary Words prior to the weekly assessment, use these clues. Have volunteers take turns reading aloud the clues. Children say and then write the word or words that best answer the clue.

1. Estas dos palabras terminan con una *s.* (*equipos, juntos*)
2. Esta palabra rima con *oso.* (*monstruoso*)
3. Esta palabra tiene el sonido de la *r* fuerte. (*rugido*)
4. Esta palabra tiene cuatro sílabas. (*sorprendente*)

You may want to display the Vocabulary Words and definitions on page 49 and have children copy them to use when they study for the vocabulary test.

INTERVENTION PRACTICE BOOK
page 22

Focus Skill Narrative Elements: Character

To review character before the weekly assessment, distribute *Intervention Practice Book* page 22. Have volunteers read aloud the first direction line and the sentences. Guide children to think about the things characters say and do.

Review Test Prep

INTERVENTION ASSESSMENT BOOK

Ask children to turn to page 149 of the *Pupil Edition*. Call attention to the Tips for answering the test questions. Tell children that paying attention to these tips can help them answer not only the test questions but also other test questions like these.

Para ti
pages 124–145

Have children follow along as you read each test question and the tip that goes with it. Discuss how good test-takers do their work calmly and quietly.

AFTER
Weekly Assessments

Self-Selected Reading

Have children select their own books to read independently. They might choose books from the classroom library shelf, or you may wish to offer a group of appropriate books from which children can choose.

- *Mantenerse abrigado* See page 149M of the *Teacher's Edition* for an Independent Reading Plan.
- *Amigos* por Loles Durán. SM, Ediciones, 1996.
- *Sapo y Sepo son amigos* por Arnold Lobel. Alfaguara, 1996.

After children have chosen their books, give each child a copy of *Mi diario de lectura,* which can be found on page R35 in the back of the *Teacher's Edition*. Have children fill in the information at the top of the form. Then have them use the log to keep track of their reading and to record their responses to the literature.

Conduct student-teacher Conferences. Arrange time for each child to meet with you individually to discuss his or her self-selected reading. Have children bring their *Diarios de lectura* to share with you at the conference. Children might also like to choose a favorite passage to read aloud to you. Ask questions designed to stimulate discussion of the book. For example, you might ask what children like to do when they are alone and how their activities might differ if they are with friends.

FLUENCY PERFORMANCE Have children read aloud to you the passage from *Solos tú y yo* that they selected and practiced with their partners. Keep track of the number of words the child reads correctly. Ask the child to rate his or her own performance on the 1–4 scale. If children are not happy with their oral reading, give them an opportunity to continue practicing and then to reread the passage to you again.

See *Evaluación de la fluidez oral de la lectura* for monitoring progress.

LESSON 6

Use with

"El nabo gigante"

BEFORE

Building Background and Vocabulary

Review Phonics: diptongos: *ia, au*

Identify the sound. Tell children to listen for the diphthong *ia* and *au* as you say the words *piano* and *autor.* Then have the children repeat the following sentences twice: *Un anciano plantó un pequeño nabo. Tolstoy es el autor del cuento El nabo gigante.* Ask them to identify the words the have the diphthongs *ia* and *au.* (*anciano y autor*)

Associate letters to sound. Write on the board: *Un anciano plantó un pequeño nabo. Tolstoy es el autor del cuento El nabo gigante. Paula toca el piano pausadamente.* Underline *ia* in *anciano* and *piano* and *au* in *autor, Paula* and *pausadamente.* Explain that these letter combinations stands for the diphthong *ia* and *au.*

Word blending. Model how to blend and read the word *piano* and *Paula.* Slide your hand under the word as you pronounce the diphthongs*/piaano/* and */Pauula/.* Then say the words naturally *piano, Paula.* Follow a similar procedure to *anciano, autor, pausadamente.*

INTERVENTION PRACTICE BOOK

page 24

Apply the skill. *Letter substitution* Write the following words on the board and have children read each aloud. Make changes necessary to form the words in parantheses. Have a volunteer read aloud new word.

Pino (piano)	**actor** (autor)	**pasa** (pausa)	**pala** (Paula)
jala (jaula)	**copa** (copia)	**casa** (causa)	**cacho** (caucho)

Introduce Vocabulary

PRETEACH lesson vocabulary. Tell children that they are going to learn nine new words that they will see again when they read a story called *El nabo gigante.* Teach each vocabulary word using the following process.

Write the word.
Say the word.
Track the word and have children repeat it.
Give the meaning or context.

Use the following suggestions or similar ideas to give the meaning or context.

gigante Relate to dinosaurs, elephants, whales.

nieta Point out the diphthong ie. Relate to *grandfather, grandson.*

jalaba Show how to pull up a chair.

plantó Point out the -ed ending. Explain that to plant something is to put in the ground.

AFTER
Building Background and Vocabulary

fuerte	Relate to people and things that are strong.
nabo	Relate to another root vegetable such as a carrot or a beet.

For vocabulary activities, see Vocabulary Games on pages 2–5.

Vocabulary Words

gigante enorme
nieta hija del hijo o hija de alguien
jalaba tiraba, arrastraba
plantó enterró una semilla para que creciera
fuerte poderoso
nabo una raíz comestible

Apply Vocabulary Strategies

Use suffixes. Write the word *crece* on chart paper. Below *crece* write *crecer* and *decrecer.* Use a colored marker to underline *crec* in *crece* and *crecer.* Use a second color to underline *de* in *decrecer.* Tell children that they can sometimes figure out the meaning of words by looking for prefixes that they know.

MODEL **El radical *crec* me es familiar porque lo he visto en palabras como *crece* y *crecer.* También yo he visto prefijos como *de* en palabras como *decrecer.* Con la palabra base, terminación y prefijo, leo la palabra *decrecer.* Guide children in using a similar procedure to decode the words *plantado* and *fuerte, fuerza* and *esfuerza.***

RETEACH **lesson vocabulary.** Have children listen to each riddle and then hold up the word card that completes the answer. Reread each riddle aloud with the correct answer. Discuss how the children made their choices.

1. Tengo buenos músculos para cargar cajas grandes. Yo soy __________ (*fuerte*)
2. ¿Quién es la hija de mi hija? Ella es mi __________ (*nieta*)
3. Soy tan alto como un árbol y amplio como una casa. Soy un __________ (*gigante*)
4. Su maleta pesaba mucho. Por eso la __________ para llevarla (*jalaba*)
5. Yo crecí debajo de la tierra y puedes comerme. Yo soy un __________ (*nabo*)
6. Era la semilla que se puso en la tierra para germinar. Hoy es el árbol que se __________ (*plantó*)

FLUENCY BUILDER Using *Intervention Practice Book* page 23, read each word in the first column aloud and have students repeat it. Then have students work in pairs to read the words in the first column aloud to each other. Follow the same procedure with each of the remaining columns. After partners have practiced reading aloud the words in each column separately, have them practice the entire list. *Save Intervention Practice Book* page 23 to use on pages 25 and 27.

BEFORE

Reading
El nabo gigante
pages 154–166

USE SKILL CARD 6A

Focus Skill Sequence

PRETEACH the skill. Tell children that events happen in a certain order. Give an example such as waking up, eating breakfast, and then going to school. Discuss why these events do not happen in a different order.

Have children look at **side A of Skill Card 6: Sequence.** Read the definition of sequence. Next, have children look at the pictures and describe what is happening in each one.

Now call attention to the diagram. Have volunteers take turns reading the sentences aloud. Ask:

- **¿Que pasaría si las oraciones no estuvieran en el mismo orden?** (*Possible response: The information would not make sense.*)
- **¿Por qué son importantes las palabras en letras rojas?** (*Help children understand how these words help make the sequence clear.*)

Explain that when events in a story are in time order, we say that the text is organized, or set up, according to sequence.

Prepare to Read: *El nabo gigante*

Para ti
pages 154–166

Preview. Tell children that they are going to read a selection called *El nabo gigante* that includes pictures with caption. *El nabo gigante* gives information in how people can help each other to get the things done.

- **Pages 154–155:** Puedo ver el título: *El nabo gigante* y los nombres de los autores. Veo el dibujo de una planta que me imagino sea un nabo. En la página 155 veo un señor mayor con una pala pequeña en la mano. Creo que está plantando una semilla en la tierra.
- **Pages 156–157:** Veo el texto y una mano tirando algo que creo es el nabo.
- **Pages 158–159:** El anciano parece que está muy cansado. Parece que está tirando de una rama con hojas. ¿Serán esas las hojas de un nabo?

Set Purpose. Model setting a purpose for reading *El nabo gigante*

MODEL Después de este vistazo que eché a las primeras páginas, puedo imaginarme que el el autor quiere que aprendamos a plantar nabos. Una de las razones para leer es aprender a hacer cosas nuevas. Bueno, comenzaré a leer para saber cómo se plantan nabos.

AFTER

Reading
El nabo gigante
pages 154–166

Reread and Summarize

Have children reread and summarize *El nabo gigante* in sections, as described below.

Pages 154–157
Vamos a releer otra vez las páginas 156–157 para recordar como es de dificil plantar nabos gigantes.

Summary: Es muy difícil porque crecen mucho debajo de la tierra. El nabo creció muchísimo y el anciano no pudo sacarlo.

Pages 158–159
Leamos estas páginas para recordar qué hizo el anciano cuando no pudo sacar el nabo.

Summary: El anciano reconoce que no puede sacar el nabo y busca la ayuda de su mujer, pero aún así los dos juntos no pudieron sacar el nabo de la tierra.

Pages 160–162
Leamos estas páginas para saber quién vino a ayudar al anciano a sacar el nabo.

Summary: Cada uno de ellos reconoce que no puede sacar el nabo. Llama al siguiente, y uno tras el otro se ponen a jalar.

Pages 163–166
Releamos estas páginas para recordar cómo finalmente pueden sacar el nabo.

Summary: Se pusieron a jalar hasta que pudieron sacar el nabo. Entendemos por qué es importante trabajar en equipo.

FLUENCY BUILDER Use *Intervention Practice Book* page 23. Call attention to the sentences on the bottom half of the page. Tell children that their goal is to read each phrase or sentence smoothly. Model appropriate pace, expression and phrasing as you read each sentence and have children read it after you. Then have children practice by reading the sentences aloud three times to a partner.

BEFORE
Making Connections
page 168–169

Directed Reading: *El cuento del nabo,* pp. 46–52

Sonidos alegres
pp. 46–52

Ask a volunteer to read aloud the title. Help children identify the turnip in the illustration on page 46. Read aloud page 46 while the children listen to find out why the turnip was so big. Ask: **¿Cómo el nabo se hizo tan grande?** (*Possible response: Él creció y creció*) **CAUSE AND EFFECT**

Make sure children understand that the water level in a well goes up and down. Read page 47 aloud while the children listen to find out what happened to the turnip. Ask: **¿Qué le sucedió al nabo ahora? ¿Qué le sucedió al nabo antes?** (*Possible response: Ahora se cayó dentro del pozo. Antes rodó y rodó colina abajo.*) Focus Skill **Sequence**

Pages 48-49

Have the children read page 48 to find out what the woman did. Ask: **¿Por qué ella no pudo sacar el nabo del pozo?** (*Possible response: El nabo estaba muy pesado.*) **DRAW CONCLUSIONS**

Read aloud the first five paragraphs on page 49 while the children listen to find out who came to help the woman. Model using the summarize strategy to make clear what happened in the story.

> MODEL **No estoy muy seguro de lo que sucedió. Voy a resumir para poder entenderlo mejor. La nieta ayudó a la señora, pero no pudieron sacar el nabo. Entonces algunos hombres dijeron que ayudarían.** Focus Strategy **Summarize**

Discuss whether the children agree with your summary. Have a volunteer read aloud the rest of page 49 while the others listen for what happened. Ask: **¿Quienes jalaban? ¿Qué sucedió?** (*Possible responses: La mujer, la nieta y los hombres tiraban pero no pudieron sacar el nabo del pozo.*) **SUMMARIZE**

Page 50

Have the children read page 50 to find out who else came to help. Ask: **¿Qué pensaba la señora del ratón?** (*Possible responses: Pensaba que no era fuerte. Creía que cargaba la peste.*) **IDENTIFY CHARACTERS' EMOTIONS**

Have the children look at the illustration on page 50 to find out how the mouse helps. Ask: **¿Crees que con echar água al pozo se podrá sacar el nabo?** (*Possible responses: sí, no*) **MAKE PREDICTIONS**

Page 51

INTERVENTION PRACTICE BOOK page 25

Have the children read page 51 to see if their prediction was correct. Ask: **¿Qué aprendió la señora con el ratón?** (*Possible responses: La ayuda a veces viene de donde menos uno la espera. La inteligencia casi siempre es mejor que la fuerza bruta.*) **DRAW CONCLUSIONS**

Summarize the selection. Ask children to think about the events in the story. Then have them complete. Comprehension BLM 25.

Page 52

Answers to *Piénsalo* Questions

1. Las respuestas pueden variar. **SUMMARIZE**
2. Ella dijo que él era pequeñito y no tenía fuerza. **INTERPRET STORY DETAILS**
3. Acepte respuestas razonables. **WRITE A STORY**

AFTER

Skill Review
page 153A

USE SKILL CARD 6B

Focus Skill Sequence

RETEACH the skill. Have children look at **side B of Skill Card 6: Sequence.** Read the skill reminder with them, and have a volunteer read the paragraph aloud.

Have a volunteer read aloud the set of directions. Explain that the children will work with partners to create their own diagrams. Remind them to write one event in each box to show the sequence. Have the children create their own graphics that model the one on the skill card.

After children have completed their diagrams, have them display and explain their work. Point out that *El cuento del nabo* is organized according to sequence. It tells in time order about the events in the story.

Focus Skill Review Phonics Skill from *El nabo gigante*

RETEACH diptongos: *ia, au.* Write the word *automóvil* on the board. Have volunteers write four more words on the board with *au.* Explain that you will say four more words with *ia.* Have the children to read aloud the list.

1. automóvil	**2. flauta**	**3. autobús**	**4. auditor**
5. lluvia	**6. gracias**	**7. furia**	**8. social**

FLUENCY BUILDER Use copies of *Intervention Practice Book* page 23. Explain that today the children will practice the sentences on the bottom half of the page by reading them aloud on tape. Assign new partners. Have the children take turns reading the sentences aloud to each other and then reading them on tape.

INTERVENTION PRACTICE BOOK page 23

BEFORE

Drafting dialogue
Pages 171C–171D

Writer's Craft: Dialogue

Build on prior knowledge. Tell children that they are going to talk and write about dialogue. Write on the board:

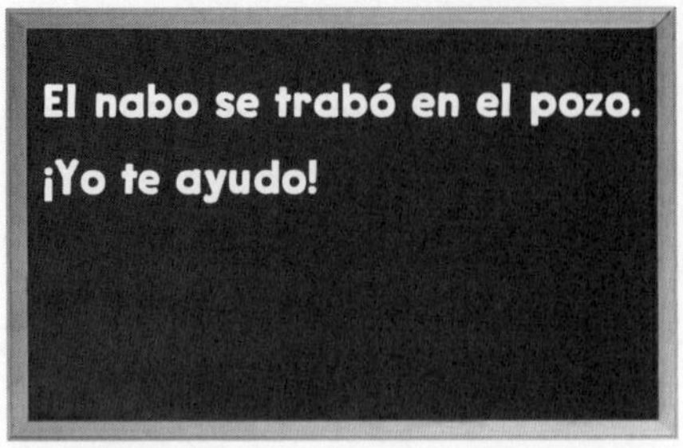

Construct the text. "Share the pen" with the children. Guide them in deciding who might have spoken each of these sentences in *El cuento del nabo.* Help them add a comma and the speaker's name to each sentence. Have them use the word *said* to show the person was speaking.

El nabo se trabó en el pozo, dijo la señora.
¡Yo te ayudo! —dijo el ratón.

Revisit the text. Go back and read the dialogue together. Ask: **¿Cómo puedo hacer que el lector sepa cuáles palabras son parte del diálogo?** (*Pon guiones antes y después de las frases de diálogo.*)

- Guide children in adding the *guiones.*

  ***—El nabo se agarró al pozo,* —dijo la señora.**
  ***—¡Yo te ayudo!* —dijo el ratón.**

- Ask: **En la segunda oración que pronombre podemos usar para sustituir la palabra *ratón*?** (*Él*) Make the appropriate change.
- Have children read the completed dialogue aloud and then copy it on their papers.

On Your Own

Have children write a sentence that tells what someone said to them today. Remind them to use the word *said* and the speaker's name. Have them use a *coma* to separate what is said from what is read. Remind them to add *guiónes* to show which words are spoken.

AFTER

Spelling Lesson
page 167I

Connect Spelling and Phonics

RETEACH **diptongos *au, ia*** Write the word *autopista* on the board. Explain that you will say three more words in which the diphthong *au* is used. Have volunteers write again the word on the board. Then write the word *familia* on the board, explain that you will say three more words in which the diphthong *ia* is used, and repeat the process.

1. automóvil	**2. autopista**	**3. autobús**	**4. auditor**
5. lluvia	**6. gracias**	**7. familia**	**8. social**

Dictate the following sentence and have children write it: *La lluvia cae sobre el automóvil y el autobús en la autopista.*

Build and Read Longer Words

Remind children that they have learned how to decode words with the diphthongs *ia* and *au.*

Write the word *pausadamente* on the board. Tell children that they can sometimes figure out long words by looking for syllables, prefixes and suffixes. Cover *mente* and have a volunteer read the word *pausada.* Then cover *da* and have a volunteer read the word *pausa.* Point out that *pausa* uses the diphthong au.

FLUENCY BUILDER Have children choose a passage from *El cuento del nabo* to read aloud to a partner. You may have children choose passages that they found particularly interesting, or have them choose one of the following options:

- Read pages 46–48. From *Una señora plantó* . . . through . . . *gritó pidiendo ayuda*. (Total: 83 palabras)
- Read pages 49–51. From *La nieta gritó* . . . through . . . *sacó aquel nabo!* (Total: 92 palabras)

Children should read the selected passage aloud to their partners three times. Have the child rate each reading on a scale from 1 to 4.

SCALE	
1	Not so good
2	Pretty good
3	Good
4	Great!

BEFORE

Weekly Assessments

Review Vocabulary

To revisit vocabulary words prior to the weekly assessment, use these true or false questions. Have volunteers take turns reading aloud the sentences. Children determine whether the definitions are true or false. Encourage them to then correct the false sentences.

1. El **nabo** es un vegetal comestible. (*verdadero*)
2. Si eres **fuerte** es que tienes mucha fuerza. (*verdadero*)
3. La **nieta** de la anciana se llama Paula y la anciana es también su abuela. (*verdadero*)
4. Un **gigante** es un hombre muy pequeñito. (*falso*)
5. El granjeto **plantó** un coche en el jardín. (*falso*)
6. La mujer **jalaba** por una cuerda el cubo de agua del pozo. (*verdadero*)

You may want to display the vocabulary words and definitions on page 59 and have children copy them to use when they study for the vocabulary test.

INTERVENTION PRACTICE BOOK
page 26

Focus Skill Review Sequence

To review sequence before the weekly assessment, distribute *Intervention Practice Book* p. 26. Have volunteers read aloud the first direction line and the sentences. Guide children to use signal words and unstated clues to put the sentences in order in the sequence diagram.

Para ti
page 171

Review Test Prep

INTERVENTION ASSESSMENT BOOK

Ask children to turn to page 171 of the *Pupil Edition.* Call attention to the Tips for answering the test questions. Tell children that paying attention to these tips can help them answer not only the test questions but also other test questions like these.

Have children follow along as you read each test question and the tip that goes with it. Discuss why the signal word ***first*** is the most important word in Question 1. Then what signal word in question 2 could help them figure out the correct answer to that question. (*last*)

Self-Selected Reading

Have children select their own books to read independently. They might choose books from the classroom library shelf, or you may wish to offer a group of appropriate books from which children can choose.

- *El gigante del desierto.* See page 17 IO of the *Teacher's Edition* for an Independent Reading Plan.
- *Guillermo Jorge Manuel José* por Mem Fox. Ekaré-banco del Libro, 1991.
- *En mi proprio jardín* por Judi Kurjian. Charlesbridge, 1994.

After children have chosen their books, give each child a copy of "Mi diario de lectura", which can be found on page R35 in the back of the *Teacher's Edition.* Have children fill in the information at the top of the form. Then have them use the log to keep track of their reading and to record their responses to the literature.

Conduct student-teacher conferences. Arrange time for each child to conference with you individually about his or her self-selected reading. Have children bring their *Diarios de Lectura* to share with you at the conference. Children might also like to share a favorite passage to read aloud to you. Ask questions about the book designed to stimulate discussion. For example, you might ask how the illustrations in a folktale helped them understand the story or how they could tell what might happen next in a short story.

FLUENCY PERFORMANCE Have children read aloud to you the passage from *El cuento del nabo* that they selected and practiced with their partners. Keep track of the number of words the child reads correctly. Ask the child to rate his or her own performance on the 1–4 scale. If children are not happy with their oral reading, give them an opportunity to continue practicing and then to reread the passage to you again.

See *Oral Reading Fluency Assessment* for monitoring progress.

LESSON 7

Use with

"Ayudar es sencillo"

BEFORE

Building Background and Vocabulary

Review Phonics: Diphthongs *ua, ue*

Identify the sound. Tell children to listen for the diphthongs *ua* and *ue* as you say the words *lengua* and *muela.* Then have the children repeat the following sentences twice: *Al niño le duele una muela. María se mordió la lengua.* Ask them to identify the words that have the diphthongs *ua* and *ue.* (*duele, muela, lengua*)

Associate letters to sound. Write on the board: *Te duele una muela pero no te pica la lengua.* Underline *ue* in *duele* and *muela* and *ua* in *lengua.* Explain that these letter combinations come together to form the one sound they hear in the words.

Word blending. Write the word *muela* on the board. Read it aloud and emphasize the syllable containing the sound /ue/. Explain to the children that in some words the sounds of two vowels blend to form a new sound. For example, the sound /u/ is blended with the sound /e/ in the word *muela.* Write the syllables *mue* and *la* separately and demonstrate how to blend them into the word *muela.* Repeat this procedure with the word *lengua*, which contains the sound /ua/.

INTERVENTION PRACTICE BOOK

page 28

Apply the skill. *Vowel and consonant substitution* Write the following words on the board, and have children read each one aloud. Make the changes necessary to form the words in parentheses. Have a volunteer read aloud each new word.

ella (huella)	**carta** (cuarto)	**nevar** (nueve)	**percha** (puerta)
gana (guante)	**nube** (nueve)	**lluvia** (llueve)	**cada** (cuadro)

Introduce Vocabulary

PRETEACH lesson vocabulary. Tell the children that they are going to learn six new words that they will see again when they read a story called *Ayudar es sencillo.* Teach each Vocabulary Word using the following process.

Write the word.

Say the word.

Track the word and have children repeat it.

Give the meaning or context.

Use the following suggestions or similar ideas to give the meaning or context.

quehaceres Point out the words *que* and *hacer.* Relate to chores that children might do at home.

satisfecho Relate to how children feel when they have successfully completed a project.

sencillo Relate two things that are easy to do such as wave your hand and things that are plain like a hotdog without condiments.

germinarán Relate to tiny plants just starting to grow.

herramienta Relate to a tool such as a screwdriver or a hammer.

sucios Relate to what their clothing is like after playing outside.

For vocabulary activities, see Vocabulary Games on pages 2–7.

Vocabulary Words

quehaceres trabajos que se hacen regularmente

satisfecho contento, feliz

sencillo fácil, simple

germinarán comenzarán a crecer

herramienta objeto que hace más fácil un trabajo

sucios manchados, no limpios

AFTER
Building Background and Vocabulary

Apply Vocabulary Strategies

Use familiar word parts. Write the word *quehaceres* on chart paper. Then write *que* and *hacer.* Use a colored marker to underline those two words in the word *quehaceres.* Tell children that they can sometimes figure out how to pronounce a word by looking for words and letter patterns that they know within the word.

MODEL **Conozco las palabras *que* y *hacer.* Si combino las dos palabras, creo que la palabra quehaceres significa algo que uno tiene *que hacer.***

Guide children in using a similar procedure to decode the words *germinarán* and *herramienta.*

RETEACH **lesson vocabulary.** Have children listen to each of the following questions. Tell them to hold up the word card that gives the correct answer. Then discuss how the meaning of the vocabulary word fits the answer.

¿Qué palabra significa que *no es difícil*? (*sencillo*)

¿Qué palabra significa *los trabajos que deben realizarse*? (*quehaceres*)

¿Qué palabra significa que *no están limpios*? (*sucios*)

¿Qué palabra significa que alguien queda *feliz* con el trabajo realizado? (*satisfecho*)

¿Qué palabra es un *objeto que hace más fácil un trabajo*? (*herramienta*)

¿Qué palabra significa que *comenzarán a crecer*? (*germinarán*)

FLUENCY BUILDER Use *Intervention Practice Book* page 27. Read each word in the first column aloud and have children repeat it. Then have children work in pairs to read the words in the first column aloud to each other. Follow the same procedure with each of the remaining columns. After partners have practiced reading aloud the words in each column separately, have them practice the entire list. Save *Intervention Practice Book* page 27 to use with pages 71 and 73.

BEFORE

Reading *Ayudar es sencillo* pages 174–186

USE SKILL CARD 7A

Focus Skill Main Idea

PRETEACH the skill. Point out to children that the main idea of a story is the most important idea. Discuss that knowing which idea is the main idea helps readers understand what the story is about.

Have children look at **side A** of **Skill Card 7: Main Idea.** Read the definition of *main idea.* Next read the paragraph aloud and then have children reread it with you. Ask:

> **¿Por qué la idea principal es que a Tim le gusta ayudar a la gente?** (*Possible response: Porque es la idea más importante.*)
>
> **¿Por qué la idea principal no puedo ser que Tim ayuda a su padre a limpiar el garage?** (*Possible response: Esta idea cuenta solamente una de las maneras en que Tim ayuda a la gente.*)
>
> **¿Qué otras ideas cuentan cómo Tim ayuda a la gente?** (*Possible response: Éll ayuda a su mamá a lavar los platos. Él ayuda su hermanita a guardar los juguetes.*)

Explain that other ideas in a story usually tell about the main idea.

Prepare to Read: *Ayudar es encillo*

Para ti pages 174–186

Preview. Tell children that they are going to read a selection entitled *Ayudar es sencillo.* Explain that this selection is a photo essay that tells about a topic using photographs and words. Tell children that *Ayudar es sencillo* gives information about how children can help others do many kinds of jobs. Then preview the selection.

- **Pages 174–175:** Yo veo el título, *Ayudar es sencillo*, en la página 174 y el nombre del fotógrafo en la página 175. Las fotos en estas páginas muestran una niña y un hombre. Yo creo que ella le está ayudando al hombre.
- **Pages 176–177:** En estas páginas veo a una niña pasando un martillo a un hombre. Creo que esta seleción trata sobre las maneras en que los niños pueden ayudar.
- **Pages 178–179:** Ahora veo a niños trabajando en una huerta y lavando un carro. Parece que se están divirtiendo mucho. Creo que esas páginas mostrarán cómo ayudar puede ser divertido.

Set Purpose. Tell children they can use what they know to set a purpose for reading. Model setting a purpose for reading *Ayudar es sencillo.*

> MODEL **Por lo que he visto hasta ahora, creo que aprenderé sobre las diferentes maneras en que un niño puede ayudar. Uno de los propósitos de la lectura es aprender ideas importantes acerca del tema. Voy a mirar las fotos para encontrar ideas importantes acerca del tema. Leeré para a aprender sobre las ideas en las fotos.**

AFTER

Reading ***Ayudar es sencillo*** ***pages 174–186***

Reread and Summarize

Have children reread and summarize *Ayudar es sencillo* in sections, as described below.

Pages 174–177
Vamos a releer las páginas 174–177 para recordar algunas de las maneras en que los niños pueden ayudar.

Summary: Los niños pueden ayudar simplemente con pasarle a alguien una herramienta.

Pages 178–181
Volvemos a leer las páginas 178–181 para descubrir otras tareas con las cuales los niños pueden ayudar.

Summary: En la primavera los niños pueden plantar semillas en el huerto. En un día muy caliente algunos quehaceres pueden ser divertidos, como lavar un carro. Algunos trabajos pueden ser sucios, como cambiar el aceite del motor de un carro.

Pages 182–183
Ahora vamos a releer las páginas 182–183 para recordar qué hemos aprendido sobre cómo ayudar.

Summary: Los niños pueden ayudar al profesor a mantener organizado el salón de clases o ayudar a un adulto a pintar. Trabajar con un adulto y hacer un buen trabajo te hace sentir muy especial.

Pages 184–186
Vamos a releer las páginas 184–186 para recordar lo mejor de ayudar.

Summary: Una vez que hayas aprendido bien los quehaceres, puede que te paguen por tu labor. Pero lo mejor de ayudar es que te acercas a otras personas.

FLUENCY BUILDER Use *Intervention Practice Book* page 27. Call attention to the sentences on the bottom half of the page. Tell children that their goal is to read each phrase or sentence smoothly. Model appropriate pace, expression, and phrasing as you read each sentence and have children read it after you. Then have children practice by reading the sentences aloud three times to a partner.

BEFORE

Making Connections
pages 190–191

Directed Reading of *Herramientas que ayudan*

Sonidos alegres
pp. 54–61

Pages 54–55

Ask a volunteer to read aloud the title. Help children understand from the illustration that this selection is told by two children who interviewed other kids about the chores they do. Read pages 54–55 aloud while children listen to find out what the interviewers learned about Ted. Ask: **¿Qué es lo más importante que aprendiste sobre Ted?** (*Possible response: A Ted le gusta ayudar a su mamá.*) **MAIN IDEA**

Pages 56–57

Have a volunteer read aloud page 56 while children listen to find out about Jim's chore. Write the word *sencillo* on the board. Model using the Decoding/Phonics strategy to decode this word.

> MODEL **Cuando leo esta página, algunas palabras son nuevas para mí. Busco sonidos conocidos de las vocales o de las consonantes para que me ayuden a decodificar esas palabras nuevas. Trato de combinar los diferentes sonidos. Veo la palabra *sencillo* y pienso en los sonidos de las letras. Pronuncio la palabra lentamente/seenciilloo/. Luego la pronuncio rápidamente. DECODING/PHONICS**

Discuss the strategies children use to help them figure out how to pronounce unfamiliar words. Have a volunteer read aloud page 57. Ask: **¿Cómo sabías cómo pronunciar la palabra *herramientas*?** (*Possible response: Miro las letras y pienso en los sonidos de cada una.*) **DECODING/PHONICS**

Pages 58–59

Read aloud page 58 while children listen and look at the illustrations to find out what job Ben just finished. Ask: **¿Qué trabajo hizo Ben?** (*Possible response: Él pintó la cerca*) **DRAW CONCLUSIONS**

Have a volunteer read aloud page 59 while children listen to find out about Pat's chore. Ask: **¿Cuál es el trabajo de Pat?** (*Possible response: pasear a su perro Campeón*) **NOTE DETAILS**

Have children look at the illustrations on page 59 to find out what tool helps Pat walk Shep. Ask: **¿Qué herramienta ayuda a Pat a pasear Campeón?** (*Possible Response: una correa*) **NOTE DETAILS**

Page 60

Read aloud page 60 while children listen for questions they can answer. Ask: **¿Cúales quehacers prefieren hacer? ¿Qué herramientas les gustan usar?** (*Accept any reasonable responses*) **EXPRESS PERSONAL OPINIONS**

INTERVENTION PRACTICE BOOK
page 29

Summarize the selection. Ask children to think about the events in the story. Have them tell you the events in the story in order. Then have them complete *Intervention Practice Book* page 29.

Answers to *Piénsalo* Questions

1. Cavar, lavar platos y arreglar motores. **SUMMARIZE**
2. En que sólo tiene que caminar y pasear. **INTERPRET STORY DETAILS**
3. Las respuestas pueden variar. **TASK**

AFTER

Skill Review
page 173A

USE SKILL CARD 7B

Focus Skill Main Idea

RETEACH the skill. Have children look at **side B of Skill Card 7: Main Idea.** Read the skill reminder with them, and have a volunteer read the paragraph aloud.

Read aloud the next direction. Remind children to think about all the ideas in the story before they decide which one is the most important.

After children have identified and written the main idea, have them share their answer with the class. Point out that the selection *Herramientas que ayudan* has a main idea and other ideas that tell something about the main idea.

Review Phonics Skill from *Ayudar es sencillo*

RETEACH diphthongs *ua, ue.* Write this sentence on the board: *El guacamayo escuchó el trueno, mientras llovía en el bosque.* Read the sentence aloud. Have volunteers point to the words with the ***/ua/ue/*** sounds. Then read this list aloud and have children raise their hands when they hear the ***/ua/ue/*** sounds: *guacamole, cuatro, vaca, guapo, casa, puente, punto.*

FLUENCY BUILDER Be sure children have copies of *Intervention Practice Book* page 27. Explain that today children will practice the sentences on the bottom half of the page by reading them aloud on tape. Assign new partners. Have children take turns reading the sentences aloud to each other and then reading them on tape.

INTERVENTION PRACTICE BOOK
page 27

BEFORE

Drafting a Personal Story
page 193C

Writer's Craft: Using Colorful Words

Build on prior knowledge. Tell children that they are going to talk and write about something that happened to them. Point out that they can use colorful words to describe their experience to make it more descriptive and interesting. Invite a volunteer to name a personal experience he or she would like to write about. Write it on the board. Then list some ideas for colorful words that might be used to describe the experience.

Experience: El primer pez que pesqué

Idea 1: Piensa en cómo estaba el lago el día en que fui a pescar: *tranquilo*

Idea 2: Pienza en qué le hizo el pez al cordel cuando mordió el anzuelo: *le dio un tirón*

Idea 3: Piensa en cómo era el pez cuando lo agarré en mis manos: *resbaladizo*

Construct the text. "Share the pen" with children. Guide them in using the colorful words to write sentences that describe catching a fish. For example:

> Cuando fui a pescar el lago estaba tranquilo. Eché mi anzuelo al agua. El cordel dio un tirón. Agarré el pez. El pez estaba resbaladizo.

Revisit the text. Go back and read the sentences together. Ask: **¿Qué puedo hacer para estar seguro de que el lector entiende el orden de los sucesos?** (*Add colorful words*)

- Guide children in adding colorful words for details. For example: *Primero* eché el anzuelo al agua. *Entonces,* el cordel dio un tirón. *Al final*, agarré el pez. Explain that words like these give details to an audience.
- Ask: **¿Qué pronombre podemos usar para reemplazar la palabra *pez*?** (*éste*) Make the appropriate change.
- Have children read the descriptive paragraph aloud and then copy it on their own papers.

On Your Own

Have children write a paragraph about something that happened to them. Remind them to use colorful words to describe the experience.

AFTER

Spelling Lesson
page 187I

Connect Spelling and Phonics

RETEACH diphthongs /*ua*/*ue*. Write the word *suave* on the board. Remind children that in some words the sound of two vowels blends to form a new sound like in the word *suave.* Explain that you will say more words with the combination /*ua*/ and /*ue*/. Have volunteers write each word on the board. Check for misspelled words and help children correct

1. averiguamos*	**2. fueron**	**3. después**	**4. Juan***
5. agua	**6. cuando**	**7. cuadro**	**8. suelo**

*** Word appears in *Herramientas que ayudan.***

Dictate the following sentence and have children write it:
Juan, *ponte los guantes y martilla el cuadro en la pared.*

Build and Read Longer Words

Remind children that they have learned how to decode words with the /sh/ sound spelled *sh.* Explain that now they will use what they have learned to help them read some longer words.

INTERVENTION ASSESSMENT BOOK

Write the word *cuentista* on the board. Cover -ista and have a volunteer read the syllable cuent-. Point out that cuent- has the /ue/ sound. Then cover cuent- and have a voluneer read -ista. Have children blend the word parts to read the longer word cuentista. Follow a similar procedure with these words *cuarteto, cuaderno, guacamayo.*

FLUENCY BUILDER Have children choose a passage from *Herramientas que ayudan* to read aloud to a partner. You may have children choose passages that they found particularly interesting, or have them choose one of the following options:

- Read pages 55–56. (From *A Ted le gusta...* through *...ayudar en casa.* Total: 57 words)
- Read pages 58–59. (From *"Papi tiene que...* through *...instrumentos como éste."* Total: 54 words)

Encourage children to read their passages aloud to their partners three times. Have the child rate his or her own reading on a scale from 1 to 4.

BEFORE
Weekly Assessments

Review Vocabulary

Write the vocabulary words on the board. Tell small groups they are going to write a list of rules that might be found at the local gas station. Below are examples to share with children if they need help getting started. Be sure to allow time for groups to read their rules.

1. Si estás vendiendo gasolina, los demás se pueden ocupar de los ________ como barrer la acera y sacar la basura. (*quehaceres*)
2. Si riegan todas las plantas todos los días, ________. (*germinarán*)
3. Trabajen en un automóvil hasta dejar ________ al cliente. (*satisfecho*)
4. Ocúpense de lavar los uniformes ________. (*sucios*)
5. Todas las pinzas y destornilladores deben ir en el cajón de las ________. (*herramientas*)
6. Este es un método ________. Si lo siguen, harán un buen trabajo. (*sencillo*)

You may want to display the vocabulary words and definitions on page 69 and have children copy them to use when they study for the vocabulary test.

INTERVENTION PRACTICE BOOK page 30

Focus Skill Review Main Idea

To review main idea before the weekly assessment, distribute *Intervention Practice Book* page 30. Have volunteers read aloud the directions and then the paragraph. Guide children to think about the most important thing that they read.

Review Test Prep

Para ti page 193

Ask children to turn to page 193 of the *Pupil Edition.* Call attention to the Tips for answering the test questions. Tell children that paying attention to these tips can help them answer not only the test questions but also other test questions like these.

INTERVENTION ASSESSMENT BOOK

Have children follow along as you read each test question and the tip that goes with it. Discuss how the first, third, and fourth sentences in question 1 tell something about the second sentence. Remind children to think about which sentence in question 2 is not as important as the others.

Self-Selected Reading

Have children select their own book to read independently. They might choose a book from the classroom library shelf, or you may wish to offer a group of appropriate books from which children can choose.

- *La banda del barrio* See page 193O of the *Teacher's Edition* for an Independent Reading Plan.
- *Trabajo con papá* por Jean Claverie, Altea, 1986.
- *Seré pintor* Grafalco, 1991.

After children have chosen their books, give each child a copy of *Mi diario de lectura*, which can be found on page R35 in the back of the *Teacher's Edition.* Have children fill in the information at the top of the form. Then have them use the log to keep track of their reading and to record their responses to the literature.

Conduct student-teacher conferences Arrange time for each child to meet with you individually to discuss his or her self-selected reading. Have children bring their *Diarios de lectura* to share with you at the conference. Children might also like to share a favorite passage to read aloud to you. Ask questions designed to stimulate discussion of the book. For example, you might ask what information the child learned from a nonfiction text or how illustrations helped him or her better understand the topic.

FLUENCY PERFORMANCE Have children read aloud to you the passage from *Herramientas que ayudan* that they selected and practiced with their partners. Keep track of the number of words the child reads correctly. Ask the child to rate his or her own performance on the 1–4 scale. If children are not happy with their oral reading, give them an opportunity to continue practicing and then to reread the passage again to you.

See *Oral Reading Fluency Assessment* for monitoring progress.

LESSON 8

BEFORE

Building Background and Vocabulary

Use with

"El Sr. Putter y Tabby vuelan el avión"

Review Phonics: Consonant Vowel Blend: ga/gue/gui/go/gu

Identify the sound. Tell children to listen for the syllables *ga, gue, gui, go, gu.* Explain to children that the *g* sound is written with the letter *g* as in the words *gato, gusano,* and *gorro.*

Associate letters to sound. Write these words on the board and ask a volunteer to circle the syllables containing the letter *g* (*ga, go, gu*).

Also tell them that the *g* sound is written with the vowel *u* as in the words *guitarra* and *juguete.* Write these words on the board and ask a volunteer to circle the syllable *gui* and the syllable *gue.* Explain that in this case the vowel *u* is silent after the *g.*

INTERVENTION PRACTICE BOOK page 32

Word blending. Write on the board the following words. Read the words as you point to each word. Later, point out the word *guitarra,* and ask for a volunteer to read them. Continue with the second word in the same manner pointing out the words *llegue, amigo, and Gonzalo.* Invite children to copy these words into their journals. Ask children to circle the syllable with the letter *g* in each word.

Apply the skill. Write on the board words that have one or two syllables (*guión, gata, luego, algún, gustar*). Read each word aloud and ask children to say if the word has one or two syllables. Invite volunteers to underline the syllable which contains the letter *g.*

Introduce Vocabulary

PRETEACH lesson vocabulary. Tell children that they are going to learn five new words that they will see again when they read a story called *El Sr. Putter y Tabby vuelan el avión.*

Teach every vocabulary word using the following process.

Write the word.
Say the word.
Track the word and have children repeat it.
Give the meaning or context.

Use the following suggestions or similar ideas to give the meaning or context.

grúas Point out the gr sound. Tell that those are machines with long, movable arms used to lift things.

instrucciones Point out the letters *cc* inside the word. The word means instructions on how to do something.

promesa Point out the pr sound. Tell it means a statement made by a person telling that he or she will do something.

retorcerse Point to *re* and to *torcer.* Tell children the word means "to bend, to turn around quickly."

preocupada Point out *pre* plus *ocupada.* Tell it is when someone is thinking that bad things may happen.

For vocabulary activities, see Vocabulary Games on pages 2–7.

Vocabulary Words

grúas máquinas con brazos largos y móviles para alzar cosas pesadas

instrucciones pasos a seguir para hacer algo

promesa declaración hecha por una persona asegurando que va a hacer algo

retorcerse torcer, moverse dando una vuelta rápida

preocupada tener la idea que podría suceder algo malo

AFTER
Building Background and Vocabulary

Apply Vocabulary Strategies

Use context clues. Write the word *retorcerse* on chart paper and explain that many times you can figure out the meaning of a word from understanding the rest of the words around it. Read the following sentence aloud, pausing at the missing word. *Los juguetes de cuerda la hacían* __________. Point to the word *retorcerse* on the chart paper and explain that this word makes sense in the sentence.

> MODEL **Sé que los juguetes de cuerda hacen que los gatos den vueltas rápidas. Así entiendo que la palabra *retorcerse* significa "moverse dando vueltas rápidas".**

RETEACH lesson vocabulary. Have children listen to each of the following sentences. Tell them to hold up the word card that gives de right answer for each question or sentence. Reread the sentence aloud with the correct word choice. Then discuss how the meaning of the Vocabulary Word fits the sentence.

1. ¿Qué palabra dice qué suele hacer un niño cuando tiene un dolor de estómago? (*retorcerse*)
2. ¿Qué palabra significa *explicaciones*? (*instrucciones*)
3. ¿Qué palabra significa *máquinas enormes*? (*grúa*)
4. ¿Qué palabra es una declaración de que harás algo sin falta? (*promesa*)
5. ¿Qué palabra dice cómo se siente tu mamá cuando piensa que podría suceder algo malo? (*preocupada*)

FLUENCY BUILDER Using *Intervention Practice Book* page 31, read each word in the first column aloud and have children repeat it. Then have children work in pairs to read the words in the first column aloud to each other. Follow the same procedure with the remaining columns. After partners have practiced reading aloud each column separately, have them practice the entire list. (Save *Intervention Practice Book* page 31 to use on pages 81 and 83.)

BEFORE

Reading *El Sr. Putter y tabby vuelan el avión pages 196–219*

USE SKILL CARD 8A

Focus Skill Predict Outcomes

PRETEACH the skill. Tell children that they can use what they already know and clues in a story to predict what will happen. Hold a piece of fruit and say "Yum." Discuss how the word *yum* is a clue that you will enjoy eating the fruit.

Have children look at **side A** of **Skill Card 8: Predict Outcomes.** Read the introduction about how readers predict outcomes. Next read the paragraph aloud, and then have children reread it with you.

Now call attention to the diagram and have volunteers take turns reading the clues aloud. Then read the prediction aloud. Ask:

- **¿Cómo las pistas te ayudan a predecir que a los perros les gusta cazar ardillas?** (*Possible response: Las pistas e indicios nos llevan aconcluir que a los perros les gustan cazar ardillas y nos llevan a concluir que los ardillas se acercan a los perros.*)
- **¿Qué ya sabes sobre los perros que podría ayudarte a hacer una predicción?** (*Possible response: Algunos perros les gusta cazar ardillas.*)

Explain that identifying clues as you read a text and predicting what will happen next can help you better understand the story.

Prepare to Read: *El Sr. Putter y Tabby vuelan el avión*

Preview. Tell children they will read the selection called *El Sr. Putter y Tabby vuelan el avión.* Explain that this story is realistic fiction. The people and places seem real, but the story is made-up. Then preview the selection.

Para ti
pages
196–219

- **Pages 196–197:** Puedo ver el título *"El señor Putter y Tabby"* con sus dibujos en la página 196 y *"vuelan el avión"* en la página 197 con los nombres de los autores. Veo dibujos del Sr. Putter, su gata, un avión y una planta que me imagino sea un nabo y el dibujo de un aeroplano.
- **Pages 198–203:** Veo el texto, una tienda de juguetes y un camión. Puedo ver al señor Putter jugando con una troca de bomberos y con un aeroplano.
- **Pages 204–205:** Por todas las páginas que vi hasta ahora parece que a la gata la asustan los juguetes. Veo la habitación de un niño con las paredes llenas de fotos de aviones. Al señor Putter sí le gustan los aviones.

AFTER

Reading ***El Sr. Putter y tabby vuelan el avión pages 196–219***

Reread and Summarize

Have children reread and summarize *El Sr. Putter y Tabby vuelan el avión* in sections, as described below.

Pages 196–201
Vamos a releer otra vez las páginas 196–201 para recordar como le gustaban los juguetes al señor Putter y como los odiaba la gata Tabby.

Summary: Al señor Putter amaba ir a la juguetería y jugaba con toda clase de juguetes. Tabby, ya vieja, se ponía tan nerviosa que le provocaba hipo.

Pages 202–207
Al releer estas páginas entendemos que al señor Putter le gustaban sobre todo los aviones de juguete.

Summary: Un día el señor Putter se enamoró de un biplano con control de radio. Tabby tuvo hipo por todo el camino a casa.

Pages 208–213
En estas páginas leemos otra vez que Tabby no tiene más hipo pero sigue sin gustarle el avión del señor Putter, que sale para volar su avión.

Summary: El señor Putter lee las instruciones. El señor Putter, muy triste, después de una serie de intentos sin éxito, se da por vencido, mientras la gata ronronea de alegría.

Pages 214–219
Leemos en estas páginas que la gata también se siente triste, le hace caricias al señor Putter. Éste se siente mejor, habla con cariño al aeroplano que prende y lentamente despega.

Summary: Entendemos que es importante trabajar en equipo. En sequencia, se ponen a trabajar juntos, hasta que pueden terminar el trabajo.

FLUENCY BUILDER Be sure children have copies of *Intervention Practice Book* page 31, which you used for the previous Fluency Builder activity. Call attention to the sentences on the bottom half of the page. Tell children that their goal is to read each phrase or sentence smoothly. Model appropriate pace, expression, and phrasing as you read each sentence and have children read it after you. Then have children practice by reading the sentences aloud three times to a partner.

BEFORE
Making Connections
pages 222–223

Directed Reading: *La promesa*

Sonidos alegres
pp. 62–69

Ask a volunteer to read aloud the title. Make sure children understand what a promise is. Help children identify the setting in the illustration as a toy shop. Read page 62 aloud while children listen to find out more about the picture. Ask: **¿Quién es el niño del dibujo?** (*Possible response: Luli*) **DRAW CONCLUSIONS**

Ask: **¿Qué Luli está comprando con su mamá?** (*un avión que volaba*) **NOTE DETAILS**

Page 63

Read aloud page 63 while children look at the picture and listen to find out what Bud buys. Ask: **¿Qué grúa Bob va a comprar?** (*Possible response: aquélla que el Sr. García está apuntando con el dedo.*) **INTERPRET STORY EVENTS**

Ask: **¿Por qué ellos van a comprar aquella grúa?** (*Possible response: porque levanta objetos y tiene*) **CAUSE AND EFFECT**

Pages 64–65

Read aloud page 64 while children listen to find out what Bigotuda does. Ask: **¿Qué crees que Bigotuda hará después?** (*Possible response: Creo que cazará el insecto porque a ella la encantan los insectos*) Focus Skill **PREDICT OUTCOMES**

Have a volunteer read aloud page 65 while children listen to find out if their prediction was correct. Ask: **¿Qué hará ahora Bigotuda? ¿Qué hará ahora el insecto?** (*Possible response: Bigotuda va a correr y saltar. El insecto va a volar.*) **NOTE DETAILS**

Page 66

Read aloud the first four paragraphs on page 66 while children listen for what happens. Write the word *aplastar* on the board. Model using the word bits and parts to understand this word.

> **MODEL** **Cuando veo una palabra que no conozco, busco por partes las palabra que ya conozco. Miro la palabra *aplastar* y veo una palabra más pequeña que es *plasta. Se que* plasta quiere decir cosa blanda, como masa o barro. Así se que el avión se quedo hecho una *plasta*.**

Discuss the strategies children use to help them figure out unfamiliar words. Read aloud the rest of page 66 while children listen to find out what Muffin did. Ask: **¿Qué palabra reconoces en la palabra *estaba*?** (*Possible response: estar*) Focus Strategy **LOOK AT WORD BITS AND PARTS**

Page 67

Have a volunteer read aloud page 67 while children listen to find out what happens to the bug. Ask: **¿Qué le sucede al insecto?** (*El Sr. García dejó libre al insecto.*) **INTERPRET STORY EVENTS**

Page 68

Read aloud page 68 while children listen to find out what happens next. Ask: **¿Qué crees que Bigotuda hará ahora? Por qué?** (*Possible response: Cazará otro insecto, porque a ella la encanta cazar insectos.*) Focus Skill **PREDICT OUTCOMES**

INTERVENTION PRACTICE BOOK

page 33

Page 69

Summarize the selection. Ask children to think about the events in the story. Then have them complete *Intervention Practice Book* page 33.

Answers to *Think About It* Questions

1. El Sr. García prometió que Bigotuda atraparía el insecto. **SUMMARIZE**
2. Acepte respuestas razonables, tales como: Bigotuda atrapa casi todos los insectos que persigue. **INTERPRET STORY EVENTS**
3. Acepte respuestas razonables. **DRAW A PICTURE**

AFTER

Skill Review
page 225C

USE SKILL CARD 8B

Focus Skill Predict Outcomes

RETEACH the skill. Have children look at **side B** of **Skill Card 8: Predict Outcomes.** Read the skill reminder and first direction line with them. Have a volunteer read the story aloud.

Read aloud the next set of directions. Explain that children will work with partners to create their own diagrams. Remind them to look in the story for important ideas that could be clues.

After children have completed their diagrams, have them display and explain their work. Point out that predicting outcomes as they read can help them better understand a story.

Review Phonics Skill from *El Sr. Putter y Tabby vuelan el avión*

RETEACH the skill. Write the following list on the board: *gato, grito, gota, gruta, gueto, greta*. As you read the list aloud, have children direct a volunteer to cross out any word that does not have the ga/gue/gui/go/gu.

FLUENCY BUILDER Be sure that children have copies of *Intervention Practice Book* page 31. Explain that today children will practice the sentences on the bottom half of the page by reading them aloud on tape. Assign new partners. Have children take turns reading the sentences aloud to each other and then reading them on tape.

INTERVENTION PRACTICE BOOK

page 31

BEFORE

Drafting a Paragraph That Describes
page 223A

Writing Process: Descriptive Sentences

Build on prior knowledge. Tell children that they are going to talk and write about one of their favorite places. Explain that by using describing words, they can help others better imagine the place. Write on the board:

> **Mi cuarto es pequeño.**
> **Mi cuarto está regado.**
> **En mi cuarto hay cosas interesantes.**

Construct the text. "Share the pen" with children. Guide them to think of descriptive words to add to each of the sentences. Ask them to describe just how small the room is. Have them tell how messy the room is. Ask them to name what kinds of interesting things are in the room. Write new sentences that include their ideas. For example:

- *Mi cuarto es tan pequeño que no puedo recibir más de una visita al mismo tiempo.*
- *Hay roperos abiertos con ropas colgadas.*
- *Hay una pecera en una esquina.*

Revisit the text. Go back and read the sentences together. Ask: ¿Cómo puedo hacer las dos últimas oraciones más descriptivas aún (Adicionando más palabras descriptivas)

- Guide children in adding more descriptive words to each sentence. For example: *Hay roperos abiertos con ropas colgando y piezas de modelos de aviones sobre la mesa de trabajo. Hay una pecera en una esquina con pecesitos tropicales de colores.*
- Ask: **¿Qué oración podríamos añadir que nos hable de cómo te sientes en tu cuarto?** (*Accept reasonable responses.*) Add an appropriate sentence such as: ***Ésta es la mejor habitación que un niño podría tener.***

Have children read the completed sentences aloud and then copy them onto their papers.

On Your Own

Have children write descriptive sentences about the classroom. Remind them to use descriptive words.

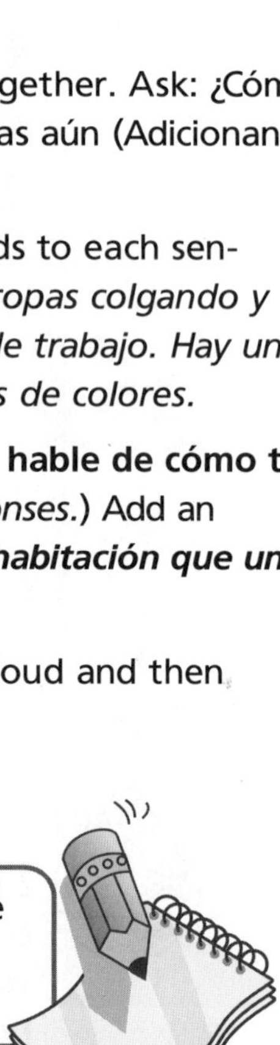

AFTER

Spelling Lesson
page 219H

Connect Spelling and Phonics

RETEACH **Consonant combination *ga, gue, gui, go, gu.*** Write the word *guitarra* on the board. Explain that you will say more words in which the *ga, gue, gui, go* is used. Have volunteers write each word on the board.

Show them objects, illustrations or photographs of such items as:

1. bigotuda*	**2. juguete***	**3. García***	**4. gata***
5. gustaban*	**6. aseguro**	**7. luego**	**8. recoger***

Word appears in *La promesa.

Dictate the following sentence and have children write it: *García compró juguetes que le gustaban a su gata bigotuda.*

Build and Read Longer Words

INTERVENTION ASSESSMENT BOOK ✓

Remind children that they have learned how to decode words with the diphthongs ia/au.

Write the word *juguetería* on the board. Tell children that they can sometimes figure out long words by looking for syllables, prefixes and suffixes. Cover *ría* and have a volunteer read the word *juguete*. Point out that juguete uses the combination gue. Follow similar procedure with these words: *recoger, desorganizar, agradecer e ingratitud*.

FLUENCY BUILDER Have children choose a passage from *La promesa* to read aloud to a partner. You may have children choose passages that they found particularly interesting, or have them choose one of the following options:

- Read pages 63–66. (From *Así que Bobi*... through ...*El insecto aterrizóen un avión; Bigotuda, también.* Total: 94 words.)
- Read pages 66–68. (From *¡Plasf! Los juguetes cayeron*... through ...*Es una promesa!* Total: 107 words.)

Children should read the selected passage aloud to their partners three times. Have the child rate each reading on a scale of 1 to 4.

BEFORE
Weekly Assessments

Review Vocabulary

To revisit Vocabulary Words prior to the weekly assessment, use these sentence frames. Have volunteers take turns reading aloud the sentence stems and choices. Children should identify the correct choice and explain why that choice makes sense in the sentence.

1. Sí, te **prometo** algo que yo
   a. puedo olvidarme de ello. **b.** tengo que cumplir.
2. Sam comenzó a **preocuparse**
   a. de que algo malo pudiera suceder. **b.** que iba a divertirse.
3. Los hombres usan la **grúa** para
   a. levantar cargas pesadas. **b.** hacer agujeros.
4. Cuando alguien empieza a **retorcerse** está
   a. contorsionándose. **b.** durmiendo.
5. Jeff lee las **instrucciones** para
   a. estornudar **b.** ensamblar un modelo de avión.

Correct responses: 1.b, 2.a, 3.a, 4.a, 5.b.

You may want to display the vocabulary words and definitions on page 79 and have children copy them to use when they study for the vocabulary test.

INTERVENTION PRACTICE BOOK
page 34

Focus Skill Review Predict Outcomes

To review predict outcomes before the weekly assessment, distribute *Intervention Practice Book* page 34. Have volunteers read aloud the first direction line and the paragraph. Guide children to look for clues as they read to help them predict the outcome.

Review Test Prep

Write on the board:

Mi tía Agatha grita cuando ve un gato.
¡Un día en mi casa un gato pasó por entre sus piernas! Tía Agatha
a. lo levantó en brazos.
b. lo acarició.
c. gritó.
d. dijo —qué gato más noble.

Para ti
page 225

INTERVENTION ASSESSMENT BOOK

Read the text and question aloud. Guide children to look for clues in the text to help them answer the question.

AFTER

Weekly Assessments

Self-Selected Reading

Have children select their own books to read independently. They might choose books from the classroom library shelf, or you may wish to offer a group of appropriate books from which children can choose.

- *Buscar animales* See page 225S of the *Teacher's Edition* for an Independent Reading Plan.
- *Todos mis juguetes* por Mary Blocksma. Children's Press, 1990.
- *Pipo y el oso* por Chris Riddell. Anaya. 1986.

After children have chosen their books, give each child a copy of *My Reading Log*, which can be found on page R35 in the back of the *Teacher's Edition*. Have children fill in the information at the top of the form. Then have them use the log to keep track of their reading and to record their responses to the literature.

Conduct student-teacher conferences. Arrange time for each child to conference with you individually about his or her self-selected reading. Have children bring their Reading Logs to share with you at the conference. Children might also like to share a favorite passage to read aloud to you. Ask questions designed to stimulate discussion about the book. For example, you might ask what the children learned about the characters in the stories or have them give a brief summary of the story.

FLUENCY PERFORMANCE Have children read aloud to you the passage from "The Promise" that they selected and practiced with their partners. Keep track of the number of words each child reads correctly. Ask the child to rate his or her own performance on the 1–4 scale. If children are not happy with their oral reading, give them an opportunity to continue practicing and then to reread the passage to you again.

See *Oral Reading Fluency Assessment* for monitoring progress.

LESSON 9

Use with

"El pastel de Erizo"

BEFORE

Building Background and Vocabulary

Review Phonics: Consonant combinations *tr*

Identify the sound. Write these words on the board and ask a volunteer to circle the syllables containing the letter blend *tr.* This sound is represented by the letters *tr* as in the words *trabajo* and *cuatro.* Write these words on the board and ask a volunteer to circle the letters *tr* which represent these sounds.

Associate letters to sound. Write on the board: *Una tropa de niños se subió al bus de la escuela.* Underline *tr* in *tropa.* Explain that these letters combinations stands for the consonant combinations *tr.* Write on the board the words *trenza, truco, cuatro.* Encourage volunteers to read these words. If it is necessary, explain or illustrate the meaning of each word. Ask children to write these words onto a sheet of paper.

Word blending. Explain to children that in some the sound /t/ blends with the sound /r/ to make the sound /tr/. Tell them this sound is written with the letters *tr* as in the words *trigo* and *tropa.*

INTERVENTION PRACTICE BOOK page 36

Apply the skill. *Letter substitution* Write the following words on the board and have children read each aloud. Make changes necessary to form the words in parantheses. Have a volunteer read aloud new word.

Tio (trío) **póster** (postre) **ten** (tren) **meto** (metro)
ente (entre)

Introduce Vocabulary

PRETEACH lesson vocabulary. Tell childrens that they are going to learn nine new words that they will see again when they read a story called *El pastel de Erizo.* Teach each vocabulary word using the following process.

Use the following suggestions or similar ideas to give the meaning or context.

Write the word.
Say the word.
Track the word and have children repeat it.
Give the meaning or context.

grumosa Point out phonic gr. It means grumous, lumpy.

hornear Point out letter h with no sound. It means bake, cook in the oven.

mantequilla Point out ll. It means butter, milk fat.

AFTER

Building Background and Vocabulary

rebanada	Point out that starting a word is only one r, inside it is two (rr). It means a slice a thin portion.
receta	Point out the word starting with one r. It means recipe set of instructions, or steps, used when cooking or baking.
tazón	Point out ending on meaning big or large. It means bowl a round, deep container used to hold liquids.

For vocabulary activities, see Vocabulary Games on pages 2–7.

Vocabulary Words

grumosa no lisa, con grumos

hornear cocinar en el horno

mantequilla grasa de la leche

rebanada porción delgada

receta conjunto de instrucciones o de pasos para hacer algo

tazón taza grande

Apply Vocabulary Strategies

Use Suffixes. Write the word *grumosa* on chart paper and underline the word *grumo* in one color and the suffix *osa* in another color. Tell children that they can sometimes figure out the meaning of a word by looking for word parts that they know.

MODEL **I already know what *grumo* is. So the word *grumosa* must mean "something that has lots of *grumos*" or "something that looks like having lots or the consistence of *grumos*." Guide children in using a similar procedure to figure out the meaning of *rebanada* and *hornear.***

RETEACH **lesson vocabulary.** Have children listen to each of the following sentences. Tell them to hold up the word card that completes each answer. Reread the sentence aloud with the correct word choice. Then discuss how the meaning of the vocabulary word fits the sentence.

1. Esta palabra comienza con la combinación *gr.* (*grumosa*)
2. Estas palabras tienen cuatro sílabas. (*mantequilla, rebanada*)
3. Esta palabra rima con *cometa.* (*receta*)
4. Esta palabra rima con *corazón.* (*tazón*)
5. Esta palabra comienza con la *h* muda. (*hornear*)

FLUENCY BUILDER Using *Intervention Practice Book* page 35, read each word in the first column aloud and have children repeat it. Then have partners read the words in the first column aloud to each other. Tell children to follow the same procedure with each of the remaining columns. After partners have practiced reading aloud the words in each column, have them practice the entire list. Save *Intervention Practice Book* page 35 to use on pages 91 and 93.

BEFORE

Reading *El pastel de Erizo* pages 228–245

USE SKILL CARD 9A

Focus Skill Synonyms

PRETEACH the skill. Explain that synonyms are words that have the same or almost the same meanings. Give the example of *triste* and *descontentol.* Discuss that knowing synonyms can help you better understand the meaning of words while reading.

Have children look at **side A** of **Skill Card 9: Synonyms.** Read the definition of synonyms. Next read the two sentences aloud. Point out that the two underlined words are synonyms. Now call attention to the exercise and have volunteers take turns reading the sentences aloud. Ask:

- **¿Cómo puedo imaginar el significado de cada palabra subrayada?** (*Possible response: Yo puedo usar las otras palabras en la oración como pista.*)
- **¿Cómo cada palabra subrayada está relacionada con la nueva palabra?** (*Possible response: Ellas son sinónima.*)
- **¿Por qué las oraciones mantienen siempre el mismo significado aún cuando se cambia la palabra subrayada?** (*Possible response: Porque la nueva palabra tiene siempre el mismo significado que la palabra subrayada.*)

Explain that one word in a synonym pair can have more meanings than the other. Give the example of *grande* and *gigante.*

Prepare to Read: *El pastel de Erizo*

Para ti
pages 228–245

Preview. Tell children that they are going to read a selection entitled *El pastel de Erizo.* Explain that this selection is a story that has made-up characters and events that happen in order (beginning, middle, end). Then preview the selection.

- **Pages 228–229:** Puedo ver el título: *El pastel de Erizo* y los nombres de los autores. Veo el dibujo de un Erizo.
- **Pages 230–231:** Veo un Erizo leyendo un libro de cocina. Se pone a buscar productos, cuando llega un conejo a su casa. Las páginas tienen texto.
- **Pages 232–233:** El conejo parece que ayuda pero deja caer un polvo blanco que creo es harina. El conejo vierte harina en un tazón.

AFTER

Reading ***El pastel de Erizo*** ***pages 228–245***

Reread and Summarize

Have children reread and summarize *El pastel de Erizo* in sections, as described below.

Pages 228–232

Vamos a releer otra vez las páginas 228–232 para recordar qué quería Erizo y quién le fue a visitar.

Summary: Erizo quería comer un pastel. Ya había sacado todos los productos que necesitaba y empezaba a leer la receta cuando que llegó de visita Conejo.

Pages 233–237

Releamos estas páginas para ver qué pasó después.

Summary: Conejo se puso a hacer el pastel pero no conseguía batir la masa. Se fue dejando Erizo batiendo la masa. Ardilla llegó, y anádió huevos al tazón con la masa. Ahora era un poco más fácil batir la masa.

Pages 238–242

Leamos otra vez para saber qué pasó en la cocina de Erizo y qué decidió él hacer.

Summary: Lechuza engrasó el molde. Ardilla y Lechuza se fueron. La casa estaba hecha un desastre. Erizo tiró la masa a la basura, cerró la puerta e hizo el pastel siguiendo la receta. Después limpió la cocina y llegó Conejo para comer el pastel.

Pages 243–247

Leamos en estas páginas para averiguar qué creían los amigos de Erizo.

Summary: Empezaron a comer el pastel. Los amigos de Erizo se creían que habían contribuído para hacer el pastel. Erizo les agradeció, con buenas maneras, pero les advirtió que lo haría solo la próxima vez.

FLUENCY BUILDER Use *Intervention Practice Book* page 35. Call attention to the sentences on the bottom half of the page. Tell children that their goal is to read each phrase or sentence smoothly. Model appropriate pace, expression and phrasing as you read each sentence and have children read it after you. Then have children practice by reading the sentences aloud three times to a partner.

BEFORE

Making Connections
pages 250–251

Directed Reading: *Muchos, muchos pastelitos,* pp. 70–75

Sonidos alegres pp. 70–75

Ask a volunteer to read aloud the title. Point out Conejo and Comadreja in the picture. Read aloud page 70 while children listen to find out what Conejo and Comadreja will do. Ask: **¿Por qué a Comadreja le encantan los pastelitos?** (Accept reasonable responses) **EXPRESS OPINIONS**

Page 71

Have a volunteer read aloud page 71 while children listen for what happened to the bowl. Ask: **¿Qué sinónimos uno puede usar para palabra se rompió?** (*Possible response: se partió*) Focus Strategy **SYNONYMS**

Pages 72–73

Read aloud page 72 while children listen for what happens when the batter is mixed. Model using the Make Inferences strategy.

> MODEL **Cuando leí que Comadreja añadió cosas a la masa, yo me pregunté por qué ella haría eso. Entonces me acordé que el cuento dice en la página 71 que ella sacó un tazón para Conejo. Sé que a mi también me gusta ayudar en la cocina, así creo que Comadreja también quería ayudar.** Focus Strategy **MAKE INFERENCES**

Discuss that readers can use what they learn from the text and what they already know to figure out things the author does not tell in the story. Have a volunteer read aloud page 73. Ask: **¿Por qué crees que Comadreja dijo que se había bañado en la masa?** (*Possible response: porque he leído en el texto que ella se había cubierto de masa.*)

Page 74

Read aloud page 74 while children listen to find out why the oven door is open. Ask: **¿Por qué la puerta del horno estaba un poquito abierta?** (*Possible response: para calentar también la masa de Comadreja.*) **CAUSE AND EFFECT**

Page 75

Have a volunteer read aloud page 75 while children listen to find out how Possum feels at the end. Ask: **¿Por qué Comadreja estaba feliz al final?** (*Possible response: Porque Conejo dijo que ella podría ser ahora una campeona en comer los pastelitos.*) **DRAW CONCLUSIONS**

INTERVENTION PRACTICE BOOK page 37

Summarize the selection. Ask children to focus on the most important events in the story.

AFTER

Skill Review
page 25 I I

USE SKILL CARD 9B

Answers to *Piénsalo* Questions

1. Hizo la masa de los pastelitos porque el tazón se rompió. **SUMMARIZE**
2. Porque sigue pensando que Conejo es el campeón de la cocina y ella no hace otra cosa que armar líos. **INTERPRET STORY EVENTS**
3. Las respuestas pueden variar. **WRITE AN INVITATION**

Focus Skill Synonyms

RETEACH the skill. Read the skill reminder with them. Then read aloud the directions. Have a volunteer read aloud the sentences and word choices. Explain that children will complete the exercise.

After children have finished, have them explain why their word choice makes sense. Explain that a word can have more than one synonym. Display children's papers in the classroom.

Review Phonics Skill from *El pastel de Erizo*

RETEACH Consonant Combination *tr.* Say aloud the following words while children listen for the *tr* sound: *trueno, trompa.* Then read aloud the following words and have children tell which word does not have the *tr* sound: *taco, trago, tipo, tropa, nuestro, trueno, atacó y trompa.*

FLUENCY BUILDER Use *Intervention Practice Book* page 35. Explain that today children will practice the sentences on the bottom half of the page by reading them aloud on tape. Assign new partners. Have children take turns reading the sentences aloud to each other and then reading them on tape.

BEFORE

Drafting a Story
Page 251A

Writing Process: Story

Build on prior knowledge. Tell children that they are going to talk about and write the beginning of a story. Display the following information:

> **Título:** ***La rana y el sapo fueron al parque acuático.***
>
> **Idea 1:** ***El sapo quería ir al parque acuático para montar en los aparatos.***
>
> **Idea 2:** ***La rana no cree que es una buena idea.***
>
> **Idea 3:** ***El sapo dijo que la rana le tenía miedo al agua.***

Construct the text. "Share the pen" with children. Guide them to use the ideas on the board to write the beginning of a story. For example:

El sapo quería ir al parque acuático. El quería montar en los aparatos. Un día invito a la rana para que fueran al parque acuático. La rana pensó que no era una buena idea. El sapo dijo que la rana le tenía miedo al agua.

Revisit the text. Go back and read the beginning of the story. Ask: **¿Cómo puedo contarle a los lectores que el sapo quiere montar en los aparatos?** (Inventa una razón y añadela a el cuento.)

- Guide children to revise the second sentence to tell why Toad wants to go on the rides. For example: *El quería montar en los aparatos porque creía que era muy excitante.*
- Ask: **¿Cómo puedo hacer saber al lector lo que se dijeron el sapo y la rana?** (*add dialogue*) For example: *El sapo le dijo a la rana: - Yo creo que mañana deberíamos ir al parque acuático.*
- Have children read the completed paragraph aloud and then copy it onto their papers.

On Your Own

Have children think of a character and write the beginning of a story about that character. Suggest that they think about what problem the character might face and solve.

AFTER

Spelling Lesson
Page 247H

Connect Spelling and Phonics

RETEACH **Consonant Combination *tr.*** Write the word tractor on the board. Explain that you will say tseven more words in which the combination tr is used. Have volunteers write each word on the board.

I. ***trozo***	2. ***tractor***	3. ***tratado***	4. ***tropa***
5. ***truco***	6. ***trabajo***	7. ***trigo***	8. ***triste***

Dictate the following sentence and have children write it: *El trabajo de recoger trigo también se hace con tractor.*

Build and Read Longer Words

Prepare the following syllable cards: *tran, qui, lo,* and arrange them in a pocket chart to form the word *tranquilo.* Ask children to read this word as you point to each syllable and then ask them to read the entire word at a normal speed. Repeat this process with the following syllable cards: *cen, tí, me, tro (centímetro), pu, pi, tre (pupitre), en, con, trar (encontrar), es, tre, nar (estrenar).* Once the children read each word, make sure they understand meaning. Ask the children to copy these words onto a sheet of paper.

FLUENCY BUILDER Have children choose a passage from *Muchos, muchos pastelitos* to read aloud to a partner. You may have childrens choose passages that they found interesting, or have them choose one of the following options:

- Read pages 72–75. (From *Conejo mezcló la masa . . .* through . . . *serás una campeona ayudándome a terminarlos.* Total: 94 words.)
- Read pages 70–72 (From *Comadreja estaba en la puerta . . .* through . . . *mezcló la masa con Conejo.* Total: 106 words.)

Encourage childrens to read their passages aloud to their partners three times. Have the child rate his or her own reading on a scale from 1 to 4.

SCALE	
1	Not so good
2	Pretty good
3	Good
4	Great!

BEFORE
Weekly Assessments

Review Vocabulary

To revisit vocabulary words prior to the weekly assessment, use these sentence frames. Have volunteers take turns reading aloud the sentence stems and choices. Children identify the correct choice and explain why that choice makes sense in the sentence.

1. Una cosa tienes que tener para hacer **pastelitos**
   a. yemas. b. maíz.
2. Puedes usar una **receta** para ayudarte a
   a. armar una tienda. b. hacer una tarta.
3. Una cosa que puedes **hornear** es
   a. leche. b. pollo.
4. La **mantequilla** además de usarla en el pastel también se unta
   a. en el pan. b. en los frijoles.
5. Me comí una **rebanada** de
   a. macarrón. b. pan.
6. La **masa** del pastel es
   a. espesa. b. fina.

Correct responses: 1.a, 2.b, 3.b, 4.b, 5.b, 6.a.

You may want to display the vocabulary words and definitions on page 89 and have children copy them to use when they study for the vocabulary test.

INTERVENTION PRACTICE BOOK
page 38

Focus Skill Review SYNONYMS

To review synonyms before the weekly assessment, distribute *Intervention Practice Book p. 38.* Have volunteers read aloud the first direction line and the sentences. Guide children to use the information in each sentence to help them understand the meaning of the underlined word.

Review Test Prep

Para ti
page 253

Ask children to turn to page 253 of the *Pupil Edition.* Call attention to the Tips for answering the test questions. Tell children that paying attention to these tips can help them answer not only the test questions but also other test questions like these.

INTERVENTION ASSESSMENT BOOK

Have children follow along as you read each test question and the tip that goes with it. Discuss that they should answer each question about the word in bold type.

Self-Selected Reading

Have children select their own books to read independently. They might choose books from the classroom library shelf, or you may wish to offer a group of appropriate books from which children can choose.

- *El mundo bajo el agua* See page 253O of the *Teacher's Edition* for a plan.
- *Un pasito...y otro pasito* por Tomie de Paola. Ekaré-Banco el Libro, 1993.
- *Sopa de piedras* por Marcia Brown. Lectorum, 1991.

After children have chosen their books, give each child a copy of *Mi diario de lectura,* which can be found on page R35 in the back of the *Teacher's Edition.* Have children fill in the information at the top of the form. Then have them use the log to keep track of their reading and to record their responses to the literature.

Conduct Student-Teacher Conferences Arrange time for each child to conference with you individually about his or her self-selected reading. Have children bring their *Diarios de lectura* to share with you at the conference. Children might also like to share a favorite passage to read aloud to you. Ask questions about the book designed to stimulate discussion. For example, you might ask what information the child learned from a nonfiction text, or how the pictures helped them understand a fiction story.

FLUENCY PERFORMANCE Have children read aloud to you the passage from *Muchos, muchos pastelitos* that they selected and practiced with their partners. Keep track of the number of words the child reads correctly. Ask the child to rate his or her own performance on the 1–4 scale. If children are not happy with their oral reading, give them an opportunity to continue practicing and then to reread the passage to you again.

See *Oral Reading Fluency Assessment* for monitoring progress.

LESSON 10

Use with

"Se vende limonada"

BEFORE

Building Background and Vocabulary

Review Phonics: Consonant combinations: *gl*, *gr*

Identify the sound. Tell children to listen for the consonant combinations *gl* and *gr* as you say the words *globo* and *negro.* Then have the children repeat the following sentences twice: *El niño tenía un globo rojo y otro negro.* Ask them to identify the words that have the combinations */gl/ gr* . (globo y inglés)

Associate letters to sound. Write on the board: *Apúntame en el globo un país donde hablen inglés. El pizarrón en nuestra escuela es negro.* Underline *gl* in *globo* and *inglés* and *gr* in *negro.* Explain that these letter combinations stand for the consonant combinations gl and gr.

Word blending. Model how to blend and read the word *globo* and *negro.* Slide your hand under the word as you elengate the sounds */ggloobbo/.* Then say the word naturally *globo.* Follow similar procedure with the word *negro.*

INTERVENTION PRACTICE BOOK

page 40

Apply the skill. *Letter substitution* Write the following words on the board and have children read each aloud. Make changes necessary to form the words in parentheses. Have a volunteer read aloud new word.

cabo (clabo)	**rega** (regla)	**nego** (negro)
gato (grato)	**gano** (grano)	**banca** (blanca)

Introduce Vocabulary

PRETEACH lesson vocabulary. Tell children that they are going to learn five new words that they will see again when they read a realistic fiction story called *Se vende limonada.* Teach each vocabulary word using the following process.

Write the word.

Say the word.

Track the word and have children repeat it.

Give the meaning or context.

Use the following suggestions or similar ideas to give the meaning or context.

anunció Point out the strong syllable with the stress. It means announced, made something known to many people.

llegó Point out ll and the strong syllable with stress. It means arrived.

tristes Point out the consonant combination *tr.* It means glum, gloomy; sad.

AFTER

Building Background and Vocabulary

miembros Point out that before *b* always use *m* and the combination *br* It means members, those who belong to a group

reconstruir Point out the prefix *re,* plus the combination *tr.* It means rebuild to make something again; build again.

For vocabulary activities, see Vocabulary Games on pages 2–7 (*Intervention Teachers Guide*).

Vocabulary Words

anunció dio a conocer algo a mucha gente

llegó vino

tristes afligidos, apenados, sombríos, descontentos

miembros los que pertenecen a un grupo

reconstruir volver a hacer

Apply Vocabulary Strategies

Use Synonyms. Write the words *triste* and *descontento* on chart paper and explain that these words are synonyms. Tell children that recognizing synonyms can help them figure out the meanings of words.

MODEL **Sé que sinónimos son palabras que tienen el mismo o casi el mismo significado. Si sé que *triste* y *descontento* son sinónimos, me será más facil recordar el signifiado de cada una de esas dos palabras.**

Guide children in a similar procedure to understand the meaning of *llegó* and *anunció.* Synonyms they could suggest are *vino* and *informó.*

RETEACH **lesson vocabulary.** Have children listen to each of the following sentences. Tell them to hold up the word card that completes each rhyme. Reread the sentence aloud with the correct word choice. Then discuss how the meaning of the vocabulary word fits the sentence.

1. Vera lloró cuando el regalo de su cumplaños *(llegó)*.
2. —Hoy no va a llover *(anunció)* la televisión.
3. La casita del perro se rompió, la tuvimos que *(reconstruir)*.
4. Luis sabía que su amigo estaba descontento y *(triste)*.
5. —Hemos tocado siempre con la misma banda —dijeron sus *(miembros)*.

FLUENCY BUILDER Using *Intervention Practice Book* page 39, read aloud each word in the first column and have children repeat it. Then have children work in pairs to read the words in the first column aloud to each other. Follow the same procedure with each of the remaining columns. After partners have practiced reading aloud the words in each separate column, have them practice the entire list. Save *Intervention Practice Book* page 39 for use on pages 101 and 103.

BEFORE

Reading *Se vende limonada* pages 256–274

(Focus Skill) COMPARE AND CONTRAST

PRETEACH the skill. Explain to children that when you compare things you tell how they are the same and when you contrast things you tell how they are different. For example: two children may be alike because they are girls and different because one has a dog and the other has a cat. Discuss why it helps readers to compare and contrast as they read.

USE SKILL CARD 10A

Have children look at **side A** of **Skill Card 10: Compare and Contrast.** Read the definition of compare and contrast. Next, read the paragraphs aloud and then have children reread them with you. Ask:

- **¿Cómo sabes que Jeremy y Fred tienen la misma edad?** (*Possible response: porque los párrafos lo dicen.*)
- **¿Cómo sabes que a Jeremy y Fred les gustan distintos deportes?** (*Possible response: porque el primer párrafo dice que a Jeremy le gustael fútbol americano y a Fred le gusta el fútbol.*)
- **¿Por qué estan *12 de años de edad* y *tiene un perro* en el círculo del medio?** (*Possible response: Porque esas son las dos cosas en que se parecen Jeremy y Fred.*)

Explain that when we compare and contrast characters in different stories, it helps us to understand both characters better.

Prepare to Read: *Se vende limonada*

Para ti pages 256–274

Preview. Tell children that they are going to read a selection entitled *Se vende limonada* Explain that it is realistic fiction. The people and places seem real, but the story is made-up. Then preview the selection.

- **Pages 256–257:** Puedo ver el título: *Se vende limonada* y los nombres de los autores. En la página 257 veo niños en una hamaca que creo son los personajes del cuento.
- **Pages 258–259:** Veo el dibujo de una casa en un árbol. Veo dos niños conversando uno en las escaleras de la entrada de una casa, el otro sentado en una hamaca con un cofre en las manos. Las dos páginas tienen texto.
- **Pages 260–261:** Veo a una niña en la página 261 escribiendo en una gráfica de barras.
- **Pages 262–263:** En la página 262, veo un puesto con un cartel que dice limonada a 25 centavos. Creo que los niños están vendiendo limonada para ganar dinero para su club. En la página 63, veo los días de la samana en un gráfico de barras. Creo que ellos van a registrar cuánto dinero ganan por día.

AFTER

Reading ***Se vende limonada pages 256–274***

Reread and Summarize

Have children reread and summarize *Se vende limonada* in sections, as described below.

Pages 256–260

Vamos a releer otra vez las páginas 256–260 para saber qué idea importante tuvieron los niños.

Summary: Los niños decidieron vender limonada para arreglar su club.

Pages 261–265

Ahora vamos a releer estas páginas para ver cómo les marchará su nuevo negocio.

Summary: Shery apuntaba en una gráfica de barras las ventas que hacían en el día. Las ventas aumentaban.

Pages 266–270

Mientras leemos otra vez estas páginas intentamos descubrir que sucedió de malo el jueves.

Summary: Las ventas subieron hasta el miércoles, pero el jueves nadie vino a comprar. Mathew descubrió que un malabarista atraía la atención del vecindario.

Pages 271–275

Vamos a releer las páginas 271–275 para recordar que solución encontraron los niños.

Sumamry: Los niños invitaron al malabarista para que hiciera su acto junto al puesto de limonada. Las ventas subieron otra vez y ya pudieron reconstruir el club, que ahora también tenía al malabarista como nuevo miembro.

FLUENCY BUILDER Use *Intervention Practice Book* page 39. Call attention to the sentences on the bottom half of the page. Tell children that their goal is to read each phrase or sentence smoothly. Model appropriate pace, expression and phrasing as you read each sentence and have children read it after you. Then have children practice by reading the sentences aloud three times to a partner.

BEFORE
Making Connections
pages 278–279

Directed Reading of *Una sorpresa de limonada*

Sonidos alegres
pages 78–84

Ask a volunteer to read aloud the title. Explain that children will find out what the surprise is as they read the story. Read page 78 aloud while children listen to find out why Barb is glum. Ask: **¿Por qué Bárbara está triste?** (*Possible response: Ella se ha mudado y extraña a sus amigos.*) **IDENTIFY CHARACTERS' EMOTIONS/ DRAW CONCLUSIONS**

Page 80

Read aloud the first two words on page 80 while children listen. Write the word *añadió* on the board. Model using the Read Ahead strategy to find the meaning for this word.

> MODEL **No estoy seguro qué quiere decir la palabra *añadió.* Voy a leer el resto de la oración para que pueda entender lo que quiere decir. Dice que Carmen añadió que no la pudieron reconstruir. Así se que *añadió* quiere decir contar otra cosa a más.** Focus Strategy **READ AHEAD**

Discuss how reading ahead can help readers figure out the meaning of a difficult word. Have a volunteer read aloud the word *reconstruir* on page 80. Then have them finish reading the sentence. Ask: **¿Cómo leer que los miembros del club no tienen dinero, me ayuda a entender lo que quiere decir el autor con la palabra *reconstruir*?** (*Possible response: Si necesitan dinero para hacer algo con la casa que se cayó, con seguridad debe ser para levantar la casa que se cayó, hacerla de nuevo. Así que* reconstruir *debe querer decir hacer algo de nuevo, construir de nuevo.*)

Pages 80–81

Have a volunteer read these pages aloud while children listen to find out what problem Mark, Kim, and Karl have. Ask: **¿Qué podemos notar hasta ahora que tienen de común este cuento y *Se vende limonada?*** (*Possible responses: Los niños tienen una casa club que tiene que ser reconstruida pero no tienen dinero suficiente para hacerlo. En ambos cuentos los niños venden limonada para ganar dinero.*) Focus Skill **COMPARE AND CONTRAST**

Pages 82–83

Ask a volunteer to read aloud page 82 while children listen to find out how the club members got started. Ask: **¿Qué están haciendo Carlos y Carmen?** (*Possible response: montando un puesto*) **NOTE DETAILS**

Page 84

Read aloud page 84 while children listen to find out how the story ends. Ask: **¿Cómo se siente Bárbara al final? ¿Por qué?** (*Possible response: Ella está feliz porque es una amiga y todos los amigos son miembros del club.*) **INTERPRET STORY EVENTS**

Summarize the selection. Ask children to focus on the most important events in the story. Then have them complete *Intervention Practice Book* page 41.

INTERVENTION PRACTICE BOOK
page 41

Answers to *Piénsalo* Questions

1. Les ofreció limonada. **SUMMARIZE**
2. Porque le dice a su mamá que está extrañando a sus amigos. **INTERPRET STORY EVENTS**
3. Accept reasonable responses. **TASK**

AFTER

Skill Review
page 281C

USE SKILL CARD 10B

Focus Skill Review Compare and Contrast

RETEACH the skill. Have children look at **side B** of **Skill Card 10: Compare and Contrast.** Read the skill reminder aloud with them and have a volunteer read the paragraphs aloud.

Read the next set of directions. Explain that children will work with partners to create their own diagrams. Remind them to reread both paragraphs to find out how the settings are alike and how they are different.

After children have completed their compare and contrast diagrams, have them display and explain their work. Point out that *Una sorpresa de limonada* has a plot that is quite like the plot in *Se vende limonada.*

Focus Skill Review Phonics Skill from *Se vende limonada*

RETEACH Consonant combinations: *gl, gr.* Write this sentence on the board: *Gregorio el glotón llevaba una camisa negra.* Read the sentence aloud. Have volunteers point to the words with the ***/gl/gr*** sound. Then read the following list aloud and have children raise their hands when they hear the */gl/ /gr/* sound: *grande, bola, glosario, carga, griego, iglesia.*

FLUENCY BUILDER Use *Intervention Practice Book* page 39. Explain that today children will practice the sentences on the bottom half of the page by reading them aloud on tape. Assign new partners. Have children take turns reading the sentences aloud to each other and then reading them on tape.

BEFORE

Drafting a Good Ending
Page 281G

Writing: Good Endings

Build on prior knowledge. Tell children that they are going to talk about and write a good ending for a story. Display the following:

Era el primer día de Bret en su escuela nueva. Él extrañaba a sus amigos. En el receso para la merienda él se quedó sólo. Él miraba los otros niños jugando al béisbol. Uno de los niños pegó con tanta fuerza a la bola que sin querer la rebotó en Bret.

Construct the text. "Share the pen" with children. Help them get ideas for a good ending to the story. Write the ideas on the board in the order they might happen in the story. For example:

- Bret agarra la bola
- Bret se la devuelve a los niños
- Los niños le invitan a jugar co ellos
- Bret está feliz

Revisit the text. Go back and read the ideas together. Ask: **¿Cómo puedo usar estas ideas para escribir un buen final?** (*ordénalas en oraciones*)

- Guide children into combining the ideas into sentences. For example: *Bret agarró la bola y se la tiro otra vez a los niños. Los niños invitaron a Bret para que se uniera a ellos. Bret está feliz.*
- Ask: **¿Qué otra cosa podemos escribir para mostrar por qué Bret está feliz?** (*porque el econtró nuevos amigos*) Make the appropriate change.
- Have children read the paragraph aloud with the ending. Have them copy the paragraph onto their own papers.

On Your Own

Have children write a new ending for *Una sorpresa de limonada.* Remind them that a good ending shows how the problem was solved.

AFTER

Spelling Lesson
Page 275H

Connect Spelling and Phonics

RETEACH **Consonant Combination *gr/gl.*** Write the word *gracias* on the board. Explain that you will say two more words in which the combination gr is used. Have volunteers write each word on the board. Then write the word *iglesia* on he board, explain that you will say two words in which the diphthong *ia* is used, and repeat the process.

1. grillo	**2. globo**	**3. iglesia**	**4. gritaron***
5. tigre	**6. gracias***	**7. alegró***	**8. blanca**

*** Word appears in *Una sorpresa de limonada.***

Dictate the following sentence and have children write it: *El grillo negro no tenía miedo del tigre grande.*

Build and Read Longer Words

Remind students that they have learned how to decode words with the combinations *gl/gr.*

Write the word *englobar* on the board. Tell children that they can sometimes figure out long words by looking for syllables, prefixes and suffixes. Cover *en* and have a volunteer read the word *globar.* Then cover *r* and have a volunteer read the word *globa.* Point out that *globa* uses the combination *gl.*

FLUENCY BUILDER Have children choose a passage from *Una sorpresa de limonada* to read aloud to a partner. You may have students choose passages that they found interesting, or have them choose one of the following options:

- Read pages 78–80. (From *Bárbara estaba…* through *…Se cayó.* Total: 95 words)
- Read pages 81–83. (From *Lo siento dijo Bárbara…* through *…podemos reconstruir la casa.* Total: 94 words)

Encourage students to read their passages aloud to their partners three times. Have children rate each of their own readings on a scale from 1 to 4.

BEFORE

Weekly Assessments

Review Vocabulary

To revisit vocabulary words prior to the weekly assessment, use these sentence frames. Have volunteers take turns reading aloud the sentence stems and choices. Children identify the correct choice and explain why that choice makes sense in the sentence.

1. Si tía Vera **llegó** a las 6 de la tarde, ella probablemente
   a. ya está en su casa. **b.** recibió un telefonema.
2. Si tenemos que **reconstruir** un Castillo de arena, él probablemente
   a. duró para siempre. **b.** se cayó.
3. Alguién que está **triste** puede estar
   a. llorando. **b.** cantando.
4. Uno de los **miembros** de su familia es
   a. su hermana. **b.** su bicicleta.
5. Si Sally **anunció** sus planes, ella probablemente quería que
   a. nadie se enterase. **b.** todos lo supieran.

Correct responses: 1.a, 2.b, 3.a, 4.a, 5.b.

You may want to display the vocabulary words and definitions on page 99 and have children copy them to use when they study for the vocabulary test.

INTERVENTION PRACTICE BOOK
page 42

Focus Skill Review Compare and Contrast

To review compare and contrast before the weekly assessment, distribute *Intervention Practice Book* page 42. Have volunteers read aloud the first direction line and the two stories. Guide children to reread the stories before filling in the graphic organizer.

Review Test Prep

Write on the board:

Jeff y Len eran amigos. Ambos tenían mascotas. Jeff tiene un gato, y Len tiene un periquito.

¿Qué respuesta hablan del parecido entre Jeff y Len?

- **Jeff tiene un gato y Len un periquito.**
- **A Jeff le gusta ciencias y a Len le gusta matemá ticas.**
- **Jeff y Len eran amigos.**

INTERVENTION ASSESSMENT BOOK

(*Jeff tiene un gato y Len un periquito*)
Read the text and question aloud. Help children look for clues in the text to answer the question. Tell children that when they take any test to be sure they understand the question before trying to choose an answer.

Self-Selected Reading

Have children select their own books to read independently. They might choose books from the classroom library shelf, or you may wish to offer a group of appropriate books such as the following from which children can choose.

- *A veces solo, a veces con amigos.* See page 281S of the *Teacher's Edition* for an Independent Reading Plan.
- *Mi calle* por Isidoro Sánchez. Parramón Ediciones, 1988.
- *El gran negocio de Franicisca* por Lillian Hoban. HarperCollins, 1996.

After children have chosen their books, give each child a copy of *Mi diario de lectura*, which can be found on page R35 in the back of the *Teacher's Edition.* Have children fill in the information at the top of the form. Then have them use the log to keep track of their reading and to record their responses to the literature.

Conduct student-teacher conferences. Arrange time for each child to conference with you individually about his or her self-selected reading. Have children bring their *Diarios de lectura* to share with you at the conference. Children might also like to choose a favorite passage to read aloud to you. Ask questions designed to stimulate discussion about the book. For example, ask how a favorite character in the book compares or contrasts with a character in *Una sorpresa de limonada.*

FLUENCY PERFORMANCE Have children read aloud to you the passage from *Una sorpresa de limonada* that they selected and practiced with their partners. Keep track of the number of words each child reads correctly. Ask the child to rate his or her own performance on the 1–4 scale. If children are not happy with their oral reading, give them an opportunity to continue practicing and then to reread the passage to you again.

See *Oral Reading Fluency Assessment* for monitoring progress.

LESSON 11

BEFORE

Building Background and Vocabulary

Use with

"Johnny Appleseed"

Review Phonics: Consonants with vowels: *ca, que, qui, co, cu*

Identify the sound. Have the children to listen closely for and distinguish the *ca* and *que* sounds when you pronounce the words *vaca* and *queso.* Say the following sentence and have them repeat it twice: *Me quedo aquí porque nadie está en casa.* Have them identify the words that have the /ka/ and /ke/ sounds. (*quedo, que, casa*)

Associate letters to sound. Write the following sentence on the board: *El chico quiere montar el caballo.* Underline -co (chico), qui- (quiere), and -ca (caballo) to explain that these letter combinations correspond to /ko/, /ke/, and /ka/ respectively.

Word blending. Demonstrate for the children how to blend the sounds in the underlined words in the previous sentence. Stress the particular sounds with exaggerated mouth movements as you reread the sentence.

INTERVENTION PRACTICE BOOK page 44

Apply the skill. The following words should be written on the board as the students pronounce each aloud. Then, make the appropriate changes on the board to create the word in parentheses. Ask for volunteers to pronounce the new words:

luna (cuna)	**sobrar** (cobrar)	**faldo** (caldo)	**hueso** (queso)
piso (quiso)	**rito** (chico)	**tone** (toque)	**Lara** (cara)

Introduce Vocabulary

PRETEACH lesson vocabulary. Tell children that they are going to learn six new words that they will see again when they read the play *Johnny Appleseed.*

Write the word.

Say the word.

Track the word and have children repeat it.

Give the meaning or context.

Use the following suggestions or similar ideas to give the meaning or context:

frontera: Relate this word to the United States and mention that the border of the US touches two other countries: *Las fronteras de los EE.UU. tocan dos países: Canadá y México.*

cacerola: Give synonyms: *olla, pote para cocinar.* Ask your students *¿Qué puedes cocinar en una cacerola?* Point out the sound *ca-* (/ka/).

hortalizas: Focus on pronunciation and ask children *¿Cuáles son las hortalizas favoritas tuyas?*

sobrevivir:	Separate the word into its two compound parts and ask for volunteers to define each (*sobre* and *vivir*) in order to figure out the meaning.
domar:	Act out the verb by making messy hair neat or by being excited and calming youreself down.
salvaje:	Give examples of animals in the wild (*elefantes, leones, monos*) and where they live (*various parts of Africa, ...*)

For vocabulary activities, see Vocabulary Games on pages 2–7.

AFTER
Building Background and Vocabulary

Apply Vocabulary Strategies

Recognizing parts of words. Write the word *"sobrevivir"* on the board. Ask a student to separate the word into two distinct parts and have her/him explain why she/he divided it this way. Ask for other examples of compound words. If the children are having troubles, help guide them by giving hints or various words and have them combine them.

MODEL **Yo dividiría *sobrevivir* en dos partes: *sobre* y *vivir* que son palabras solas. Otras palabras como ésta son *maltratar* y *menospreciar.***

RETEACH **lesson vocabulary.** Read aloud each of the following words and have the children hold up the word card that is the given word's closest synonym. Reread each pair aloud with the correct word choice and explain why this word fits best.

1. olla: __________ (*cacerola*)
2. vegetales, legumbres: __________ (*hortalizas*)
3. borde de un país: __________ (*frontera*)
4. controlar: __________ (*domar*)
5. la selva: __________ (*salvaje*)
6. estar vivo: __________ (*sobrevivir*)

FLUENCY BUILDER Use *Intervention Practice Book* page 43. Read each word in the first column aloud and have children repeat it. Then have children work in pairs to read the words in the first column aloud to each other. Follow the same procedure with each of the remaining columns. After partners have practiced reading aloud the words in each column separately, have them practice the entire list.

Save *Intervention Practice Book* page 43 to use on pages 111 and 113.

BEFORE

Reading *Johnny Appleseed* pages 286–304

USE SKILL CARD 11A

Focus Skill Details

PRETEACH the skill. Point out to children that details help give information about the main idea or topic of a sentence or story. Discuss how details help readers picture things in their minds and understand things better.

Have children look at **side A** of **Skill Card 11: Details.** Read the explanation of details. Next, read the paragraph and have children reread it with you.

Call attention to the web and ask children to give details about the topic. Ask:

- **¿Qué ocurriría si la mamá hiciera un pastel con pasas en vez de manzanas?** (*Possible response: Los detalles serían diferentes.*)
- **¿Qué pasaría si el cuento dijera que la mamá solamente estaba cocinando? Quedaría claro que ella estaba cocinando un pastel?** (*Possible response: No, la mamá podría estar cocinando cualquier cosa porque no hay un detalle que diga que ella está cocinando un pastel.*)

Prepare to Read: *Johnny Appleseed*

Preview. Tell children that they are going to read a selection entitled *Johnny Appleseed.* Explain that this selection is a play, or a story that can be acted out. Tell children that *Johnny Appleseed* tells about a true American hero named John Chapman. Then preview the selection.

Para ti
pages 286–304

- **Page 286:** Yo veo a todos los personajes de la obra de teatro y, a la izquierda, se explica qué significa una obra de teatro y cosas que hay que buscar mientras la leo.
- **Page 287:** Leo el título con los autores. Es el primer acto y dice la época y dónde ocurre. Me doy cuenta que ocurrió hace mucho tiempo. Veo un personaje con una manzana, que debe ser de Johnny.
- **Pages 288–289:** Hablan el narrador y el coro y hay unos dibujos del coro. Creo que hay mucha gente en el coro.
- **Pages 290–295:** Me parece que Johnny es más viejo. Lleva ropas muy graciosa. Me parece que está disfrutando su aventura y está conociendo a mucha gente durante su recorrido.

Set Purpose. Model setting a purpose for reading *Johnny Appleseed.*

MODEL **Por lo que he visto, creo que voy a leer sobre las aventuras de Johnny Appleseed que se refieren a la vida de John Chapman. Voy a leer para averiguar por qué le llamaban Johnny Appleseed.**

AFTER

Reading *Johnny Appleseed* pages 286–304

Reread and Summarize

Have children reread and summarize Johnny Appleseed in sections, as described below.

Pages 287–289

Vamos a revisar las páginas 287–289 para enterarnos por qué Johnny Appleseed quiere mudarse al oeste y plantar semillas de manzana.

Summary: Johnny Appleseed hace lo mismo que hicieron sus vecinos: irse al Oeste. Él siembra semillas de manzana para que todos puedan comer manzanas cada vez que lo deseen.

Pages 290–295

Vamos a revisar las páginas 290–295 para saber por qué la Familia de la frontera le hace tantas preguntas a Johnny.

Summary: La familia está sorprendida de que Johnny haya vivido al aire libre tanto tiempo y no le haya temido al frío y a la soledad.

Pages 296–299

Vamos a revisar las páginas 296–299 para ver a dónde va la Familia y porqué.

Summary: La Familia de la frontera regresa a la carreta porque los hijos tienen miedo de los osos aunque sean amigos de Johnny.

Pages 300–304

Vamos a revisar las páginas 300–304, el segundo acto. Johnny ya tiene 70 años. ¿Por qué es un heróe?

Summary: Johnny fue un pionero que se sentía feliz plantando manzanos para todos los que llegaban al oeste.

FLUENCY BUILDER Be sure children have copies of *Intervention Practice Book* page 43, which you used for the previous Fluency Builder activity. Call attention to the sentences on the bottom half of the page. The slashes break the sentences into phrases to allow you to work on phrasing. Tell children that their goal is to read each phrase or sentence smoothly. Model appropriate pace, expression and phrasing as you read each sentence. Then have children read it after you. Have children practice reading the sentences aloud three times to a partner.

BEFORE

Making Connections
pages 308–309

Directed Reading of *Ana y sus muñecas de manzana*

Sonidos alegres
pages 86–92

***Ana y sus muñecas de manzana* page 86–93** Ask your children to volunteer to read the title of the story aloud. Read pages 86–87 aloud while the children listen to figure out the setting. Ask: **¿Cuáles son las palabras que indican que Ana y la Mamá están preparando la comida?** (*Possible responses: hortalizas, cacerola, cesta, manzanas*) **LITERARY ANALYSIS**

Ask: **¿Porqué Ana exclama al principio "¡Mamá!"?** (*Possible responses: Ana está emocionada por salir a jugar afuera, para ver a sus amigos. El tono de su voz nos dice eso.*) Focus Skill **RECOGNIZING IMPORTANT DETAILS**

Pages 88–89

Help the children read pages 88–89 to find out more about Ana and her family. Ask them: **¿Por qué se burlan los chicos de Ana?** (*Possible response: Ella es su hermana menor.*) **MAIN IDEA**

Encourage volunteers to read aloud. Choose one of the children to read page 89, the first 9 lines (through Jorge).

> MODEL **Cuando yo oía esta sección, no sabía si Carlos, Enrique, y Miguel estaban gritando a Ana o si iban a meterle miedo. Pero, pensé en mis hermanos mayores y cómo se burlan de mí de vez en cuando.** Focus Strategy **CREATE MENTAL IMAGES**

Invite other students to give their percepcions of the reading. Ask for another volunteer to read the rest of page 89. Ask: **¿A dónde va Ana y cómo va a hacer lo que dice?** (*Possible response: Cuando Ana respondió que iba a recoger manzanas, pensé en de donde vienen las manzanas y después pude entender mejor lo que ella intentaba a hacer.*) **IMPORTANT DETAILS**

Pages 90–91

Guide the children to read pages 90–91 to find out what Ana does with one of the apples that Jorge picks for her. Ask: **¿Qué hace Ana con una de las manzanas que Jorge le dio?** (*Possible response: Ana la convierte en una muñeca con ojos de semillas.*) **DRAW CONCLUSIONS**

Conclude by inviting the children to finish the story, page 92. Ask: **¿Por qué toda la familia está tan alegre con Ana?** (*Possible response: ¡La familia le da a Ana su apoyo por su creatividad en crear una muñeca de una manzana!*) **MAIN IDEA**

INTERVENTION PRACTICE BOOK
page 45

AFTER

Skill Review
pages 285A

USE SKILL CARD 11B

Summarize the selection. Ask children to think about what happened first, next, and last in *Ana y sus muñecas de manzana*.

Answers to *Think About It* Questions

1. Ana hizo su muñeca de una manzana con ojos de semillas. **SUMMARY**
2. Carlos, Enrique, y Miguel se burlaron de Ana antes de hacer su muñeca porque es la hermana menor y es muy joven. **INTERPRETATION**
3. Accept various and reasonable responses. **TASKS**

Focus Skill Details

RETEACH the skill. Have children look at **side B** of **Skill Card 11: Details**. Read the skill reminder with them, and have a volunteer read the paragraph aloud.

Read aloud the set of directions. Explain that children will work with partners to create their own detail web. When they have completed their webs, have them explain and display their work.

Focus Skill Phonics Skill: *ca, que*

RETEACH the skill. Read aloud the following sentence and have them listen for the *ca* and *que* sounds: *Anica llora porque no hay más queso en casa.* Then read the sentence aloud slowly, pausing after each word. Direct children to stand after each word if they hear the /ka/ and /ke/ sounds.

FLUENCY BUILDER Be sure that children have copies of *Intervention Practice Book* page 43. Explain that today children will practice the sentences on the bottom half of the page by reading them aloud on tape. Assign new partners. Have children take turns reading the sentences aloud to each other and then reading them on tape.

INTERVENTION PRACTICE BOOK
page 43

BEFORE

Drafting an Informative Paragraph
Page 311G

Writer's Craft: Giving Facts and Reasons

Build on prior knowledge. Tell children that they are going to talk and write about giving detailed information about something. Discuss that when you inform someone about something, you want to include facts and reasons so that your sentence is clear. Guide children to see that a good informative sentence should include a clear topic or main idea. Display and read aloud the following list:

Sentence Topic: Un lobo.

Detail 1: Un lobo se parece a un perro.

Detail 2: Un lobo no está domesticado.

Detail 3: Un lobo no sería un animal doméstico muy bueno.

Construct the text. "Share the pen" with children. Guide them in writing an informative sentence based on the topic *Un lobo* and the list of details. For example:

- *Un lobo se parece a un perro, pero no sería un animal doméstico muy bueno.*

Revisit the text. Go back and read the informative sentence. Ask: **Si no tuviera yo los detalles, ¿que ocurriria con mi frase?** (*No te da información clara.*) Ask: **¿Dónde puedo añadir otro detalle para hacerla más interesante?** (*Responses will vary.*)

Have children read the completed informative sentence aloud and then copy it on their papers.

On Your Own

Have children choose a favorite weekend hobby or activity and write an informative sentence about it. Ask them to take turns reading their sentences to a partner, checking to see if the details and meaning are clear. Then have them revise their sentences as needed and share them aloud with the class.

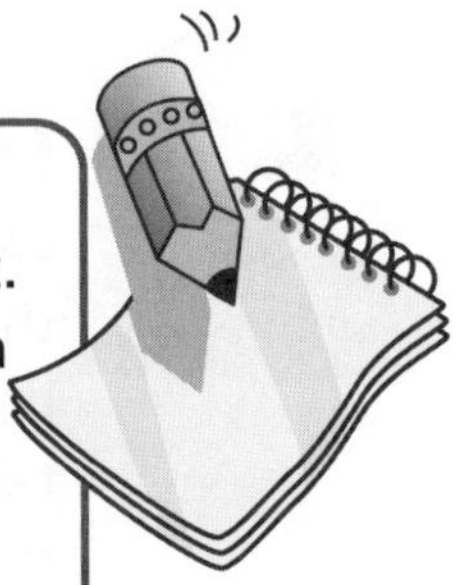

AFTER

Spelling Lesson
page 305H

Connect Spelling and Phonics

RETEACH Combination of consonant with vowel: *ca que, qui, co, cu*
Begin by writing the word *queso* on the blackboard. Explain to the class that you will give them one more word with the combination of consonant + vowel: *que (bosque).* Invite volunteers to the board to write the words you say on the board. Repeat the process with *ca, qui, co, cu* using the following words:

1. cabaña*	**2. encuentra***	**3. recoger***	**4. quien***
5. oscuro*	**6. muñeca***	**7. tranquila***	**8. querer***
9. cueva	**10. cuidado***	**11. gráfica**	

*** Word appears in *Solos tú y yo.***

Ask the children to write the following sentence as you dictate it aloud to them: *Necesitas cocinar queso aquí en la cueva.*

Build and Read Longer Words

Comment to the children to remind them that they have learned how to distinguish between many sounds made with the consonant + vowel combination: *ca, que, qui, co, cu.*

Write the word *cualquiera* on the board. Tell the children that they can figure out meanings of words by looking at its parts. If you cover *cual* in front of the class, invite a student to read what is not covered: *quiera.* Do the same by covering *quiera.* Here are two words forming one. Can they figure out what the word *cualquiera* means? Repeat the process with more compound words that have the consonant + vowel combinations studied in this lesson. (*Possible choices: cuatrocientos, cortaplumas, casamentero, quitanieves*)

FLUENCY BUILDER Ask for volunteers to play the parts of every character in *Ana y sus muñecas de manzana.* Have them take their parts and read the play outloud. Divide the reading up into sections and switch roles. Encourage participation by all by alternating roles and parts.

- Read pages 87–89. (From *Mama!*... through ...*Esperen y verán.* Total: 110 words.)
- Read page 91. (From *Estos árboles*... through ...*Le gustarás a la familia!* Total: 109 words.)

Children should read the selected passage aloud to their partners three times. Have the child rate each reading on a scale from 1 to 4.

BEFORE
Weekly Assessments

Review Vocabulary

To revisit Vocabulary Words prior to the weekly assessment, use these sentence frames. Have volunteers take turns reading aloud the sentence frames and answer choices. children identify the correct choice and explain why that choice makes sense in the sentence.

1. Un animal **salvaje** debe mantenerse en
   a. una jaula   **b.** en la cocina
2. Una **frontera** divide a
   a. dos ríos   **b.** dos países
3. Para **sobrevivir**, tu cuerpo tiene que tener
   a. agua   **b.** leche
4. Para **domar** una fiera hay que
   a. ser pintor   **b.** ser domador
5. La **cacerola** se usa para cocinar
   a. ladrillos   **b.** patatas
6. Las **hortalizas** son
   a. animales   **b.** vegetales

Correct responses: 1.a, 2.b, 3.a, 4.a, 5.b, 6.b.

If the above are read aloud, you may want to review them a second time so that the children may write them in a notebook prior to the assessment.

INTERVENTION PRACTICE BOOK
page 46

Focus Skill Recognizing Important Details

Before the weekly assessment, review this skill by distributing *Intervention Practice Book* page 46. Have volunteers read aloud the first directionline and the sentences. Guide the children to list as many details as they can by asking questions such as: **Si este detalle no estuviera aquí, ¿cambiaria el cuento? ¿Para qué existe este detalle aqui?**

Review Test Prep

Have children turn to page 311 of the *Student Edition.* Guide the children through the tips for answering the test questions. Help them understand the purpose of the tips and that they will assist them in answering test questions such as these on this test as well as others.

Para ti
pages 310–311

Have the children read along as you read each test question aloud and the tip that goes along with it. Discuss all of the details in each.

INTERVENTION ASSESSMENT BOOK

Self-Selected Reading

Have children select their own books to read independently. They might choose books from the classroom library shelf, or you may wish to offer a group of appropriate books from which children can choose.

- *La casa en el árbol* see page 31 IS of the *Teacher's Edition* for the Independent Reading Plan.
- *Un libro ilustrado sobre Martin Luther King,* por David A. Adler. Holiday House, 1992.
- *El alfabeto a toda vela.* Aims International, 1989.

After children have chosen their books, give each child a copy of *Mi diario de lectura*, which can be found on page R35 in the back of the *Teacher's Edition.* Have children fill in the information at the top of the form. Then have them use the log to keep track of their reading and to record their responses to the literature.

Conduct student-teacher conferences. Arrange time for each child to conference with you individually about his or her self-selected reading. Have children bring their Reading Logs to share with you at the conference. Children might also like to share a favorite passage to read aloud to you. Ask questions about the book designed to stimulate discussion. For example, you might ask why the book is a folk tale, and if there are any similarities between the story and information learned in *Johnny Appleseed.*

FLUENCY PERFORMANCE Have children read aloud to you the passage from *Ana y sus munecas de manzana* that they selected and practiced with their partners. Keep track of the number of words the child reads correctly. Ask the child to rate his or her own performance on the 1–4 scale. If children are not happy with their oral reading, give them an opportunity to continue practicing and then to reread the passage to you again.

See *Oral Reading Fluency Assessment* for monitoring progress.

LESSON 12

BEFORE

Building Background and Vocabulary

Use with

"De semilla a planta"

Review Phonics: Combination of Consonants: *pl, pr*

Identify the sound. Lead the children by instructing them to listen for the combination of consonants *pl* and *pr* in the words *playa* and *probar*. Teach them the following sentence and have them repeat it twice: *Usaba una pluma para escribir su prosa.* Can they identify the words that have these *pl* and *pr* sounds (*próximo*, *plástico*, *proceso*, *plata*)?

Associate letters to sound. Write the following sentence on the board: *Su collar de plata es precioso.* Highlight the initial *pr-* and *pl-* sounds by sounding them out slowly when repeating the sentence aloud.

Word building: syllables Use the words *plata* and *precioso* from above to stress the combination of the letter *p* with other consonants: *pl* and *pr*. For *plata*, show the children how the tongue presses against the anterior part of the roof of the mouth when pronouncing it. As for *precioso*, as you move from *p* to *r* in pronouncing the word, roll the letter *r.*

Apply the skill. *Syllable Substitution* Ask each child to think of a word. Go around the room asking each child to say his/her word. Then, ask the class if they can rhyme that word with one that begins with *pl-* or *pr-*. (Examples might be: *puma-pluma*, *lata-plata*, *lana-plana*, *risa-prisa*)

Introduce Vocabulary

PRETEACH lesson vocabulary. Tell children that they are going to learn five new words that they will see again when they read a story called *De semilla a planta.* Teach every Vocabulary Word using the following process.

Write the word.
Say the word.
Track the word and have children repeat it.
Give the meaning or context.

Use the following suggestions or similar ideas to give the meaning or context.

hermoso: Use this adjective to describe people. Tell the children: *Mi abuela es muy hermosa*.

nutrientes: Relate this word to the new food pyramid in the US and contrast it with those countries with citizens who lack in regular nourishment such as parts of Africa. Ask a child: *¿Qué tipos de nutrientes tiene tu almuerzo hoy?*

protege: Tell the children this comes from the verb *proteger*. Ask them: *¿Qué haces tú para proteger el ambiente?*

madura: This word can refer to people and fruits and vegetables. Ask them: *¿Cuál es el color de un plátano maduro?*

arroyos: Point out the rolling *rr* sound in this word. Explain to them what you can find in arroyos. (Examples: little crayfish-*cangrejo de río*, minnows-*pececillo de agua dulce*, rocks-*piedras*)

Vocabulary Words

hermoso muy bonito

nutrientes parte del alimento que se necesita para vivir y crecer

protege mantiene a salvo

madura lista para comer

arroyos pequeños ríos

For vocabulary activities, see Vocabulary Games on pages 2–7.

AFTER

Building Background and Vocabulary

Apply Vocabulary Strategies

Use familiar words parts. Write the words *bello* y *belleza* on the board, and explain that they are nearly the same. Tell children that noticing words that come from each other will help them figure out the meaning of words.

MODEL **Yo sé que *hermoso* tiene que ver con bonito o bello. Me doy cuenta que *hermoso* y *belleza* están relacionados o significan casi lo mismo.**

Guide children in a similar procedure to find the meaning of *protección* and *maduro.*

RETEACH **lesson vocabulary.** Read aloud each of the following sentences. After each one invite the class to hold up the word card that completes each best. Reread the complete sentence and ask encourage volunteers to explain why the word fits.

1. La novia lleva un collar de perlas muy _________. (*hermoso*)
2. Todos debieran usar poco el coche pues de esa forma se _________ el ambiente. (*protege*)
3. Amelia bebió agua de los _________ durante el paseo. (*arroyo*)
4. Mi hermanito se comió una pera _________. (*madura*)
5. Las verdura frescas tienen muchos _________. (*nutrientes*)

FLUENCY BUILDER Using *Intervention Practice Book* page 47, read aloud each word in the first column and have children repeat it. Then have children work in pairs to read aloud to each other the words in the first column. Follow the same procedure with the words in each of the remaining columns. After partners have practiced reading aloud the words in each column separately, have them practice the entire list.

(See *Intervention Practice Book* page 47 to use on pages 121 and 123.)

BEFORE

Reading *De semilla a planta pages 314–331*

USE SKILL CARD 12A

Focus Skill Read Diagrams

PRETEACH the skill. Point out to children that diagrams are pictures with labels that give information. Tell them that diagrams help give a clear picture of what a selection is about and help readers learn the right words to name the parts of something.

Have children look at **side A** of **Skill Card 12: Leer Diagramas.** Read the definition of *diagrams.* Next read the paragraph and then have the children reread it with you.

Now call attention to the diagram and have volunteers take turns reading the labels aloud. Ask:

- **¿Qué ocurriría si la idea central de este párafo se tratara de construir una casa en vez de plantar una semilla?** (*Possible response: El diagrama sería diferente; mostraría las partes de una casa.*)
- **¿Por qué un diagrama te ayudaría si lo incluyes cuando escribes?** (*Possible response: Le ayudaría al lector para entender sobre lo que escribes.*)

Prepare to Read: *De semilla a planta*

Para ti pages 314–331

Preview. Animate the children by telling them the title of the next story, *De semilla a planta.* Comment to the class that this story explains how a tiny seed can grow into a large tree, one that you might climb or play on. Preview the selection with your class.

- **Page 314:** Yo veo el título, *De semilla a planta*. Hay un dibujo de una semilla debajo de la tierra y una planta que sube de ésta.
- **Pages 315–316:** Hay unos dibujos de un roble, un girasol, un manzano, una cinnia, un diente de león, y un aster. Son palabras y cosas nuevas para mi.
- **Page 317:** En esta página hay un diagrama de una flor y sus partes. Creo que he visto estas partes de la flor pero no sabía sus nombres.

Set Purpose. Model setting a purpose for reading *De semilla a planta*.

MODEL **Del vistazo a la lección he aprendido nuevas palabras para algunas flores que ya conocía y otras que no. También, me di cuenta que voy a aprender las partes de una flor.**

AFTER

Reading ***De semilla a planta pages 314–331***

Reread and Summarize

Have children reread and summarize *De semilla a planta* in sections, as described below.

Pages 315–319

Vamos a revisar las páginas 315–319 para saber más sobre las semillas y las partes de la flor.

Summary: En la flor está la semilla. Pero antes de que comience a crecer tiene que ocurrir la polinización. Esto ocurre cuando los granos de polen caen de los pistilos de las flores a causa del viento, los pájaros o las abejas.

Pages 320–322

Vamos a revisar las páginas 320–322 para averiguar cómo se forma una semilla.

Summary: La semmilla se forma cuando el polen de una flor cae en el pistilo de otra flor de su mismo tipo y llega hasta el óvulo de ésta. La semilla crece mientras la flor muere y un fruto crece alrededor de la semilla para protegerla. Las semillas salen de sus frutos cuando éstos maduran, cuando un pájaro se los come o debido al viento y la lluvia.

Pages 323–325

Vamos a revisar las páginas 323–325. En ellas se dice como se dispersan las semillas y más información sobre ellas.

Summary: El viento y los animales dispersan las semillas. Puedes comprar semillas en pequeños sobre y sembrarlas en tu jardín. La semilla consiste en una capa exterior dura que la protege, con el alimento en el centro donde está la yema.

Pages 326–330

Vamos a revisar las páginas 326–330 para saber más sobre la germinación de una semilla.

Summary: La germinación requiere ciertas condiciones para que ocurra, éstas son: tierra, agua sol y nutrientes minerales. La semilla se transformará en una planta donde nuevas semillas se formarán.

FLUENCY BUILDER Be sure children have copies of *Intervention Practice Book* page 47. Call attention to the sentences on the bottom half of the page. The slashes break the sentences into phrases to allow you to work on natural phrasing. Tell children that their goal is to read each phrase or sentence smoothly. Model appropriate pace, expression and phrasing as you read each sentence and have children read it after you. Then have children practice by reading the sentences aloud three times to a partner.

BEFORE

Making Connections
pages 334–335

Directed Reading of *Un día en la vida de una semilla*

Sonidos alegres
pp. 94–101

Ask your children to volunteer to read the title of the story aloud. Read pages 94–95 aloud while the children listen to figure out what the story is going to be about. Ask: **¿Qué sucede dentro del girasol y por qué?** (*Possible responses: Las semillas crecen dentro y se van a formar otras plantas de estas semillas.*) **LITERARY ANALYSIS**

Ask: **¿Porqué cae una semilla del girasol?** (*Possible responses: Cae porque va a crear otra flor en la tierra.*) Focus Skill **RECOGNIZING IMPORTANT DETAILS**

Pages 96–97

Help the children read pages 96–97 to find out more about the seed that fell from the sunflower. Ask them: **¿Cómo llegó la semilla en uno de los arroyos?** (*Possible response: El ratón la suelta allí.*) **MAIN IDEA**

Encourage volunteers to read aloud. Choose one of the children to read page 97 to the class.

> MODEL **Yo leí el recorrido de la semilla por el arroyo. Al fin se quedó atascada en unos pastos y espinas. Por haber leído en voz alta otra vez pude saber su recorrido.** Focus Strategy **REREAD ALOUD**

Invite other students to give their percepcions of the reading. Ask for another volunteer to read page 97. Ask: **¿Por qué crees que se quedó la semilla en unos pastos y espinas?** (*Possible response: Tal vez chocó con las patas de los caballos y su camino cambió de dirección.*) **IMPORTANT DETAILS**

Pages 98–99

Guide the children to read page 98 as the journey of the seed continues. Ask: **¿Cómo termina el viaje de la semilla?** (*Possible response: La semilla llega a la tierra.*) **DRAW CONCLUSIONS**

Invite the children to continue the story and direct them to page 99. Ask: **¿Y qué pasa con la semilla?** (*Possible response: Encuentra las condiciones necesarias para crecer y convertirse en planta.*) **MAIN IDEA**

Page 100

Guide students to conclude the story on page 100. Ask the children: **¿La semilla crece y en qué se transforma?** (*Possible response: Crece y se convierrte en un girasol igual al que le dio origen.*) **MAKE JUDGEMENTS**

Summarize the selection. Encourage the children to think about how other seeds may find a place to germinate and grow.

INTERVENTION PRACTICE BOOK
page 49

Page 101

Answers to *Think About It* Questions

1. La semilla llega a la tierra viajando a través del arroyo y del pasto, hasta llegar al suelo húmedo. **SUMMARY**
2. Cuando la semilla brota se forman raíces, luego el tallo, las hojas y finalmente las flores. **INTERPRETATION**
3. Accept various and reasonable responses. **FORMULATE QUESTIONS**

AFTER

Skill Review
pages 335I

USE SKILL CARD 12B

Focus Skill Read Diagrams

RETEACH the skill. Have children look at **side B** of **Skill Card 12: Read Diagrams.** Read the skill reminder with them, and have a volunteer read the paragraph aloud.

Read the directions. Explain that children will work with partners to label the parts of the sports shoe. Tell them that once the picture has labels, it is called a diagram.

After children have labeled their drawings and added color and other details, have them display their diagrams. Point out that the selection *Un día en la vida de una semilla* has pictures that could be labeled to become diagrams. Ask volunteers to give some examples from the story illustrations.

Review Phonics Skill: *pl, pr*

RETEACH the skill. Read aloud the following sentence: *Los plátanos son apreciados en Praga.* Then read each word one at a time. Tell children to say "Yes" if they hear the sound made by /pl/ and /pr/ and "No" if they do not.

FLUENCY BUILDER Be sure that children have copies of *Intervention Practice Book* page 47. Explain that today children will practice the sentences on the bottom half of the page by reading them aloud on tape. Assign partners. Have children take turns reading the sentences aloud to each other and then reading them on tape.

INTERVENTION PRACTICE BOOK
page 47

BEFORE

Drafting an Informative Paragraph
page 337C

Writer's Craft: Informative Sentence

Build on prior knowledge. Tell children that they are going to talk about and write a sentence that informs or tells someone about something. Explain that it is important to stay focused on the topic. Provide the following example on the board:

Sentence topic: Un enemigo de una planta comestible

Detail 1: Los insectos les hacen daño.

Detail 2: Los animales mastican las plantas.

Detail 3: Los días secos las marchitan.

Construct the text. "Share the pen" with children. Guide them in writing an informative sentence based on the topic and the list of details. For example:

> Una planta comestible tiene enemigos que son los insectos, los animales, y los días secos.

Revisit the text. Reread the informative sentence. Ask: **¿Si incluyo datos sobre otro tema, como el tema de los árboles grandes o animales domésticos favoritos, que ocurriría a mi frase?** (*No tendría sentido.*)

- Have children discuss what they could write about in a paragraph that started with the sentence above.

On Your Own

Have children write possible topics for an informative sentence. Ask them to choose one topic and write a list of details about it. Then have children write an informative sentence that focuses on one topic.

AFTER

Spelling Lesson
page 33 II

Connect Spelling and Phonics

RETEACH combination consonants *pl* and *pr*. Begin by writing the word *privado* on the blackboard. Explain to the class that you will give them one more word with the combination of consonant + vowel: *pr* (*prendar*). Invite volunteers to the board to write the words you say on the blackboard. Repeat the process with *pl* using the following words:

1. plátano	**2. pluma**	**3. plantas***	**4. planeta**
5. plancha	**6. presidente**	**7. príncipe**	**8. protege***

Word appears in *Un día en la vida de una semilla.

Ask the children to write the following sentence as you dictate it aloud to them: *Al presidente le gustan los plátanos durante la primavera.*

Build and Read Longer Words

Remind the children of the distinct sound of words with the letter combination of *pl* and of *pr*.

INTERVENTION ASSESSMENT BOOK

Write the word *prevenir* on the board. Tell the children that they can figure out meanings of words by looking at its parts, particularly suffixes and prefixes. Encourage volunteers by asking the children if they can detect the prefix in this word, *pre*. By taking out the prefix, what word to we have? (*venir*) Can they figure out what the word *prevenir* means? Repeat the process with more words with the pl/pr combinations that have prefixes or suffixes. (Possible choices: *placentero, prejuzgar, preocupación*)

FLUENCY BUILDER Ask for volunteers to read aloud parts of *Un día en la vida de una semilla.* Divide the reading up into sections and change volunteers often.

- Read pages 94–96. (*En el jardín*... through ...*en el arroyo.* Total: 72 words.)
- Read pages 97–99. (From *Ahora la semilla*... through ...*de la planta.* Total: 95 words.)

Children should read the selected passage aloud to their partners three times. Have the reader rate each reading on a scale from 1 to 4.

SCALE
1 Not so good
2 Pretty good
3 Good
4 Great!

BEFORE
Weekly Assessments

Review Vocabulary

To revisit Vocabulary Words prior to the weekly assessment, use the following synonym pair format. Have volunteers take turns reading the given word. Ask them to identify the correct choice to create a synonym pair and then explain why the two belong together.

1. **hermoso**
   a. picante
   b. bonito
2. **nutrientes**
   a. alimentos
   b. medicinas
3. **protege**
   a. contamina
   b. mantiene seguro
4. **madura**
   a. podrida
   b. fruta lista para comer
5. **arroyo**
   a. corriente de agua
   b. cascada

Correct responses: 1.b, 2.a, 3.b, 4.b, 5.a.

You may extend this activity to write or dictate to the children other words and encourage them to place these words in the same syllable chart.

Focus Skill Review Diagrams

INTERVENTION PRACTICE BOOK
page 50

Before the weekly assessment, review this focus skill by distributing *Intervention Practice Book* page 50. Invite the children to volunteer to read aloud the first direction line and the sentences. Guide the children to interpret the visuals and ask them what they are saying. Encourage them to ask themselves: **¿Qué significado tienen los gráficos y los diagramas? ¿Cómo puedo explicar lo que significan con palabras?**

Review Test Prep

Para ti
page 337

Ask children to turn to page 337 of the *Pupil Edition*. Call attention to the tips for answering the test questions. Tell children that paying attention to these tips can help them answer not only the test questions on this page but also other test questions like these.

INTERVENTION ASSESSMENT BOOK

Have children follow along as you read each test question and the tip that goes with it. Discuss how each choice in question 1 asks about the words used to label the diagram. Tell them to look closely at the line connecting the word and the picture for a clue about what the diagram is showing. Then have them read each choice and ask themselves if it makes sense in the diagram. Remind them to look back at the diagram when they answer question 2.

Self-Selected Reading

Have children select their own books to read independently. They might choose books from the classroom library shelf, or you may wish to offer a group of appropriate books from which children can choose.

- *La sorpresa sobre la semilla* See page 377 of the *Teacher's Edition* for an Independent Reading Lesson Plan.
- *Cómo crece una semilla* por Helen J. Jorda. HarperCollins, 1996.
- *Las semillas* por Susan Kuchalla. Sistemas Técnicos de Edición, 1990.

After children have chosen their books, give each child a copy of *My Reading Log,* which can be found on page R35 in the back of the *Teacher's Edition*. Have children fill in the information at the top of the form. Then have them use the log to keep track of their reading and to record their responses to the literature.

Conduct student-teacher conferences. Arrange time for each child to conference with you individually about his or her self-selected reading. Have children bring their Reading Logs to share with you at the conference. Children might also like to share a favorite passage to read aloud to you. Ask questions designed to stimulate discussion about the book. For example, you might ask if there were any diagrams included in the selections, or if they learned enough information to draw a diagram of the focus topic.

FLUENCY PERFORMANCE Have children read aloud to you the passage from *Un día en la vida de una semilla* that they selected and practiced with their partners. Keep track of the number of words the child reads correctly. Ask the child to rate his or her own performance on the 1–4 scale. If children are not happy with their oral reading, give them an opportunity to continue practicing and then to reread the passage to you.

See *Oral Reading Fluency Assessment* for monitoring progress.

LESSON 13

BEFORE

Building Background and Vocabulary

Use with

"La vida secreta de los árboles"

Review Phonics: Words Stressed on the Second-to-Last Syllable

Identify the sound. Review the objective of the phonics lesson: words stressed on the second-to-last syllable. Read to children the words *señora* and *niño*. Ask them to listen for the stress on the second to last syllable. Write the following sentence on the board and have children identify words that fall into this category: *El joven tiene un gato precioso.* (Answers: *joven, tiene, gato, precioso*)

Associate letters to sound. Write the words *automóvil, lápiz*, and *árbol* on the board. Have children say these words aloud and stress with them that the spoken accent falls on the written accent. Then write the words *niña, viejo,* and *loro* on the board. Say these words aloud with children stressing that the spoken accent also falls on the second-to-last syllable in these words, but there is no written accent.

INTERVENTION PRACTICE BOOK

page 52

Word blending. Model for children how to blend words that are accented on the second-to-last syllable. Write the following words on the board and say them with obvious stress on the second-to-last syllable: *perro, rosa, trébol.*

Apply the skill. *Syllable Substitution* Write the following words on the board: *gato, lápiz, árbol*. Have children read each word aloud, applying the appropriate stress.

Introduce Vocabulary

PRETEACH lesson vocabulary. Tell children that they are going to learn five new words that they will see again when they read a story called *La vida secreta de los arboles.* Teach each vocabulary word using the following process.

Write the word.
Say the word.
Track the word and have children repeat it.
Give the meaning or context.

Use these suggestions or similiar ideas to help children better understand the meaning or context.

descubrir Relate to finding something that was lost or learning how to do something in school.

energía This is a multiple-meaning word. Point to a light or something electrical and explain that it takes power, or energy, to make it work. Children may be more familiar with the energy they get from food or rest.

pronosticar Use the synoym *predecir* to explain this word. Ask children: *¿Creen que puedan pronosticar el futuro?*

esparce This word comes from the infinitive *esparcir.* Ask children: *¿Qué pasa con un perro con mucho pelo cuando viene el verano y hace más calor?* (*Possible answer: El perro esparce su pelo.*)

fuente Turn on the faucet in the room. Ask: *¿De dónde viene el agua?* (*Possible answer: del arroyo o río*) Explain that *fuente* is where something comes from.

Vocabulary Words

descubrir hallar

aprender por primera vez

energía el poder de hacer cosas

pronosticar predecir

esparce arroja, desparrama

fuente el lugar de donde viene algo

For vocabulary activities, see Vocabulary Games on pages 2–7.

AFTER

Building Background and Vocabulary

Apply Vocabulary Strategies

Use synonyms. Write the words *descubrir* y *encontrar* on the board. Explain that these words are synonyms. Tell them that recognizing synonyms will help them remember the meaning of words.

> MODEL **Yo sé que los sinónimos son palabras que tiene igual o parecido significado. Si yo sé que *descubrir* y *encontrar* son sinónimos, entonces entenderé y recordaré qué significa cada palabra.**

Guide children in a similar procedure to understand the meaning of *esparce* and *fuente.*

RETEACH **lesson vocabulary.** Have children listen to each of the following clues. Tell them to hold up the card that shows the correct match. Reread the clue aloud and say the correct answer. Have children verify their words and discuss how they made their choices.

1. Cuando vas a aprender algo por primera vez, tú vas a <u>(descubrir)</u> algo nuevo.
2. Un buen desayuno me da <u>(energía)</u> para todo el día.
3. El reporte del tiempo va a <u>(pronosticar)</u> una tormenta para mañana.
4. Desconozco esa <u>(fuente)</u> de información.
5. Cual algo se riega en una supericie decimos que se <u>(esparce)</u>.

FLUENCY BUILDER Using *Intervention Practice Book* page 51, read aloud each word in the first column and have children repeat it. Then have children work in pairs to read aloud to each other the words in the first column. Follow the same procedure with each of the remaining columns. After partners have practiced reading aloud the words in each column separately, have them practice the entire list.

(See *Intervention Practice Book* page 61 to use with pages 131 and 133.)

BEFORE

Reading ***La vida secreta de los árboles*** ***pages 340–359***

USE SKILL CARD 13A

Focus Skill Fact and Fiction

PRETEACH the skill. Point out to children that a fact gives information about a real thing or event and that fiction tells a story that is meant to entertain. Explain that books with facts often have photographs, diagrams, and charts. Discuss how fiction tells stories that are made up.

Have children look at **side A** of ***Tarjeta de destreza 13: Hecho y ficción/*** **Skill Card 13: Fact and Fiction**. Read the definition of *fact* and *fiction.* Next read the paragraph and then have children reread it with you.

Now call attention to the chart and have volunteers take turns reading the information aloud. Ask:

- **¿Este cuento sería de ficción o no?** (*Possible response: Aunque algunas cosas son datos y hechos, sería ficción porque muchas cosas están inventadas.*)
- **¿Cómo se puede destacar si estás leyendo ficción o no?** (*Possible response: Busca las fotos, los diagramas, y las cosas que pueden ser datos y hechos. Busca las cosas que están inventadas para ficción.*)

Prepare to Read *La vida secreta de los árboles*

Para ti
pages 340–359

Preview. Tell children that they are going to read a selection entitled *La vida secreta de los árboles.* Explain that this is a non-fiction selection that gives factual information about trees. Then preview the selection.

- **Pages 340–341:** En estas páginas veo el título, *La vida secreta de los árboles.* Hay una serie de preguntas en la página 341 que me motivan a saber más sobre el mundo de los árboles.
- **Pages 342–343:** Hay un subtítulo que anuncia lo que tratan las siguientes páginas: La vida del árbol. También hay un dibujo del tronco y las ramas de un árbol.
- **Pages 344–345:** El subtítulo sigue. Hay un dibujo/una foto de las raíces del árbol y sus hojas. Me imagino que vamos a aprender más sobre las partes del árbol en esta sección.

Set Purpose. Set a purpose for reading *La vida secreta de los árboles.*

MODEL **El vistazo al cuento me indica que vamos a aprender cosas generales y específicas sobre los árboles. ¡Me gustaría saber más porque por donde quiera que miro, veo un árbol!**

AFTER

La vida secreta de los árboles pages 340–359

Reread and Summarize

Have the children reread and summarize sections of *La vida secreta de los árboles* as described below.

Pages 342–345

Vamos a revisar las páginas 342–345 para saber más sobre la corteza y las raíces de los árboles y lo que necesitan para vivir.

Summary: La corteza protege a los árboles, mientras que la parte que no vemos, las raíces, ¡constituyen la otra midad del árbol! Los árboles viven más que cualquier otro ser viviente y necesitan sol y agua para crecer.

Pages 346–349

Vamos a revisar las páginas 346–349 para ver los tipos de animales que usan el árbol como su casa. También revisamos las clases de árboles que hay.

Summary: Los pájaros y los insectos habitan el árbol tanto en su exterior como en su interior, mientras que los ratones y tejones encuentran su hogar debajo de la tierra entre sus raíces. Los dos tipos principales de árboles son los que tienen las ramas dispersas y las llamadas coníferas.

Pages 355–359

Vamos a revisar las páginas 355–359 para averiguar sobre las frutas de los árboles tropicales y para enterarnos de lo que está en tu casa que también vino de un árbol.

Summary: Los aguacates, los dátiles y los mangos proceden de árboles tropicales. Las semillas de un cocotero se encuentran dentro del mismo coco. La madera y el papel, a madera de tu mesa de trabajo y las páginas del libro que estás leyendo, ¡viene de los árboles!

FLUENCY BUILDER Be sure children have copies of *Intervention Practice Book* page 51, which you used for the previous Fluency Builder activity. Call attention to the sentences on the bottom half of the page. Tell children that their goal is to read each phrase or sentence smoothly. Model appropriate pace, expression and phrasing as you read each sentence, and have children read it after you. Then have children practice by reading the sentences aloud three times to a partner.

BEFORE

Making Connections
pages 362–363

Directed Reading: *El viejo árbol*

Sonidos alegres
pp. 102–107

Ask a volunteer to read aloud the title. Read page 102 aloud while the children listen to figure out what the story is going to be about.

Ask: **¿Por qué cambia el árbol durante las diferentes estaciones?** (*Possible responses: El tiempo lo hace cambiar para sobrevivir.*) **DRAW CONCLUSIONS**

Ask: **¿Crees que es un cuento de ficción o no? ¿Por qué?** (*Possible response: No es ficción porque dice cosas sobre el árbol que son verdad.*) Focus Skill **FACT AND FICTION**

Pages 103–104

Help children read pages 103–104 to see what happens to the tree as the season changes. Ask them: **¿Por qué ni los musgos ni los helechos crecen alrededor del tronco durante el invierno?** (*Possible response: El tiempo es demasiado frío para que crezcan las plantas. Esperan hasta la primavera para crecer.*) **MAIN IDEA**

Encourage volunteers to read aloud. Choose one of the children to go back and reread page 103 to the class.

> MODEL **Muchos animales dependen de los árboles para su comida y su casa. Comen sus cortezas y hojas. No sabía que los pájaros duermen en sus ramas. Una vez yo vi una ardilla que hacía su casa en el tronco de un árbol.** Focus Strategy **LOOK AT WORD BITS AND PARTS**

Pages 105–106

Ask a volunteer to read page 105 aloud. Ask: **¿Por qué el tronco atrae tantos animales e insectos?** (*Porque es un ciclo: llegan las hormigas, y después llegan los que se comen a las hormigas, y llegan otros que se van a comer a los que se comieron a las hormigas y continúan...*) **IMPORTANT DETAILS**

Guide children to read page 106. Ask: **¿Por qué tienen que huir la coneja y su familia?** (*Possible response: Llega la mamá zorra para encontrar una casa. Tienen que huir porque los zorros se comen a los conejos.*) **DRAW CONCLUSIONS**

Page 107

Invite the children to continue the story and direct them to page 107. Ask: **¿Por qué tienen que huir la coneja y su familia?** (*Possible response: Ha sido el refugio para muchos y también ofrece alimento.*) **MAIN IDEA**

Ask children: **¿Por qué dice el narrador que todavía el tronco es una fuente?** (*Possible response: El cíclo continúa y van a llegar otros por el alimento y también para buscar refugio.*) **MAKE JUDGMENTS**

INTERVENTION PRACTICE BOOK
page 53

Summarize the selection Ask children to think about how all living things are important. Then have them complete *Intervention Practice Book* page 53.

AFTER

Skill Review
page 363I

USE SKILL CARD 13B

Answers to *Think About It* Questions

1. Lo usan como Casa y como alimento. **SUMMARY**
2. Es algo bueno para el bosque tener árboles muertos porque aún así siguen ofreciendo albergue y alimento a los animales del bosque. **INTERPRETATION**
3. Accept reasonable responses. **TASK**

Focus Skill Review Fact and Fiction

RETEACH the skill. Have children look at **side B** of ***Tarjeta de destreza 13: Hecho y ficción*/Skill Card 13: Fact and Fiction**. Read the skill reminder with them, and select a volunteer to read the paragraph aloud.

Read aloud the directions. Explain that children will work with partners to complete the chart. Remind them to look for clues that tell if something could really happen or if it is pretend.

After children have completed their charts, have them share them with other partner groups. Tell them to compare the details that they recorded. Ask volunteers to give reasons why they labeled the paragraph *fact* or *fiction.*

Review Phonics Skill from *La vida secreta de los árboles*

RETEACH words that are stressed on the second-to-last syllable. Read aloud the following sentence: *El gato de ella no me trata muy bien.* Have children listen for the stress on the second-to-last syllable. Then read this list aloud and have children raise their hands when they hear the words that are stressed on the second-to-last syllable sound: *gato, ella, trata.*

FLUENCY BUILDER Be sure children have copies of *Intervention Practice Book* page 51. Explain that today children will practice the sentences on the bottom half of the page by reading them aloud on tape. Assign new partners. Have children take turns reading the sentences aloud to each other and then reading them on tape.

INTERVENTION PRACTICE BOOK
page 51

BEFORE

Drafting a Research Report
page 365C

Research Report: Writing a Factual Paragraph

Build on prior knowledge. Tell children that they are going to write a paragraph that contains facts about one topic. Discuss with them examples of factual texts they have read, such as the two selections about trees. Guide them to see that the paragraph has one focus or main idea and that the facts give detailed information about the topic. Display and read aloud the following list:

Topic: Nido de un pájaro
Fact 1: Hecho de hojas y tierra
Fact 2: Hecho en un árbol
Fact 3: Usado para empollar a los pichones y para protección

Construct the text. "Share the pen" with children. Guide them in writing a factual paragraph based on the topic *El nido de un pájaro* and the list of facts. For example:

> Donde vive un pájaro es su nido. Los pájaros construyen sus nidos de hojas y tierra. Los pájaros los construyen en los árboles. Empollan a sus pichones en el nido y hacen un lugar para ellos allí.

Revisit the text. Read the paragraph aloud together. Ask: **Si no tuviera yo un tema, ¿qué ocurriría con mi párrafo?** (*Contaría sobre cosas diferentes.*)

- Guide children to be sure that all the sentences are about the same topic. Have them omit any sentences that stray from this topic.

On Your Own

Have children write a short factual paragraph about a topic that interests them. Urge them to include two or three important facts in their writing.

AFTER

Spelling Lesson
page 359H

Connect Spelling and Phonics

RETEACH words accented on the second-to-last syllable. Write the word *delicado* on the board. Explain to children that this word is stressed on the second-to-last syllable. Ask children to divide this word into syllables. Now, invite volunteers to write the words on the board, separate them by syllables, and circle the stressed syllable. (All words are stressed on the second-to-last syllable.)

1. bosque*	**2. fuente***	**3. ramas ***	**4. insectos***	**5. frutos***
6. hojas*	**7. estaciones***	**8. esparce***	**9. planta***	**10. viejo***

Dictate the following sentence and have children write it: *Mi hermana mayor siempre dice que le tocan más dulces porque tiene más edad.*

Build and Read Longer Words

INTERVENTION ASSESSMENT BOOK

Remind the children that every word has a stressed syllable even though there is not a written accent.

Write the word *arboleda* on the board. This word can be divided into four syllables and is stressed on the second-to-last syllable. Have children identify other words that are four or more syllables and that are stressed on the second-to-last syllable. (*caramelo, americano, puertorriqueña, interesante*)

FLUENCY BUILDER Tell the class they will read aloud parts of *El viejo árbol*. Have the children pair up. In each pair they should find their favorite passage of the story (10–15 lines long each child). Encourage the children to read aloud their passages to their partner and then switch. Each child will read his/her passage aloud 3 times. Then, ask each child to rate his/her last reading from a scale of 1–4

- Read pages 102–103. (From *En el bosque…* through *…pierde su corteza.* Total: 118 words.)
- Read page 105. (From *Las hormigas…* through *…las hormigas.* Total: 72 words.)

SCALE	
1	Not so good
2	Pretty good
3	Good
4	Great!

Children should read the selected passage aloud to their partners three times. Have the partner rate each reading on a scale from 1 to 4.

BEFORE
Weekly Assessments

Review Vocabulary

Play the following word game with the children. The vocabulary word they learned in this lesson appears in bold. Have volunteers choose the correct response.

1. Si tienes **energía**, tienes poco
   a. cansancio.
   b. ánimo.
2. Si **descubres** un tesoro, ya no está
   a. entendido.
   b. escondido.
3. Cuando **pronosticas** el futuro, no estás totalmente
   a. decidido.
   b. seguro.
4. El animal **esparce** su pelo cuando
   a. hace frío.
   b. llueva.
5. El sol es una **fuente** de energía
   a. peligrosa.
   b. utilizable.

Focus Skill Review Fact and Fiction

INTERVENTION PRACTICE BOOK page 54

To review fact and fiction before the weekly assessment, distribute *Intervention Practice Book* page 54. Have volunteers read aloud the first direction line and the sentences. Guide children to remember that a fact tells about a real thing or event. Tell them to look for clues to decide if something is fiction, or made up.

Review Test Prep

Para ti page 365

Ask children to turn to page 365 of the *Pupil Edition*. Call attention to the tips for answering the test questions. Tell children that paying attention to these tips can help them answer not only the questions on this page, but other test questions.

INTERVENTION ASSESSMENT BOOK

Have children follow along as you read the directions, each test question, and the tip. Discuss the clues to what each book is about. Then discuss the kind of book each question is asking for: a book of facts or a book of fiction. Then make sure that children choose the book title that matches what they are looking for.

AFTER

Weekly Assessments

Self-Selected Reading

Have children select their own books to read independently. They might choose books from the classroom library shelf, or you may wish to offer a group of appropriate books from which children can choose.

- *Las ardillas hacen cosas de ardillas* (See page 365O in the *Teacher's Edition* for an Independent Reading Plan.)
- *El agua* por Nichoe Girón. Patria, 1989.
- *Un árbol es hermoso* por Janice May Udry. HarperCollins, 1995.

Using "My Reading Log" After children have chosen their books, give each child a copy of *Mi diario,* which can be found on page R35 in the back of the *Teacher's Edition*. Have children fill in the information at the top of the form. Then have them use the log to keep track of their reading and to record their responses to the literature.

Conduct student-teacher conferences. Arrange time for each child to confer with you individually about his or her self-selected reading. Have children bring their Reading Logs to share with you at the conference. Children might also like to choose a favorite passage to read aloud to you. Ask questions designed to stimulate discussion about the book. For example, you might ask whether the selection is fiction or nonfiction, and what details in the story are fact or madeup.

FLUENCY PERFORMANCE Have children read aloud to you the passage from *El viejo árbol* that they selected and practiced with their partners. Keep track of the number of words the child reads correctly. Ask the child to rate his or her own performance on the 1–4 scale. If children are not happy with their oral reading, give them an opportunity to continue practicing and then to reread the passage to you.

See *Evaluación de la fluidez oral de la lectura* for monitoring progress.

LESSON 14

Use with

"El día de la sandía"

BEFORE

Building Background and Vocabulary

Introduce: /fl/, /fr/

Identify the sound. Ask children to listen for the /fl/ and /fr/ sounds as you say the words *flojo and fresa.* Then have children repeat the following sentence twice: *Ella me parece floja cuando está cogiendo las fresas.* Ask them to identify the three words that have the /fr/ and/or /fl/ sounds.

Associate letters to sound. Write on the board: *Ella me parece floja cuando está cogiendo las fresas.* Underline the *fl* in *floja* and the *fr* in *fresas.* Explain that the *fl* and *fr* sounds are quite distinct from one another. Have the children say these words stressing the *fl* and *fr* sounds.

Word building – syllables. Write on the board the spelling words that have the *fl (flaco, flama, flauta, flecha, flotaba)* and the *fr (refresco, franjas, fría, frescas, frijol).* Read each word aloud and ask children how many syllables each word has. Invite volunteers to underline the syllables which contain *fr.* Then repeat the process with the *fl* words.

Apply the skill. Write the spelling words on the board in random order. Form two columns with the heads */fl/* and */fr/.* Pronounce for them each of the column heads. Then, ask the children to come to the board and write the words in the correct column.

Introduce Vocabulary

PRETEACH lesson vocabulary. Tell children that they are going to learn seven new words that they will see again when they read a story called *El día de la sandía.* Teach each vocabulary word using the following process.

Write the word.
Say the word.
Track the word and have children repeat it.
Give the meaning or context.

Use the following suggestions or similar ideas to give the meaning or context.

carreras de relevos Point out that there are three words here. Explain that this is a type of *carrera* that maybe 3 or 4 team members run in. Choose a few children to role-play this word with for the class.

arrodillaba Demonstrate this word by getting down on your knees.

escondían Tell the children that they do this when they are playing the game hide-and-go-seek. Explain that this is done so that the one who is looking for you cannot find you.

destellos Explain that this means *brillos.* Point out some things that shine in the room.

acomodada Give the children a synonym such as *cómoda.*

arrugó Point out a wrinkled shirt or cloth in the class. Scrunch up some cloth and show them that the result is the meaning of this word.

For vocabulary activities, see Vocabulary Games on pages 2–7.

Vocabulary Words

carreras de relevos carreras en las que se reemplaza a los corredores

arrodillaba ponía las rodillas en el suelo

escondían disimulaban, sacaban de la vista

destellos brillos

acomodada cómoda

arrugó formó muchos pliegues pequeños

AFTER

Building Background and Vocabulary

Apply Vocabulary Strategies

Use synonyms/antonyms. Ask children to look at the words *destellos* and *brillos.* Have volunteers define each word. Explain that the words have similar meanings and are therefore, synonyms. Challenge children to name synonyms for the words *acomodada* (cómoda) and *escondían* (disimulaban).

RETEACH lesson vocabulary. Have children listen to each of the following questions. Tell them to hold up the word card that answers each question. You may want to write the questions on the board to help visual learners.

1. ¿Qué palabra significa *cómoda?* (*acomodada*)
2. ¿Qué palabra explica lo que le pasó a la ropa que se lavó y no se planchó? (*arrugó*)
3. ¿Qué palabra se refiere a las carreras donde los corredores son sustituidos cada cierta distancia? (*carreras de relevos*)
4. ¿Qué hacía ella cuando ponía sus rodillas en el piso? (*se arrodillaba*)
5. ¿Qué palabra se relaciona con las cosas que brillan? (*destellos*)
6. ¿Qué palabra significa lo mismo que ocultaban? (*escondían*)

FLUENCY BUILDER Using *Intervention Practice Book* page 55. Read aloud each word in the first column and have children repeat it. Then have children work in pairs to read the words in the first column aloud to each other. Follow the same procedure with each of the remaining columns. After partners have practiced reading aloud the words in each separate column, have them practice reading the entire list.

(See *Intervention Practice Book* page 55 to use on pages 141 and 143.)

BEFORE

Reading
***El día de la sandía* pages 368–388**

USE SKILL CARD 14A

Focus Skill Make Inferences

PRETEACH the skill. Tell children that we often use something we already know to understand new things that happen. For example, by knowing that Billy scraped his knee, we can make guesses about why Billy is crying. Point out that making inferences is a useful strategy to use when reading.

Have children look at **side A** of **Skill Card 14: Make Inferences**. Read the definition of an inference. Next read the paragraph and then have children reread it with you.

Now call attention to the chart and select volunteers to take turns reading the clues aloud. Ask:

- **¿Cómo sabes que Jaime no se siente muy bien?** (*Possible response: El está en la cama estornudando.*)
- **¿Qué pasaría si el autor no nos diera información sobre Jaime?** (*Possible response: Tal vez no sabríamos cómo se siente Jaime.*)

Prepare to Read *El día de la sandía*

Para ti
pages
368–388

Preview. Read the title of the story aloud. Explain that this is "realistic fiction". Make certain that the children understand what this means.

- **Pages 368–369:** En estas dos primeras páginas del cuento veo el título y también el dibujo de una chica con las semillas de una sandía detrás. ¿Qué va a pasar con la sandía?
- **Pages 370–371:** Ahora veo que hay dos personajes, la chica y un hombre. Jesse busca la sandía y se la muestra al hombre que pudiera ser su papá o un granjero ¿Qué van a hacer con la sandia?
- **Pages 372–374:** En la pág, 372, la ilustración me hacer pensar en una fiesta o festival. Puede ser que va a haber un festival del melón. Luego veo ilustraciones de la muchacha que parece cuidar una enorme planta de melón.
- **Pages 375–379:** Parece ser que una sandía está creciendo mucho. En la página 379 parece que el hombre piensa que ya se puede recoger la sandía.

Set purpose. Model setting a purpose for reading *El día de la sandía.*

MODEL De lo que he visto en estos dibujos, me parece que *El día de la sandía* deberá tratar sobre una muchacha que cultiva una sandía hasta que está lista para comer. Parece ser que hay una fiesta de sandías. Un propósito para leer es descubrir y aprender más sobre este día. Voy a leer para enterarme.

AFTER

Reading
Watermelon Day pages 368–388

Reread and Summarize

Have children work in pairs to reread and summarize *El día de la sandía* as described below.

Pages 368–371
Leamos estas páginas para recordar los personajes y porqué hay una sandía en el cuento.

Summary: La muchacha se llama Jesse y el hombre se llama Pappy. Jessy encontró una sandía en la parcela que será usada para el Día de la sandía.

Pages 372–377
Leamos para recordar qué es el Día de la sandía y qué tuvo que hacer Jesse para estar lista.

Summary: El Día de la sandía es una fiesta muy grande con mucha comida y juegos. Jesse quiere llevar su sandía pero ésta tiene que crecer primero. Ella tiene que cuidarla mucho hasta que esté lista.

Pages 378–383
Recordemos qué sucedió cuando la sandía estuvo finalmente lista para ser recogida.

Summary: Pappy cortó la sandía de su enredadera, pero aún no estaba lista para ser abierta. Ésta tenía que flotar durante un día en agua con hielo, durante la fiesta. Jesse estaba muy impaciente y no soportaba la espera.

Pages 384–387
Leamos estas páginas para saber qué sucedió cuando la sandía estuvo lista para ser abierta.

Summary: Pappy golpeó la sandía y la abrió. Estaba muy dulce, fría y jugosa. Jesse cantó una canción de la sandía mientras se comía un trozo de ella.

FLUENCY BUILDER Be sure children have copies of *Intervention Practice Book* page 55, which you used for the previous Fluency Builder activity. Call attention to the sentences on the bottom half of the page. The slashes break the sentences into phrases to allow you to work on natural phrasing. Tell children that their goal is to read each phrase or sentence smoothly. Model appropriate pace, expression, and phrasing as you read each sentence. Have children read it after you. Then have children practice by reading the sentences aloud three times to a partner.

BEFORE

Making Connections
pages 390–391

Directed Reading of *Las zanahorias del Sr. Carver*

Sonidos alegres
pages 110–115

Read the title of the story aloud. Remind the children that it is realistic fiction and ask them to explain what this means. Encourage them to use what they learned from reading *El día de la sandía.* Ask: **¿Quién sabe qué significa ficción realista? ¿Por qué *Las zanahorias del Sr. Carver* es ficción realista?** (*Possible response: Porque habla de los personajes que están cerca de las personas de la vida actual.*) **NARRATIVE ELEMENTS**

Page 110

Have children read page 110. Point out the words *escondían, mojados, verano.* Ask: **¿Qué significan éstas palabras? ¿A qué se refieren estas palabras? ¿De esta explicacion, qué crees que va a ocurrir en el cuento?** (*Possible response: El calor va a influenciar en las plantas y las frutas de un jardín.*) **MAKING INFERENCES**

Model using the secuence/Summarize strategy:

> **MODEL** **Cuando quiero recordar lo que sucede en un cuento, trato de recordar el orden en que suceden los hechos. Mantener los sucesos en orden también me ayuda a hacer inferencias y predicciones.**

Ask: **¿Qué hacen el Sr. Carver y el Sr. Ben?** (*Possible response: El Sr. Carver afloja la tierra con la pala y el Sr. Ben panta semillas de zanahorias y las cubre con tierra.*)

Pages 111–113

Discuss how Ben and Sr. Carver are planting their garden of *zanahorias.* Ask the children to tell you about Ben's feelings. Ask them: **¿Cómo está Ben y como reacciona en éstas páginas?** (*Possible response: Ben se sorprendió cuando llegó la tormenta pero después se sintio muy orgulloso.*) **IMPORTANT DETAILS**

Continue this thought by asking the children why Ben had this sudden change of emotions. Ask: **¿Por qué se sintió muy orgulloso Ben?** (*Possible response: Porque había preparado muy bien su jardín y no se habían ido flotando las semillas como resultado de la tormenta?*) **DRAW CONCLUSION**

Pages 114–115

Have the children read pages 114 and 115 to see what Ben does with the carrots when they are ready to be taken from the soil. Ask them: **¿Qué puedes aprender de las zanahorias de esta página y sobre cómo y dónde crecen?** (*Possible response: Las zanahorias crecen debajo de la tierra.*) **MAIN IDEA**

INTERVENTION PRACTICE BOOK
page 57

Summarize the selection. Ask children to think about what happened first, next, and last in *Las zanahorias del Sr. Carver.* Help them summarize the story in three or four sentences.

Answers to *Piénsalo* Questions

1. Sembraron unas semillitas y luego las cuidaron hasta que Ben tiró de la parte de arriba y salieron las zanahorias.
2. El agua las ayudó a crecer.
3. Las respuestas pueden variar.

AFTER

Skill Review
page 39II

USE SKILL CARD 14B

Focus Skill Make Inferences

RETEACH the skill. Have children look at **side B** of **Skill Card 14: Make Inferences**. Read the skill reminder with them, and have a volunteer read the paragraph aloud.

Read aloud the set of directions. Explain that children will work with partners to create their own charts. Remind them to think about the things that they know in the story to help them make an inference.

After children have completed their inference charts, have them share their charts with other partner pairs and compare the inference they made and the details they recorded that helped them.

Review Phonics Skill: /fl/, /fr/

RETEACH the skill. Read aloud the following sentence. *Las fresas son muy frescas.* Have children listen for the /fr/ sound. Then read each word one at a time and have children put their thumbs up if they hear the sound, and thumbs down if they do not.

FLUENCY BUILDER Be sure that children have copies of *Intervention Practice Book* page 55. Explain that today children will practice the sentences on the bottom half of the page by reading them aloud on tape. Assign new partners. Have children take turns reading the sentences aloud to each other and reading them on tape.

BEFORE

Drafting a Paragraph of Explanation page 391A

Writing Process: Paragraph of Explanation

Build on prior knowledge. Tell children that they are going to work together to write sentences that explain something. Remind them that explanations tell why or how something happens. Guide children to see that details in the sentence help give information. Display and read aloud the following list of details:

Sentence Topic: Los tulipanes de Ana

Detail: crecieron muy fuertes

Detail: los protegió de las enfermedades

Detail: los regó todos los días

Detail: los puso al sol

Construct the text. "Share the pen" with children. Guide them in writing an explanatory sentence based on the topic *Los tulipanes de Ana* and the list of details. For example:

- Los tulipanes de Ana crecieron muy fuertes porque los cuidó muy bien.

Revisit the text. Go back and read the explanatory sentence. Ask: **¿Si yo no dijera por qué los tulipanes crecieron muy fuertes, ¿daría una explicación la frase?** (*Possible response: No, la explicación dice porqué algo ocurrió. Necesitamos saber que creció porque los cuidó muy bien.*)

- Ask: **¿Qué te dicen todos los detalles de la lista?** (*Possible response: Te dicen lo que hizo Ana para que crecieran los tulipanes.*)

On Your Own

Have children write a list of sentence topics that explain why or how something happened. Ask them to choose a topic and brainstorm details about it. Then have children write a sentence that explains how or why something happens.

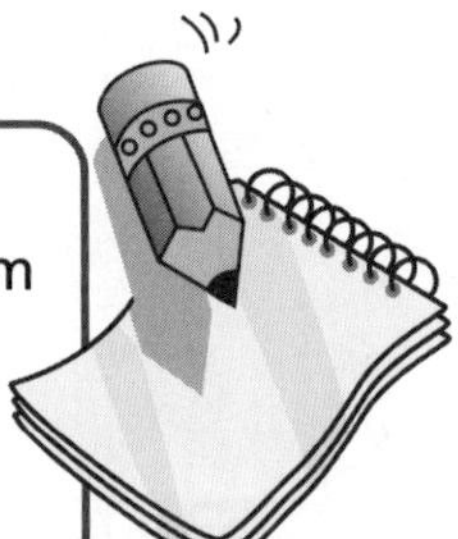

AFTER

Spelling Lesson
page 389I

Connect Spelling and Phonics

RETEACH combination of consonants: *fl* and *fr*. Write the word *fresa* on the board. Explain that you will say four more words in which the /fr/ sound is used. Have volunteers write each word on the board. Then write the word *flor* on the board, explain that you will say four words in which the /fl/ sound is used, and repeat the process.

1. frambuesa	**2. flotando***	**3. flores***	**4. fraile**
5. flaco	**6. flamenco**	**7. fractura**	**8. frijol**

Word appears in *Las zanahorias del Sr. Carver

Dictate the following sentence and have children write it: *La flaca sufrió una fractura cuando bailaba el flamenco.*

Build and Read Longer Words

Remind children that they have learned how to decode words with the /fl/ and /fr/ sounds.

Write the word *frutero* on the board. Tell children that they can sometimes figure out long words by looking for syllables, prefixes and suffixes. Cover *ero* and have a volunteer read the word *frut.* What word does this resemble? (*fruta*) Can anyone figure out what frutero means? (*dish for fruit*) Point out that *frutero* uses the /fr/ sound and spelling.

FLUENCY BUILDER Have children choose a passage from *Las zanahorias del Sr. Carver* to read aloud to a partner. You may have children choose passages that they found interesting, or have them choose one of the following options:

- Read pages 110–112. (From *Quiero comer zanahorias...* through *...Ben estaba orgulloso.* Total: 98 words.)
- Read pages 114–115. (From *Por fin llego!...* through *...¿Y qué esperamos?* Total: 82 words.)

Encourage children to read their passages aloud to their partners three times. Have the child rate his or her own reading on a scale from 1 to 4.

BEFORE

Weekly Assessments

Review Vocabulary

To revisit Vocabulary Words prior to the weekly assessment, use these true or false questions. Have volunteers take turns reading aloud the sentences. Children determine whether the definitions are true or false. Encourage them to then correct the false sentences.

1. Una **carrera de relevos** es una carrera en la que se reemplazan a los corredores. (*verdadero*)
2. Si una tela se **arrugó**, formó muchos pliegues pequeños. (*verdadero*)
3. La persona que se **arrodillaba** arrodillaba no se doblaba las piernas para hacerlo. (*falso*)
4. Estoy muy cómoda en este mullido sillón.
5. Cuando ellos **escondían** escondían los regalos, los ponían para que los vieran todos (*falso*)
6. El **destello** de la luz en los metales se produce cuando sus superficies no están pulidas. (*falso*)

You may want to display the Vocabulary Words and definitions on page 139 and have children copy them to use when they study for the vocabulary test.

INTERVENTION PRACTICE BOOK page 58

Focus Skill Review Make Inferences

To review Making Inferences before the weekly assessment, distribute *Intervention Practice Book* p. 58. Have volunteers read aloud the first direction line and the sentences. Guide children to notice details and think about what is happening to help them make a reasonable inference.

Review Test Prep

Para ti pages 392–393

Ask children to turn to page 393 of the *Pupil Edition*. Call attention to the Tips for answering the test questions. Tell children that paying attention to these tips can help them answer not only the test questions but also other test questions like these.

INTERVENTION ASSESSMENT BOOK

Have children follow along as you read each test question and the tip that goes with it. Discuss how it is sometimes helpful to reread a paragraph to make sure you find the important information. Tell children to think about the clues and read each answer choice. Direct them to look at the words in the paragraph to see if the clues match the choice.

Self-Selected Reading

Have children select their own books to read independently. They might choose books from the classroom library shelf, or you may wish to offer a group of appropriate books from which children can choose.

- *Alrededor de la hoguera* See page 393 in the *Teacher's Edition* for an Independent Reading Plan
- *¿Cómo sabes que es invierno? Por* Allan Fowler. Children's Press, 1994.
- *Por fin es carnaval* por Arthur Dorros. Dutton, 1991.

After children have chosen their books, give each child a copy of *Mi diario de lectura,* which can be found on page R35 in the back of the *Teacher's Edition*. Have children fill in the information at the top of the form. Then have them use the log to keep track of their reading and to record their responses to the literature.

Conduct student-teacher conferences. Arrange time for each child to conference with you individually about his or her self-selected reading. Have children bring their *Reading Logs* to share with you at the conference. Children might also choose a favorite passage to read aloud to you. Ask questions about the book designed to stimulate discussion. For example, you might ask the child if it was necessary to make inferences in the story and what information helped him or her to make the inferences.

FLUENCY PERFORMANCE Have children read aloud to you the passage from *Mr. Carver's Carrots* that they selected and practiced with their partners. Keep track of the number of words each child reads correctly. Ask the child to rate his or her own performance on the 1–4 scale. If children are not happy with their oral reading, give them an opportunity to continue practicing and then to read the passage to you again.

See *Oral Reading Fluency Assessment* for monitoring progress.

LESSON 15

BEFORE

Building Background and Vocabulary

Use with

"Fiesta de calabazas"

Review Phonics: Identify and read words accented on last syllable

Identify the sound. Ask children to listen for the spoken accent on the last syllable as you say the words *limón* and *pastel.* Then have children repeat the following sentence twice: *¡El pastel de limón casi me dio un ataque del corazón! Ask them to identify the words that have spoken accents on the last syllable.*

Associate letters to sound. Write on the board: *Yo quiero escribir una carta de amor que nazca de mi corazón.* Underline the following words: *escribir, amor, corazón.* Explain that the spoken accent on these words falls on the last syllable. Point out that while *corazón* has a written accent on the last syllable, the others do not. Have the children say these words.

INTERVENTION PRACTICE BOOK page 60

Word building – syllables. Write on the board the spelling words that have a spoken accent on the last syllable: (*salón, caracol, mantel, festival, azul*). Read each word aloud and ask children how many syllables each word has. Invite volunteers to underline the syllables which contain the spoken accent.

Apply the skill. Write the spelling words on the board in random order mixed in with 5 words that have spoken accents on the penultimate syllable (*mesa, examen, casa, maestra, plata*). Form two columns with the heads *accent on last syllable, accent on second to last syllable.* Ask the children to come to the board and write the words in the correct column.

Introduce Vocabulary

PRETEACH lesson vocabulary. Tell children that they are going to learn five new words that they will see again when they read a story called *Fiesta de calabazas.* Teach each Vocabulary Word using the process shown in the box.

Write the word.
Say the word.
Track the word and have children repeat it.
Give the meaning or context.

Use these suggestions or similar ideas to give the meaning or context.

arrastró Explain that when something is extremely heavy, you tend to transport it in this way. Demonstrate with a prop for the class.

presumidamente Tell the children that this can describe someone with too much pride.

corona	Describe this word by refering to the crown that a princess wears.
aldea	Compare this to a city that is smaller, consisting of a group of houses.
enredaderas	Tell the children that a plant has this characteristic when it climbs a wall or wraps around posts for support.

For vocabulary activities, see Vocabulary Games on pages 2–7.

Vocabulary Words

arrastró jaló, transportó por el suelo

presumidamente con demasiado orgullo

corona círculo de metal para la cabeza, a menudo con puntas

aldea grupo de casas más pequeño que una ciudad

enredaderas plantas con tallos largos que necesitan sostén

AFTER

Building Background and Vocabulary

Apply Vocabulary Strategies

Use synonyms/antonyms. Write the words *aldea* and *caserío* on the board, and explain that these words are synonyms. Tell the children that recognizing synonyms will help them figure out the meanings of words.

> MODEL **Yo sé que los sinónimos son palabras que tiene el mismo o muy parecidos significados. Si yo sé que *caserío* y *aldea* son sinónimos, esto me ayudará a recordar sus significados. Guíe a los niños en un procedimiento similar a entender el significado de la palabra *arrastró.* Relaciónela con jaló, y con *deslizó.***

RETEACH **lesson vocabulary.** Have children listen to each of the following questions. Tell them to hold up the word card that answers each question. You may want to write the questions on the board to help visual learners.

1. **¿Qué nombre recibe un pequeño grupo de casas?** (*aldea*)
2. **¿Cómo se llaman las plantas que no tienen su propio apoyo?** (*enredaderas*)
3. **¿Qué hizo Juan para mover un pesado saco de papas a la cocina?** (*lo arrastró*)
4. **¿Cómo vive la gente que no es modesta?** (*presumidamente*)
5. **¿Qué usan los reyes sobre su cabeza?** (*corona*)

FLUENCY BUILDER Use *Intervention Practice Book* page 59. Read aloud each word in the first column and have children repeat it. Then have children work in pairs to read the words in the first column aloud to each other. Follow the same procedure with each of the remaining columns. After partners have practiced reading aloud the words in each column separately, have them practice the entire list.

Save *Intervention Practice Book* page 59 to use on pages 151 and 153.

BEFORE

Reading
Fiesta de calabazas
pages 396–419

USE SKILL CARD 15A

Focus Skill Predict Outcomes

PRETEACH the skill. Point out to children that readers use what they learn at the beginning of a story to predict what will happen later on. Explain that it is important to pay attention to clues in the story because it will help them make predictions.

Have children look at **side A** of ***Tarjeta de destrezas 15: Predecir resultados*/Skill Card 15: Predict Outcomes**. Read the description of *predicting.* Then read the paragraph with children. Now call attention to the web and have volunteers take turns reading the prediction and clues aloud. Ask:

- **¿Qué pasaría si no tuvieras la información de que el ganador del año pasado practicaba cada mañana por una hora antes de ir a la escuela?** (*Possible response: No supieras qué información te da la pista de que ella puso 6 por la mañana en su despertador.*)
- **¿Por qué crees que Melba ganará el concurso?** (*Possible response: Porque ella tiene la determinación para ganar.*)

Prepare to Read: *Fiesta de Calabazas*

Preview. Read the title of the story aloud. Explain that this is a fantasy story that takes place in a make believe world. Make certain that the children understand what this means.

Para ti
pages 396–419

- **Pages 396–397:** En estas dos primeras páginas del cuento veo el título y también el dibujo de unas personas, animales y un montón de calabazas. Yo sé que va a occurir una fiesta de calabazas, pero estoy intentando imaginar len qué consiste.
- **Pages 398–400:** Ahora veo unos dibujos de unos personajes que están relajados, en su casa y afuera. ¿Irán ellos a la fiesta de calabazas?
- **Pages 401–403:** Los personajes empiezan a animarse. En la página 403 parece que el hombre está sorprendido. Voy a leer para enterarme por qué tiene esa expresión.

Set purpose. Model setting a purpose for reading *Fiesta de Calabazas.*

MODEL Por lo que he visto en estos dibujos, me gustaría leer sobre la *Fiesta de calabazas.* Quiero saber más sobre la cultura de la gente del cuento y también qué hacen con las calabazas.

AFTER

Reading
Fiesta de calabazas
pages 396–419

Reread and Summarize

Have children reread and summarize *Fiesta de calabazas* in sections, as described below.

Pages 398–402
Leamos estas páginas para recordar qué hace la vieja Juana con las calabazas y quién pudiera ser el nombre.

Summary: La vieja Juana gana el concurso todos los años, cosechando las calabazas más grandes. El nombre del hombrecillo es Fernando el Fanfarrón. Él quiere ganar el concurso también.

Pages 403–412
Leamos las páginas 403–412 para saber qué hacen Juana y Fernando para estar listos para el concurso.

Summary: Juana riega y le habla dulcemente a sus calabazas. Fernando la espía y trata de copiar lo que ella hace. Cuando sus calabazas no crecen, el se las roba.

Pages 413–419
Leamos para saber qué sucede en la fiesta.

Summary: Juana se da cuenta que las calabazas ganadoras son las de ella y puede probarlo trayendo las ramas de donde fueron cortadas. El presidente del concurso la nombra ganadora de la corona. Fernando le pide disculpas y Juana le dice que le enseñará a cosechar unas hermosas calabazas.

FLUENCY BUILDER Be sure children have copies of *Intervention Practice Book* page 59, which you used for the previous Fluency Builder activity. Call attention to the sentences on the bottom half of the page. The slashes break the sentences into phrases to allow you to work on natural phrasing. Tell children that their goal is to read each phrase or sentence smoothly. Model appropriate pace, expression and phrasing as you read each sentence and have children read it after you. Then have children practice by reading the sentences aloud to a partner three times.

BEFORE

Making Connections
pages 422–423

Directed Reading of *El secreto de la señorita Lechuza* pp. 118–124

Sonidos alegres
pp. 118–124

Pages 118–119

Have children read page 118. Point out the characters and setting. Ask: **¿Sobre qué hablan ellos? Al ver esta página, ¿qué crees que va a ocurrir en el cuento?** (*Possible response:* Hablan sobre los melones de la Srta. Lechuza, quien parece ser amiga de ellos. Yo creo que ellos van a ayudarla con el Concurso del Mejor Melón.) **PREDICTING OUTCOMES**

Ask the children to continue and read page 119. Model using the Self-Correction strategy:

> MODEL **Al principio, pensé que los animales de la primera página iban a comerse todos los melones del jardín de la Srta. Lechuza. Pero, después de leerlo más de una vez, me dí cuenta de que ellos son amigos de ella y quieren ayudarla. Pues, los amigos se dan cuenta de que la tierra no está buena para los melones este año y la Srta. está envejeciendo.** Focus Strategy **SELF-CORRECT**

Pages 120–121

Discuss with the children that the animals are making a plan. Ask them: **¿Por qué ellos están ayudándola en secreto?** (*Possible answer: Porque la Srta. Lechuza es muy orgullosa para pedir ayuda.*) **IMPORTANT DETAILS**

Continue reading with the children through page 121. Ask: **¿Por qué ellos trabajaban por la noche?** (*Possible response: Para que la Srta. Lechuza no pudiera verlos.*) **DRAW CONCLUSION**

Pages 122

Have the children read page 122 to see what the result of the three friends work is. Ask them: **¿Cuál es el resultado de su duro trabajo y cómo responde la Srta.?** (*Possible response: El resultado es grandes melones. La Srta. Lechuza está sorprendida.*) **MAIN IDEA**

Pages 123–124

Encourage the children to read page 123 together. Ask: **¿Sabe la Srta. que ellos la habían ayudado con los melones?** (*Possible response: Sí porque ella les responde al fin de la página que sus melones son los mejores porque tiene amigos.*) Conclude the story with the children on page 124. Ask: **¿Cómo sabe ella que ellos la ayudaron?** (*Possible response: Porque la Srta. es un búho y ¡los búhos pueden ver en la oscuridad!*) **MAKE JUDGEMENTS**

Summarize the selection. Encourage children to explain what the friends do with the melons at the end of the story.

Answers to *Think About It* Questions

1. Los animales palean, rastrillan y espantan los conejos en el huerto para cosechar los melones. Ella lo descubre porque puede ver en la oscuridad y los vio trabajando en su huerto.
2. Sienten mucho afecto. Se sabe porque van a ayudarle con la cosecha de los melones para que gane el premio otra vez
3. Acepta las respuestas apropriadas.

AFTER

Skill Review
page 425C

USE SKILL CARD 15B

Focus Skill Review Predict Outcomes

RETEACH the skill. Have children look at **side B** of ***Tarjeta de destreza 15: Predecir resultados*/Skill Card 15: Predict Outcomes.** Read the skill reminder with them, and have a volunteer read the paragraph aloud.

Read aloud the set of directions. Explain that children will work with partners to create their own webs. Remind them to use clues they read to predict the outcome.

After children have completed their webs, have them display them and explain their predicted outcome and the clues they found to help them. Point out that *El secreto de la señorita Lechuza* has clues that help them predict what the animals did. Ask volunteers to identify the clues.

Review Phonics Skill: Spoken accent on the last syllable

RETEACH the skill. Read aloud the following sentence: *Miguel me regaló un pastel para mi cumpleaños.* Have children listen for the spoken accent on the last syllable. Then read this list aloud and have children raise their hands when they hear the accent fall on the last syllable: *Miguel, regaló, pastel.*

FLUENCY BUILDER Be sure that children have copies of *Intervention Practice Book* page 59. Explain that today children will practice the sentences on the bottom half of the page by reading them aloud on tape. Assign new partners. Have children take turns reading the sentences aloud to each other and then reading them on tape.

BEFORE

Drafting a Book Report
page 394M

Book Report: Identify Story Elements

Build on prior knowledge. Tell children that they are going to prepare notes that will help them write a book report. Explain that a book report tells someone about a book. Remind children of the important parts of a story: character, plot, setting. Explain that these details should be found in the story and written down to include later in the book report.

Lo que recuerdo de un cuento:
perro
María—triste
Una calle llena en la ciudad
Camión blanco
El perro se salió

Construct the text. "Share the pen" with children. Guide them in making notes of what they remember from the story to help them later when they write their book report. For example:

- María tenía un perro grande. Ellos estaban caminando por una calle llena en la ciudad. Un camión blanco se dirigía a ella y el perro. El perro se le fue a María. Ella estaba triste.

Revisit the text. Go back and read the notes together. Ask: **¿Qué pasaría si se me olvidara hacer unos apuntes sobre los personajes, dónde ocurrió el cuento, o algo de lo que ocurrió?** (*Necesitas incluir cosas sobre los personajes, el ambiente, y el tema en un trabajo de un libro o corres el riesgo de olvidar algo importante.*)

- Guide children to combine details and organize them by placing what they remember about the characters together, the plot together, and the setting together. For example: Personajes: María y su perro; Ambiente: una calle llena en la ciudad; Tema: un camión blanco viene y el perro se escapa.

On Your Own

Have children write notes about a story they have read. Ask them to make notes about the characters, setting, and plot.

AFTER

Spelling Lesson
page 42 II

Connect Spelling and Phonics

RETEACH words accented on the last syllable. Write the word *hotel* on the board. Explain that you will say eight more words where the accent is spoken on the last syllable. Have volunteers write each word on the board.

1. corazón	**2. detrás**	**3. Azul**	**4. pastel**
5. reloj	**6. acción**	**7. salón**	**8. caminar**

Dictate the following sentence and have children write it down in their notebooks: *¡El pastel salió azul del horno, el color de mi reloj!*

Build and Read Longer Words

Remind children that they have learned how to recognize words that have the spoken accent on the last syllable.

Write the word *fanfarronear* on the board. Tell children that they can sometimes figure out long words by looking for syllables, prefixes and suffixes. Cover *-near* and have a volunteer read the word *fanfarron*. What word does this word mean? Can anyone figure out what *fanfarronear* means? (It is the verb form, meaning to brag or bluster.) Point out that *fanfarronear* and *fanfarron* both have spoken accents on the last syllable.

FLUENCY BUILDER Have children choose a passage from *El secreto de la señorita Lechuza* to read aloud to a partner. You may have children choose passages that they found interesting, or have them choose one of the following options:

- Read pages 120–121. (From *Más tarde...* through *...Shhhh! dijo Zorro Kit.* Total: 91 words.)
- Read pages 123–124. (From *Usted ganará...* through *... MUCHÍSIMA razón.* Total: 111 words.)

Encourage children to read their passages aloud to their partners three times. Have the child rate his or her own reading on a scale from 1 to 4.

BEFORE
Weekly Assessments

Review Vocabulary

To revisit Vocabulary Words prior to the weekly assessment, use these true or false questions. Have volunteers take turns reading aloud the sentences. Children determine whether the definitions are true or false. Encourage them to then correct the false sentences.

1. Una corona puede ser un premio. (*verdadero*)
2. Las plantas con enredaderas tienen tallos largos y necesitan sostén. (*verdadero*)
3. Cuando Elisa arrastró el saco, lo hizo por el aire. (*falso*)
4. Es tan orgulloso. Es tan presumido. (*verdadero*)
5. Los Ángeles es una aldea. (*falso*)

You may want to display the Vocabulary Words and definitions on page 149 and have children copy them to use when they study for the vocabulary test.

Focus Skill Review Predict Outcomes

To review the predicting outcomes before the weekly assessment, distribute *Intervention Practice Book*, p. 62. Have volunteers read aloud the first direction line and the sentences. Guide children to identify what predicting an outcome means.

Review Test Prep

Ask children to turn to page 425 of the *Pupil Edition*. Call attention to the Tips for answering the test questions. Tell children that paying attention to these tips can help them answer not only the test questions but also other test questions like these.

Have children follow along as you read each test question and the tip that goes with it. Explain that clues are usually given to help you figure out what will happen. Remind children to look back at the text for clues to see if a choice makes sense.

Self-Selected Reading

Have children select their own books to read independently. They might choose books from the classroom library shelf, or you may wish to offer a group of appropriate books from which children can choose.

- *Buscar animales*. (See page 425S of the *Teacher's Edition* for an Independent Reading Plan.)
- *¡Fiesta!* Por June Behrens. Children's Press, 1986.
- *¿Quién llegará primero?* Por Beatriz Dumerc. SM, Ediciones, 1990.

After children have chosen their books, give each child a copy of *Mi diario de lectura*, which can be found on page R35 in the back of the *Teacher's Edition*. Have children fill in the information at the top of the form. Then have them use the log to keep track of their reading and to record their responses to the literature.

Conduct student-teacher conferences. Arrange time for each child to confer with you individually about his or her self-selected reading. Have children bring their *Diarios de lectura* to share with you at the conference. Children might also like to choose a favorite passage to read aloud to you. Ask questions designed to stimulate discussion about the book. For example, you might ask children to locate details about the plot and ask if what happened in the story could happen in real life.

FLUENCY PERFORMANCE Have children read aloud to you the passage from "Miss Owl's Secret" that they selected and practiced with their partners. Keep track of the number of words the child reads correctly. Ask the child to rate his or her own performance on the 1–4 scale. If children are not happy with their oral reading, give them an opportunity to continue practicing and then to read the passage to you again.

See *Oral Reading Fluency Assessment* for monitoring progress.

Use with

"El día que la boa de Jimmy se comió la ropa"

Review Phonics: Acento Enfático (Cómo, Qué, Por qué, Quién, Sí)

Identify the sound. Have children repeat the following sentence three times: *¿Por qué él no me saludó?* Ask them which words in the sentence have the acento enfático that they hear in (*qué, por qué, él, saludó*)

Associate letters to sound. On the board, write: *¿Por qué él no me saludó?* Circle the words *por qué, saludó* and *l.* Explain that these words have a written accent, a *tilde.* Underline the letters that carry the written accent and tell them that the accent represents where the emphasis is placed when speaking the word. Ask them if they know of any other words that carry the *tilde* (*sí, cómo, quién*).

Word blending. Model how to blend and read the word *por qué.* Slide your hand under the letters as you slowly elongate the sounds making emphasis where the accent falls. Point out that the accent is emphasized in this word when it is used in a question. Then read *por qué* naturally. Follow a similar procedure for *quién, qué, sí.*

INTERVENTION PRACTICE BOOK

page 64

Apply the skill. *Vowel Substitution.* Write the following words on the board, and have children read them aloud. Make the changes necessary to form the words in parentheses. All those words outside of parenthesis (with the exception of *sí*) are interrogative words. Have children read each new word.

por qué (porque)	**sí** (si)	**cómo** (como)
quién (quien)	**qué** (que)	**dónde** (donde)

Introduce Vocabulary

PRETEACH lesson vocabulary. Tell children that they are going to learn five new words that they will see again when they read a story called *El día que la boa de Jimmy se comió la ropa.* Teach every Vocabulary Word using the strategies in the box below.

Write the word.

Say the word.

Track the word and have children repeat it.

Give the meaning or context.

Use the following suggestions or similar ideas to give the meaning or context.

aburrida Point out the *-a* ending. Relate by role-playing appropriate facial expression.

agachó Point out the *-ó* ending. Relate

	by role-playing the act of bending down suddenly under your desk.
alborotó	Relate by saying something that stirs you up, gets you excited and agitated.
excursión	Suggest related words: *viajecito, paseo.* Explain that this could be a day or weekend trip.
tractor	Show a picture of a *tractor.*

For vocabulary activities, see Vocabulary Games on pages 2–7.

Vocabulary Words

aburrida no es interesante

agachó de repente doblan las rodillas para hacerse más pequeños

alborotó estar emocionado, agitado

excursión un viajecito

tractor una máquina en la finca

AFTER

Building Background and Vocabulary

Apply Vocabulary Strategies

RETEACH lesson vocabulary. Write the word *aburrida* on chart paper and help children define it. Tell children that they can sometimes figure out the meaning of the word if they know its antonym. An antonym is a word that means the opposite of another word.

> **MODEL** **La palabra *aburrida* significa que algo no es interesante. Si saco la palabra *no* de estas palabras, me quedo con *es interesante.* Ser interesante es lo opuesto de ser aburrido. Interesante y aburrido son antónimos.**

Guide children in using a similar procedure to decode the words *agachó* and *alborotó.*

Vocabulary activity. Have children listen to each of the following sentences. Tell them to hold up the word card that completes each rhyme. Reread the sentence aloud with the correct answer.

1. En la finca, no soy un actor cuando el granjero me conduce, sino soy un *(tractor)*.
2. Ella es divertida, así que no es *(aburrida)*.
3. Vamos a un paseo por el campo, vamos de *(excursión)*.
4. Para hablar con el niño se *(agachó)*.
5. La clase empezó a gritar, o sea se con la noticia *(alborotó)*.

FLUENCY BUILDER Using *Intervention Practice Book* page 63, read each word in the first column aloud and have children repeat it. Then have partners to read the words in the first column aloud to each other. After partners have practiced reading aloud the words in each column separately, have them practice the entire list. Save *Intervention Practice Book* page 63 on pages 161 and 163.

BEFORE

Reading
El día que la boa de Jimmy se comió la ropa
pages 16–31

USE SKILL CARD 16A

Focus Skill Cause and Effect

PRETEACH the skill. Point out to children there are reasons why things happen in a story. Why something happens is *la causa.* What happens is *el efecto.* Explain that sometimes it is easy to see why things happen in a story, and other times, readers need to ask themselves why they think something happened.

Have children look at **side A** of **Skill Card 16: La Causa y el Efecto.** Read the definition of cause and effect. Next read the story with children.

Now call attention to the chart and have volunteers take turns reading the information aloud. Ask:

- **¿Por qué se divertieron durante la excursión?** (*Porque el caballo empezó a reírse.*)
- **¿Por qué hay frases por los dos lados del cuadro?** (*Possible response: Algo causa un efecto, que causa otra reacción.*)

Prepare to Read: *El día que la boa de Jimmy se comió la ropa*

Preview. Tell children that they are going to read a selection entitled *El día que la boa de Jimmy se comió la ropa.* Explain that this is a fantasy selection about a girl who describes things that probably did not really happen on her class trip. Then preview the selection.

Días maravillosos
pages
16–31

- **Pages 16–17:** Veo el título, **El día que la boa de Jimmy se comió la ropa**, y el nombre de la autora. También veo un dibujo de una serpiente grande. Creo que la serpiente es la boa de Jimmy.
- **Pages 18–19:** Veo la ilustración de una chica que vuelve de la escuela. Los personajes y el ambiente de los dibujos me parecen que son reales. La chica le dice a su madre que una vaca lloró porque un fardo de heno se la cayó encima. Creo que ella inventó estas cosas.
- **Pages 20–23:** Veo a los cerdos que saltan y tiran los almuerzos en un autobús escolar. Yo sé que los cerdos no pueden hacer eso. También veo otras cosas fantásticas que ocurrieron según la chica, durante el viaje de la clase. Pienso que la chica está exagerando lo que realmente ocurrió.

Set purpose. Model setting a purpose for *reading El día que la boa de Jimmy se comió la ropa.*

MODEL **Por lo que he visto hasta ahora, creo que voy a enterarme sobre una serpiente que se comió la ropa durante una excursión escolar. Voy a leer este cuento que parece muy gracioso.**

AFTER

Reading
El día que la boa de Jimmy se comió la ropa
pages 16–31

Reread and Summarize

Have children reread and summarize *El día que la boa de Jimmy se comió la ropa* in sections, as described below.

Pages 18–21 **Vamos a releer las páginas 18–21 y recordar como la chica cuenta lo sucedido en la excursión.**

Summary: Ella dijo que una vaca lloró porque le cayó encima un fardo de heno. Un granjero lo chocó con su tractor, mientras le gritaba a los cerdos para que salieran del autobus escolar, donde se comían el almuerzo de los niños.

Pages 22–23 **Al releamosr las páginas 22–23 para saber por qué los cerdos se estaban comiendo los almuerzos de los niños.**

Summary: Porque los niños les quitaron el maiz, que era su comida. Los niños se tiraban el maiz, porque se les había acabado los huevos.

Pages 24–27 **Vamos a releer las páginas 24–27 para recordar que pasó cuando Jimmy trajo su boa a la finca.**

Summary: A los pollos, no les gustó la boa, se alborotaron y una gallina puso un huevo que cayó en la cabeza de Juanita. Pensando que Tomás se lo había tirado, le tiró otro a él, que se agachó. Él repondió con otro huevo. En un momento todos se estaban tirando huevos y Jimmy dejó caer la boa.

Pages 28–31 **Vamos a leer las páginas 28–31 para recordar que pasó al final del cuento.**

Summary: La boa se comió la ropa que estaba en el cordel de la granjera y los niños tuvieron que salir corriendo, Jimmy tuvo que dejar la boa, pero se quedó con un cerdo, que estaba en el autobús que ahora es su mascota. La boa se comió la ropa que estaba en el cordel de la granjera y los niños tuvieron que salir corriendo, Jimmy tuvo que dejar la boa, pero se quedó con un cerdo, que estaba en el autobús que ahora es su mascota.

FLUENCY BUILDER Use *Intervention Practice Book* page 63. Call attention to the sentences on the bottom half of the page. The slashes break the sentences into phrases to allow you to work on natural phrasing. Model appropriate pace, expression and phrasing as you read each sentence and have children read it after you. Then have children practice by reading the sentences aloud three times to a partner.

BEFORE

Making Connections
pages 36–37

Directed Reading: *La noche no tan aburrida*, pp. 126–132

Sonidos alegres
pp. 126–132

Ask a volunteer to read aloud the title. Help children to see that Saúl is bored. Read pages 126–127 while children listen to find out how Saúl feels about the night.

Pages 126–127

Ask: **¿Cómo se siente Saúl sobre la noche?** (*Possible response: Está aburrido.*) **NOTE DETAILS**

Ask: **¿Por qué sale Saúl?** (*Possible response: Dobi, para salir, le ladra a Saúl, que también necesitaba un paseo.*) Focus Skill **CAUSE AND EFFECT**

Pages 128–129

Have children read pages 128-129 to find out where Saúl and Dobi go on their walk. Ask: **¿Dónde ocurre el cuento? ¿Cómo es allí?** (*Possible response: Está en una cala, donde hay dunas y un lago.*) **SETTING**

Pages 130–131

Read aloud page 130 to children. Model using the Make and Confirm Predictions strategy in order for children to predict why the fisherman is throwing all the fish back.

> MODEL **Mientras leo, intento a averiguar qué va a ocurrir en el cuento. No entiendo por qué el granjero pescaba, pero devolvía los peces al agua. Leo que los peces son rojos, y llevan números. Me parece que Rosa está jugando. Pienso que el granjero también está jugando. Sigo leyendo para saber si estoy en lo cierto.** Focus Strategy **MAKE AND CONFIRM PREDICTIONS**

Page 132

Have children read page 132 to find out what really happened to Saúl. Ask: **¿Saúl vio el granjero pescando en la cala? ¿Qué pasó?** (*Possible response: No, Saúl estaba durmiendo y soñó sobre el granjero.*) **DRAW CONCLUSIONS**

Summarize the selection. Ask children to think about why some people might think a game is boring and other people think it is fun.

INTERVENTION PRACTICE BOOK
page 65

Answers to *Piénsalo* Questions

1. Se quedó dormido y soño que había ido a dar un paseo con Dobi y estaba viendo pescar al granjero vecino en la orilla. **SUMMARY**
2. Porque recordó el sueño que tuvo y le pareció divertido. **INTERPRETATION**
3. Las respuestas pueden variar. **WRITE LIST OF GAMES**

AFTER

Skill Review
page 37I

USE SKILL CARD 16B

Focus Skill Review: Cause and Effect

RETEACH the skill. Have children look at **side B** of **Skill Card 16: Cause and Effect**. Read the skill reminder with them, and have a volunteer read the story aloud.

Read aloud the set of directions. Explain that children will work with partners to create their own charts. Remind them to look for the things that happen and the reasons that these things happen.

After children have completed their cause and effect charts, have them display and explain their work. Point out that the selection *La noche no tan aburrida* has causes and effects. Ask volunteers to name some of the things that happen and the reasons that they happen.

Review Phonics Skill from *El día que la boa de Jimmy se comó la ropa*

RETEACH acento enfático. Read aloud the following sentence: *Llegó de día en autobús.* Have children listen for the emphasis placed on each word. Then read this list aloud and have children raise their hands when they hear a word with *un acento enfático: llegó, día, autobús, cómo, qué.*

FLUENCY BUILDER Use *Intervention Practice Book* page 63. Explain that today children will practice the sentences on the bottom half of the page by recording them on tape. Assign new partners. Have children take turns reading the sentences aloud to each other and then recording them on tape.

INTERVENTION PRACTICE BOOK
page 63

BEFORE

Drafting a Good Beginning
page 39C

Writer's Craft: Writing a Good Beginning

Build on prior knowledge. Tell children that they are going to talk and write about good beginnings found in stories. Explain that a good beginning may help readers understand what the story will be about, or it may tell about something surprising that will make the reader interested or curious about the story. Ask children to share good beginnings of their favorite stories.

una excursión de la clase
finca
niños
animales de una finca
dinosaurio

Construct the text. "Share the pen" with children. Tell them the list of words that are in a story. Help children to organize some or all of the items on the list into a good beginning. For example:

> *Hoy fui de excursión con mi clase a una finca. Vi muchos animales en la finca. Vi un dinosaurio. Los otros niños le tuvieron miedo al dinosaurio.*

Revisit the text. Go back and read the story beginning together. Ask: **¿Qué te dice el comienzo del cuento?** (*Trata de una excurisión de la clase a una finca; hay muchos animales en la finca, entre ellos un dinosaurio.*)

- Guide children to make the story beginning more lively. Ask: **¿Cómo puedo cambiar el comienzo para convencer el lector de que no hay un dinosaurio en la finca?** (*No digas al principio que hay un dinosaurio en la finca.*) Make appropriate changes.
- Ask: **¿Puedo tener alguien narrando al principio? ¿Qué podría decir sobre la excursión de la clase?** Make appropriate changes.
- Have children read the completed story beginning aloud and then copy it on their papers.

On Your Own

Have children write one sentence that could be a beginning for the story. Invite them to read their sentences aloud.

AFTER

Spelling Lesson
page 33I

Connect Spelling and Phonics

RETEACH **acento enfático.** Tell children to number their papers 1–7. Dictate the following words, and have children write them. Then, write each word on the board and ask children to compare and make corrections. They should draw a line through a misspelled word and write the correct spelling below it.

1. palmoteó*	**2. también***	**3. alegré***	**4. maíz***
5. pregunté*	**6. mamá***	**7. lógico***	**5. agarró**

*** Word appears in *La noche no tan aburrida.***

Dictate the following sentence and have children write it: *Es lógico que me alegré porque mi mamá llegó rápido en autobús.*

Build and Read Longer Words

INTERVENTION ASSESSMENT BOOK

Remind children that they have learned how to decode words with the acento enfático. Explain that now they will use what they have learned to help them read some longer words.

Write the word *rápidamente* on the board. Remind children that they can often figure out longer words by looking for parts they know. Cover *mente,* and point out the *acento enfático* spelling pattern. Have children use the pattern to help them read the word part. Then cover *rápida*, and have children read *mente.* Model how to blend the word parts to read aloud the longer word *rápidamete.* Do the same to have children blend word parts to read these longer words: *autobús, excursión.*

FLUENCY BUILDER Have children choose a passage from *La noche no tan aburrida* to read aloud to a partner. You may have children choose passages that they found particularly interesting, or have them choose one of the following options:

- Read pages 126–127. (*From Era una calurosa*... through ...*de un rato.* Total: 84 words.)
- Read page 128–129. (*From ¡Gracias, Dobi*... through ...*con la mano.* Total: 106 words.)

SCALE	
1	Not good
2	Pretty good
3	Good
4	Great!

Children should read the selected passage aloud to their partners three times. Have the child rate each reading on a scale from 1 to 4.

BEFORE

Weekly Assessments

Review Vocabulary

1. Cuando ella se **agachó**, ella
a. estaba muy alta — b. estaba con las rodillas en suelo.

2. La película estaba **aburrida**, pues
a. la vi enterita. — b. me dormí.

3. Si la clase se va de **excursión**, hace
a. un viaje. — b. una fiesta.

4. Si algo te **alborotó**, estás
a. muy relajado. — b. excitado.

5. Los que conducen los **tractores** de ordinario son los
a. pescadores. — b. granjeros.

Correct responses: 1.b, 2.b, 3.a, 4.b, 5.b.

You may want to display the vocabulary words and definitions on page 159 and have children copy them to use when they study for the vocabulary test.

INTERVENTION PRACTICE BOOK page 66

Focus Skill Review Cause and Effect

To review compare and contrast before the weekly assessment, distribute *Intervention Practice Book* p. 66. Have volunteers read aloud the first direction line and the sentences. Guide children to think about the reasons why things happen.

Review Test Prep

Días maravillosos page 39

Ask children to turn to page 39 of the *Pupil Edition*. Call attention to the Tips for answering the test questions. Tell children that paying attention to these tips can help them answer not only the test questions but also other test questions like these.

INTERVENTION ASSESSMENT BOOK

Have children follow along as you read each test question and the tip that goes with it. Remind children that they can reread the story before they make their choices.

Self-Selected Reading

Have children select their own books to read independently. They might choose books from the classroom library shelf, or you may wish to offer a group of appropriate books from which children can choose.

- *Los animales del zoo.* Harcourt *Teacher's Edition*
- *Borreguita y el coyote* por Verna Aardema. Scholastic, 1993.
- *Harold y el lápiz color morado* por Crockett Johnson. Arco Iris, 1995.

After children have chosen their books, give each child a copy of *Mi diario de lectura,* which can be found on page R35 in the back of the *Teacher's Edition.* Have children fill in the information at the top of the form. Then have them use the log to keep track of their reading and to record their responses to the literature.

Conduct student-teacher conferences. Arrange time for each child to conference with you individually about his or her self-selected reading. Have children bring their *Diarios de lectura* to share with you at the conference. Children might also like to choose a favorite passage to read aloud to you. Ask questions designed to stimulate discussion about the book. For example, you might ask children to describe a humorous event in the story and to tell what caused it to happen.

FLUENCY PERFORMANCE Have children read aloud to you the passage from "La noche no tan aburrida" that they selected and practiced with their partners. Keep track of the number of words each child reads correctly. Ask the child to rate his or her own performance on the 1–4 scale. If children are not happy with their oral reading, give them an opportunity to continue practicing and then to read the passage to you again.

See *Oral Reading Fluency Assessment* for monitoring progress.

LESSON

17

BEFORE

Building Background and Vocabulary

Use with

"Use with Camilón, Comilón"

Review Phonics: *Suffixes -ón, -oso, -osa*

Identify the sound. Have children repeat the following sentence three times: *El perezoso es un gritón.* Ask them which words in the sentence have the *-ón* and/or *-oso/a* ending that they hear in *tablón* or *miedoso.* (*perezoso, gritón*)

Associate letters to sound. On the board, write: *El tristón siempre utiliza su cinturón.* Circle the words *tristón,* and *cinturón.* Explain that both have an *-ón* ending. Underline the letters *-ón* in *tristón* and *cinturón* and tell children that they stand for the /ón/ sound.

Word blending. Model how to blend and read the word *ruidoso.* Slide your hand under the letters as you slowly elongate the sounds. Then read *ruidoso* naturally. Follow a similar procedure for *tramposo, perezoso, tablón, gritón.*

INTERVENTION PRACTICE BOOK page 68

Apply the skill. *Vowel Substitution* Write the following words on the board, and have children read them aloud. Make the changes necessary to form the words in parentheses. Have children read each new word.

triste (tristón)	**ruido** (ruidoso)	**tabla** (tablón)
empalaga (empalagoso)	**grito** (gritón)	**trampa** (tramposo)
pereza (perezoso)	**miedo** (miedoso)	

Introduce Vocabulary

PRETEACH lesson vocabulary. Tell children that they are going to learn seven new words that they will see again when they read a story called *Camilón, Comilón.* Teach each Vocabulary Word using the strategies in the box below.

Write the word.
Say the word.
Track the word and have children repeat it.
Give the meaning or context.

Use the following suggestions or similar ideas to give the meaning or context.

atareadísima	Point out the *-ísima* ending. Relate to the phrase *muy ocupado*.
cesta	Show a picture of a basket. Explain this is where Easter eggs are placed.
corral	Relate to where horses are kept on a ranch.
glotonería	Relate to someone who eats too much.

merienda	Show a small snack.
perezoso	Role-play how to take it easy.
requesón	Point out various types of cheeses. Explain that this type is much more liquified.

For vocabulary activities, see Vocabulary Games on pages 2–7.

Vocabulary Words

atareadísima muy atareada, con mucho trabajo

cesta recipiente tejido con mimbre o juncos

corral lugar para los animales

glotonería las ganas de algo con exceso

merienda comida ligera

perezoso que no quiere trabajar

requesón leche cuajada

AFTER

Building Background and Vocabulary

Apply Vocabulary Strategies

Use familiar patterns. Write the word *glotonería* on chart paper and underline the letters *gloton* (*glotón*). Tell children that they can sometimes figure out the meaning of the word by looking for letter patterns that they know.

MODEL **La combinación de letras *glotón* me suena porque es una palabra que significa una persona que come en exceso y con ansia. El sufijo *-ería* convierte la palabra en sustantivo. Combino *glotón* con *-ería,* y veo que la palabra es *glotonería.***

Guide children in using a similar procedure to decode the words *merienda* and *perezoso*.

RETEACH **lesson vocabulary.** Have children listen to each of the following riddles. Tell them to hold up the word card that answers each riddle. Reread the riddles aloud with the correct answer. Then ask children how they made their choices.

1. Yo no hago nada. (*perezoso*)
2. Estoy muy ocupada. (*atareadísima*)
3. Estoy rodeada por una cerca. (*corral*)
4. Me puedes llenar de comida para un picnic. (*cesta*)
5. Soy una comidita pequeñita. (*merienda*)
6. Soy un tipo de queso cuajado. (*requesón*)
7. Yo como demasiado. (*glotonería*)

FLUENCY BUILDER Use *Intervention Practice Book* page 67. Read each word in the first column aloud and have children repeat it. Then have children work in pairs to read the words in the first column aloud to each other. Follow the same procedure with each of the remaining columns. After partners have practiced reading aloud the words in each column separately, have them practice the entire list. Save *Intervention Practice Book* page 67 to use on pages 171 and 173.

BEFORE

Reading *Camilón, comilón* pages 42–59

Focus Skill Cause and Effect

PRETEACH the skill. Point out to children that there are reasons why things happen in a story. Why something happens is the cause. What happens is the effect. Explain that sometimes it is easy to see why things happen in a story, and other times, readers need to ask themselves why they think something happened.

USE SKILL CARD 17A

Have children look at **side A** of **Skill Card 17: Cause and Effect.** Read the definition of *cause* and *effect*. Next, read the story with children.

Now call attention to the chart and have volunteers take turns reading the information aloud. Ask:

- **¿Porqué estaba triste el torero?** (*Possible response: Perdió su capa.*)
- **¿Qué pasa cuando el torero quiere recordar donde está su capa?** (*Possible response: Escribe una lista de todos los sitios donde había estado durante la mañana.*)

Prepare to Read: *Camilón, comilón*

Días maravillosos
pages 42–59

Preview. Tell children that they are going to read a selection entitled *Camilón, comilón*. Explain that this is a fantasy selection. Tell children that *Camilón, comilón* tells about a pig who was lazy and gluttonous. Then preview the selection.

- **Pages 42–43:** Veo el título, *Camilón, comilón* y el nombre del autor en la página 42. Veo unos dibujos de un cerdito relajándose en la tierra y en su cama. Por los dibujos, sé que es un cuento de fantasía.
- **Pages 44–45:** En las páginas 44–45, veo un dibujo de la casa del cerdito. El cerdito sale de la casa con una cesta. También hay un dibujo del cerdito y un perro quien tiene una sandía. Creo que el cerdito quiere que el perro ponga la sandía en su cesta.
- **Pages 46–47:** En estas páginas veo el cerdito con otros animales. El cerdito está con un caballo que tiene muchas calabazas. También visita a una vaca que le da botellas de leche.
- **Pages 48–49:** En estas páginas leo que el cerdito sigue pidiendo más comida para poner en su cesta. Lleva cada vez más comida en la cesta.

Set purpose. Model setting a purpose for reading *Camilón, comilón.*

MODEL **Por lo que he leído y visto, creo que voy a seguir al cerdito en su paseo para buscar comida. Voy a ver lo que hace con toda la comida. Leeré para entretenerme con este cuento divertido.**

AFTER

Reading ***Camilón, comilón*** ***pages 42–59***

Reread and Summarize

Have children reread and summarize *Camilón, comilón* in sections, as described below.

Pages 44–48

Vamos a leer las paginas 44–48 para recordar por qué el cerdito sale de su casa con una cesta vacía.

Summary: Camilón no quiere trabajar para obtener su comida. Así que se la pide a sus amigos.

Pages 49–51

Vamos a leer las páginas 49–51 para recordar lo que hace Camilón y lo que pide de sus amigos.

Summary: Sigue metiendo toda la comida en la cesta: plátanos, miel, lechugas, y zanahorias.

Pages 52–55

Vamos a leer las páginas 52–55 para saber por qué no estaba satisfecho Camilón.

Summary: Camilón sale con toda la comida para cenar en casa. Pero, vemos que algo diferente va a pasar.

Pages 56–58

Vamos a leer las páginas 56–58 para recordar lo que pasa al final del cuento.

Summary: Camilón era un glotón pero también a él le gustaba compartir todo. Por eso, invitó a todos sus amigos a una fiesta y compartió toda la comida.

FLUENCY BUILDER Be sure children have copies of *Intervention Practice Book* page 67, which you used for yesterday's Fluency Builder activity. Call attention to the sentences on the bottom half of the page. The slashes break the sentences into phrases to allow you to work on natural phrasing. Tell children that their goal is to read each phrase or sentence smoothly. Model appropriate pace, expression, and phrasing as you read each sentence, and have children read it after you. Then have children practice by reading the sentences aloud three times to a partner.

BEFORE

Making Connections
pages 62–63

Directed Reading of *El torero y yo*

Sonidos alegres
pages 134–139

Ask a volunteer to read aloud the title. Ask what a *torero* is. (*alguien que lucha contra los toros*) Have children read page 134. Ask: **¿Adónde va la chica de vacaciones?** (*Possible response: Va a visitar a su tía Clementina.*) **NOTE DETAILS**

Page 134

¿Qué significa "estoy usando mucho la imaginación"? (*Possible response: Inventar cosas.*) **SPECULATE**

Page 135

Have children read page 135 to find out about *la tía Clementina.* Ask: **¿Porqué a la tía no le importan tanto los modales ni las reglas?** (*Possible response: La tía cree que las reglas son para los padres y para la escuela.*) Focus Skill **CAUSE AND EFFECT** **¿Qué es lo único que falta en la casa de la tía?** (*Possible response: Un amigo con quien jugar*) **UNDERSTAND AUTHOR'S USE OF LANGUAGE** **¿Cuál crees que va a ser la sorpresa?** (*Possible response: un amigo con quien jugar*) **MAKE PREDICTIONS**

Page 136

Have children read page 136. Ask: **¿Cuál es la sorpresa?** (*Possible response: Un niño grande vestido de torero*) **CONFIRM PREDICTIONS**

Pages 137–138

Read aloud pages 137–138 to children. Model using the Make Inferences strategy in order for children to infer whether the big kid in the story is really a matador.

> **MODEL** **Mientras leo, tengo que pensar en lo que está pasando. Utilizo lo que ya sé sobre los toros y lo que me dice el autor y lo que veo en los dibujos. Yo creo que el chico grande no es un torero verdadero, pero tal vez quiere ser un torero cuando sea mayor.**
> Focus Strategy **MAKE INFERENCES**

Page 139

Have children read page 139. Ask: **¿Cómo la niña le ayuda al niño a decidir qué hacer?** (*Possible response: Ella nombra otras cosas que él puede hacer.*) **SUMMARIZE** **¿Qué decide el chico?** (*Possible response: Decide no ser un torero sino un granjero.*) **INTERPRET STORY EVENTS** **¿Crees que el cuento es real?** (*Acepta una variedad de respuestas.*) **EXPRESS OPINIONS**

Summarize the selection. Ask children to think about why people use their imaginations to tell about experiences they have not really had.

INTERVENTION PRACTICE BOOK
page 69

AFTER

Skill Review
page 65C

USE SKILL CARD 17B

Answers to *Piénsalo* Questions

1. Se va en tren a visitar a su tía. **SUMMARY**
2. Las respuestas pueden variar. Parecía que no practicaba desde hacía mucho tiempo. **INTERPRETATION**
3. Las respuestas pueden variar: Les contaría sus aventuras en casa de su tía Clementina. **SPECULATION**

Focus Skill Cause and Effect

RETEACH the skill. Have children look at **side B** of **Skill Card 17: Cause and Effect**. Read the skill reminder with them, and have a volunteer read the story aloud.

Read aloud the directions. Explain that children will work with partners to create their own charts. Remind them to look for the things that happen and the reasons that these things happen.

After children have completed their cause and effect charts, have them display and explain their work. Point out that the selection *El torero y yo* has causes and effects. Ask volunteers to name some of the things that happen and the reasons that they happen.

Focus Skill Review Phonics Skill from *Camilón, comilón*

RETEACH Suffixes: *-ón, -oso, -osa* Read aloud the following sentence: *Luis es un dormilón gracioso*. Have children listen for *-ón* and *-oso* endings. Then read this list aloud and have children raise their hands when they hear the *-ón* sound: *cabezón, juguetón, glotón*. Repeat for the *-oso* sound: *ruidoso, chismoso, miedoso.*

FLUENCY BUILDER Be sure that children have copies of *Intervention Practice Book* page 67. Explain that today children will practice the sentences on the bottom half of the page by reading them aloud on tape. Assign new partners. Have children take turns reading the sentences aloud to each other and then reading them on tape.

INTERVENTION PRACTICE BOOK
page 67

BEFORE

Drafting a Friendly Letter
page 65G

Writer's Craft: Audience and Purpose

Build on prior knowledge. Tell children that they are going to write a letter. Explain that writers write to different people, and have many different reasons for writing. Ask children to discuss letters they have written or received. Discuss and list reasons why writers write friendly letters.

> contar sobre unas vacaciónes
>
> dar direcciones
>
> invitar a alguien
>
> dar las gracias a alguien

Construct the text. "Share the pen" with children. Tell them that the list names purposes for writing a friendly letter. Help children to choose a purpose from the list and think of an audience for whom this purpose would be appropriate. Then help them construct a friendly letter. For example:

> **Querida tía Ángela,**
>
> **Estoy de vacaciones con mis amigos, los vaqueros. La estoy pasando muy bien durante las vacaciones. Aprendí como montar a caballo durante las vacaciones.**
>
> **Su sobrino,**
>
> **Paulo**

Revisit the text. Go back and read the friendly letter together. Ask: **¿Cuál es es propósito de esta carta?** (*Contar sobre unas vacaciónes.*)

- Guide children to make the letter read more smoothly. Ask: **¿Cuáles palabras puedo eliminar para que la carta fluya mejor?** (*durante las vacaciones.*) Make appropriate changes.
- Ask: **¿A quién más se puede dirigir esta carta?** (*padres, abuelos, amigos, profesores*)
- Have children read the completed friendly letter aloud and then have them copy it on their papers.

On Your Own

Have children list two purposes and two audiences for friendly letters they would like to write.

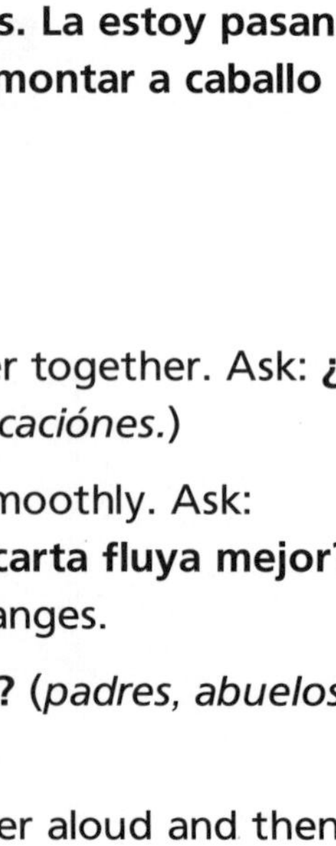

AFTER

Spelling Lesson
page 59I

Connect Spelling and Phonics

RETEACH **Suffixes *-ón, -oso, -osa.*** Tell children to number their papers 1–8. Dictate the following words, and have children write them. After each word is written, write it on the board so children can proofread their work. They should draw a line through a misspelled word and write the correct spelling below it.

1. glotón	**2. hermosa**	**3. perezoso***	**4. caprichoso**
5. camión	**6. tristón***	**7. llorón**	**8. carretón**

*** Word appears in *El torero y yo.***

Dictate the following sentence and have children write it: *El muchacho llorón es muy chismoso.*

Build and Read Longer Words

Remind children that they have learned how to decode words with the *-ón* and *-oso/a* endings. Explain that now they will use what they have learned to help them read some longer words.

INTERVENTION ASSESSMENT BOOK

Write the word *maravilloso* on the board. Remind children that they can often figure out longer words by looking for smaller words in them. Cover *-oso*, and have children read the smaller word *maravilla*. Follow a similar procedure to have them read the suffix *-oso*. Model how to blend the two smaller words to read aloud the longer word *maravilloso.* Do the same to have children blend word parts to read these longer words: *mentiroso* and *bondadoso*.

FLUENCY BUILDER Have children choose a passage from *El torero y yo* to read aloud to a partner. You may have children choose passages that they found particularly interesting, or have them choose one of the following options:

- Read pages 134–135. (*From Cuando llegan las vacaciones… through …¡sorpresa!* Total: 132 words.)
- Read pages 136–137. (*From Cuando ensillé mi caballo… through …a mi sombrero.* Total: 112 words.)

Children should read the selected passage aloud to their partners three times. Have the child rate each reading on a scale from 1 to 4.

BEFORE
Weekly Assessments

Review Vocabulary

1. Cuando eres un **perezoso**, puedes estar
a. de vacaciones. **b.** trabajando mucho.

2. En una **cesta**, puedes
a. sentarse. **b.** poner la comida.

3. En un **corral**, puedes encontrar
a. coches. **b.** animales.

4. Si sufres de **glotonería**,
a. comes un mucho. **b.** no comes nada.

5. Si comes **requesón**, comes
a. queso. **b.** frutas.

6. Una persona **atareadísima** es una persona
a. orgullosa. **b.** ocupada.

7. Si comes una **merienda**, comes
a. un poquito de comida. **b.** mucho.

Correct responses: 1.a, 2.b, 3.b, 4.a, 5.a, 6.b, 7.a.

You may want to display the Vocabulary Words and definitions on page 169 and have children copy them to use when they study for the vocabulary test.

INTERVENTION PRACTICE BOOK
page 70

Focus Skill Review Cause and Effect

To review compare and contrast before the weekly assessment, distribute *Intervention Practice Book* page 70. Have volunteers read aloud the first direction line and the sentences. Guide children to think about the reasons why things happen.

Review Test Prep

INTERVENTION ASSESSMENT BOOK

Días maravillosos
page 65

Ask children to turn to page 65 of the *Pupil Edition*. Call attention to the tips for answering the test questions. Tell children that paying attention to these tips can help them answer not only the test questions but also other test questions.

Have children follow along as you read each test question and the tip that goes with it. Remind children that they can say each word softly to themselves before making their choice.

Self-Selected Reading

Have children select their own books to read independently. They might choose books from the classroom library shelf, or you may wish to offer a group of appropriate books from which children can choose.

- *El vaquero que monta las cebras.* See page 655 in the Teacher's Edition.
- *La oruga muy hambrienta por Eric Carte.* Philomel, 1989.
- *¡La verdadera historia de los tres creditos!* Por Jon Scieszka. Viking Penguin, 1991.

After children have chosen their books, give each child a copy of *Mi diario de lectura*, which can be found on page R35 in the back of the *Teacher's Edition*. Have children fill in the information at the top of the form. Then have them use the log to keep track of their reading and to record their responses to the literature.

Conduct student-teacher conferences. Arrange time for each child to confer with you individually about his or her self-selected reading. Have children bring their Reading Logs to share with you at the conference. Children might also like to choose a favorite passage to read aloud to you. Ask questions to stimulate discussion about the book. For example, you might ask what children like to do when they are alone and how their activities might differ if they are with friends.

FLUENCY PERFORMANCE Have children read aloud to you the passages from *El torero y yo* that they selected and practiced with their partners. Keep track of the number of words each child reads correctly. Ask the child to rate his or her own performance on the 1–4 scale. If children are not happy with their oral reading, give them an opportunity to continue practicing and then to read the passage to you again.

See *Oral Reading Fluency Assessment* for monitoring progress.

LESSON 18

Use with "Querido Sr. Arándano"

BEFORE

Building Background and Vocabulary

Review Phonics: Palabras con /ll/ñ

Identify the sound. Have children repeat the following sentence three times: *La mamá llama a los niños.* Ask them which words in the sentence have the /y/ sound that they hear in *llave.* (*llama*) Repeat for /ñ/. (*niños*)

Associate letters to sound. On the board, write: *Las llaves abren la puerta de la casa.* Circle the word *llaves.* Underline the letters *ll* in *llaves* and tell children that they stand for the /y/ sound.

Word blending. Model how to blend and read the word *llamar.* Slide your hand under the letters as you slowly elongate the sounds /y/. Then read *llamar* naturally. Follow a similar procedure for *niño, sueño.*

Apply the skill. *Vowel Substitution* Write the following words on the board, and have children read them aloud. Make the changes necessary to form the words in parentheses. Have children read each new word.

llama (llamar)	**ñoñería** (ñoño)	**llevada** (llevar)	**llorón** (llorar)
llueve (llover)	**niñez** (niño)	**llanta** (llanto)	**niña** (niñería)

Introduce Vocabulary

PRETEACH lesson vocabulary. Tell children that they are going to learn six new words that they will see again when they read a story called *Querido Sr. Arándano.* Teach every vocabulary word using the following process.

Write the word.

Say the word.

Track the word and have children repeat it.

Give the meaning or context.

Use the following suggestions or similar ideas to give the meaning or context.

decepcionar Related words: *desilusionar.* Verb that means how someone feels when something isn't happening as expected.

estanque Related words: *alberca, poza, charca.* An artificial fish habitat. Explain it is smaller than a lake.

migratorias Explain that birds possess this character; they will go south in the winter and north in the summer.

información Point out and discuss the small word *informar.*

océano	Point out and discuss oceans on a world map or globe.
acariciar	Use a stuffed animal to role-play how to stroke a pet.

For vocabulary activities, see Vocabulary Games on pages 2–7.

AFTER

Building Background and Vocabulary

Apply Vocabulary Strategies

Use synonyms. Write the word *decepcionar* on chart paper and help children define it. Tell children that they can sometimes figure out the meaning of the word if they know its synonyms. A synonym is a word that means nearly the same as another word.

MODEL **Si quiero entender lo que significa la palabra *decepcionar,* puedo encontrar sinónimos, u otras palabras que tienen un significado parecido. *Desilusionar* y *defraudar* son sinónimos. Yo sé lo que significa *desilusionar;* así, sé también lo que significa *decepcionar.***

Vocabulary Words

decepcionar entristecer a alguien porque algo esperado no sucedió.

estanque alberca, depósito de agua, balsa de agua donde se crian peces

migratorias que se transladan periodicamente.

información datos sobre una persona, una cosa, un lugar

océano grandes masas de agua salada, donde viven la ballena y otros peces.

acariciar tocar suavemente una cosa.

RETEACH **lesson vocabulary.** Have children listen to each of the following sentences. Tell them to hold up the word card that tells the opposite of what is being described. Reread the sentences aloud with the correct answer. Then discuss how children made their choices.

1. Somos pequeños cuerpos de agua. (*océanos*)
2. Soy el Atlántico. (*estanque*)
3. Estoy muy alegre porque recibo lo que quiero. (*decepcionar*)
4. Nos quedamos aquí para siempre, por todo el año. (*migratorias*)
5. Pego con fuerza. (*acariciar*)
6. Yo no explico nada. (*información*)

FLUENCY BUILDER Use *Intervention Practice Book* page 71. Read each word in the first column aloud, and have children repeat it. Then have children work in pairs to read the words in the first column aloud to each other. Follow the same procedure with each of the remaining columns. After partners have practiced reading aloud the words in each column separately, have them practice the entire list. Save *Intervention Practice Book* page 71 for use with pages 179 and 181.

INTERVENTION PRACTICE BOOK

page 71

BEFORE

Reading *Querido Sr. Arándano pages 68–88*

Make Inferences

Focus Skill

PRETEACH the skill. Point out to children that readers use clues in what they read and what they already know to understand what happens in a story. Explain that sometimes readers need to use their own personal experience as well as story clues to figure out why something happens. Discuss how children use what they know from real life to make sense of things that happen in a story.

USE SKILL CARD 18A

Have children look at **side A** of ***Tarjeta de destreza 18: Hacer inferencias/* Skill Card 18: Make Inferences**. Read the definition of make inferences. Next read the story aloud while children read along with you.

Now call attention to the chart and have volunteers take turns reading the information aloud. Ask:

- **¿Qué te dice el cuento sobre los osos blancos?** (*Possible response: Viven en el Polo Norte.*)
- **¿Cómo se aprende sobre los osos blancos?** (*Possible response: Leyendo libros sobre los osos blancos.*)

Prepare to Read *Querido Sr. Arándano*

Preview. Tell children that they are going to read a selection entitled *Querido Sr. Arándano.* Explain that this is an informational story. Tell children that *Querido Sr. Arándano* tells about a girl who learns about whales from her teacher. Then preview the selection.

Días maravillosos
pp. 68–88

- **Pages 68–69:** Veo el título *Querido Sr. Arándano* y el nombre del autor en las páginas 68–69. Veo un dibujo de una chica escribiendo cartas. Creo que está escribiendo al Sr. Arándano.
- **Pages 70–71:** En la página 70, veo una carta escrita por una niña llamada Emilia a su maestro, el Sr. Arándano. En la página 71 veo una ballena nadando en un estanque. Creo que Emilia está imaginando esto.
- **Pages 72–73:** En estas páginas, veo la carta que el Sr. Arándano le escribió a Emilia. Veo un dibujo de Emilia leyendo su carta. Creo que ellos van a seguir escribiéndose a lo largo del cuento.
- **Pages 74–75:** En estas páginas veo otra carta de Emilia al Sr. Arándano y su carta de respuesta. Me doy cuenta de quién está escribiendo la carta al mirar a la firma.

Set purpose. Model setting a purpose for reading *Querido Sr. Arándano*

MODEL **Por lo visto, creo que leeré más cartas sobre las ballenas. Leeré para tener más información sobre las ballenas y también para divertirme con la imaginación de Emilia.**

AFTER

Reading
Querido Sr. Arándano pages 68–88

Reread and Summarize

Have children reread and summarize *Querido Sr. Arándano* in sections, as described below.

Pages 70–73
Volvamos a leer las páginas 70–73 para recordar quién es Emilia, por qué ella está escribiendo al Sr. Arándano y quién es el Sr. Arándano.

Summary: Emilia es una niña. Ella está escribiendo a su maestro, Sr. Arándano, porque piensa que ve una ballena en el estanque.

Pages 74–78
Volvamos a leer las páginas 74–78 para recordar lo que el Sr. Arándano le enseña a Emilia sobre las ballenas.

Summary: Las ballenas no se pierden y siempre saben dónde están en los océanos. Las ballenas azules son azules y comen pequeñas criaturas en el mar. Las ballenas azules son demasiado grandes para vivir en un estanque.

Pages 79–81
Volvamos a leer las páginas 79–81 para saber lo que Emilia hace.

Summary: Emilia leyó la carta del Sr. Arándano a la ballena. Después, ella acarició la cabeza de la ballena. En secreto, le trajo cereal y migas de pan. Nombra a la ballena Artur.

Pages 82–88
Volvamos a leer las páginas 82–88 para recordar lo que el Sr. Arándano le enseña a Emilia sobre las ballenas y lo que pasa al final del cuento.

Summary: El Sr. Arándano le enseña a Emilia que las ballenas son migratorias y viajan grandes distancias. Artur sale del estanque para ser migratoria otra vez. Después, Emilia va a la playa y ve a Artur en el mar. Le dice a Artur que la quiere y que el Sr. Arándano la quiere también.

FLUENCY BUILDER Use *Intervention Practice Book* page 71. Call attention to the sentences on the bottom half of the page. Tell children that their goal is to read each phrase or sentence smoothly. Model appropriate pacing, expression and phrasing as you read each sentence and have children read it after you. Then have children practice by reading the sentences aloud three times to a partner.

BEFORE

Making Connections
pages 92–93

Directed Reading of *Sr. Bigotes*

Sonidos alegres
pages
142–148

Ask a volunteer to read aloud the title. Ask children who they think Sr. Bigotes is. Have children read page 142 to find out. Ask: **¿Quién es el Sr. Bigotes? ¿Dónde vive el Sr. Bigotes?** (*Possible response: El Sr. Bigotes es una foca que vive en el mar.*) **NOTE DETAILS** Ask: **¿Qué aprende Pablo con el Sr. Bigotes?** (*Possible response: Aprende sobre los otros animales que viven en el mar.*) **INTERPRET STORY EVENTS**

Page 143 Have children read page 143 to find out if Sr. Bigotes really teaches Pablo. Ask: **¿Crees que el Sr. Bigotes habla con Pablo cuando le enseña? ¿Por qué?** (*Possible response: No, porque las focas no pueden hablar con los humanos.*) Focus Skill **MAKE INFERENCES**

Page 144 Have children read page 144 to find out more about seals. Ask: **¿Cuáles son las tres cosas que has leído sobre las focas?** (*Possible response: Las focas pueden nadar muy bien; usan sus aletas y nadan muy rápidamente.*) **SUMMARIZE**

Page 145 Read aloud page 145 to children. Model using the Read Ahead strategy in order for children to understand the swimming contest.

> **MODEL** **Mientras leo, a veces no entiendo lo que está ocurriendo en el cuento. Leer un poco adelante tal vez me ayudará. Si no sé lo que está ocurriendo durante la competencia de natación, puedo enterarme más si sigo leyendo.** Focus Strategy **READ AHEAD**

Pages 146–147 Have children read pages 146–147 to find out more about Sr Bigotes and Pablo. Ask: **¿Cómo recibió su nombre el Sr. Bigotes?** (*Possible response: Tiene unos bigotes muy largos.*) **DRAW CONCLUSIONS** Ask: **¿Cómo le ayudan los bigotes?** (*Possible response: Les ayudan a palpar el agua para encontrar comida.*) **NOTE DETAILS** Ask: **¿Es un buen animal doméstico la foca? ¿Por qué?** (*Possible response: No, porque no caminan muy bien en la tierra y son animales salvajes.*) **DRAW CONCLUSIONS** Ask: **¿Crees que Pablo sí quiere ser una foca?** (*Possible response: Acepta una variedad de respuestas.*) **SPECULATE**

Page 148 Have children read page 148 to find out what Neal's parents think about Sr Bigotes. Ask: **¿Los padres de Pablo han visto al Sr. Bigotes?** (*Possible response: No.*) **NOTE DETAILS** **¿Qué creen los padres sobre el Sr. Bigotes?** (*Possible response: No creen que él es real.*) **DRAW CONCLUSIONS** **¿Crees tú que es real?** (*Possible response: Acepta una variedad de respuestas.*) **EXPRESS PERSONAL OPINIONS**

Summarize the selection. Ask children to think about why it is important to learn facts about animals.

INTERVENTION PRACTICE BOOK
page 73

AFTER

Skill Review
pages 93I

USE SKILL CARD 18B

Answers to *Think About It* Questions

1. Que son buenas nadadoras y nadan rápido y lejos. También que usan dientes afilados para comer peces. **SUMMARY**
2. Porque no ven al Sr. Bigotes. El niño imagina que conversa con él cuando se va dormir. **INTERPRETATION**
3. Acepte dibujas razonables. **TASK**

Focus Skill Make Inferences

RETEACH the skill. Have children look at **side B** of ***Tarjeta de destreza 18: Hacer inferencias*/Skill Card 18: Make Inferences**. Read the skill reminder with them, and have a volunteer read the story aloud.

Read aloud the set of directions. Explain that children will work with partners to create their own charts. Remind them to look for word clues as they listen to the story being read aloud.

After children have completed their inference charts, have them display and explain their work. Point out that inferences can also be made about the selection *Sr. Bigotes.* Ask volunteers to make an inference about Pablo.

Focus Skill Review Phonics Skill from *Sr. Bigotes*

RETEACH words with *ll* and *ñ*. Read aloud the following sentence: *No voy a llorar como el niño ñoñoso*. Have children listen for the /y/ sound. Then read this list aloud and have children raise their hands when they hear the /y/: *llorar*. Repeat for the /ñ/ sound. (niño, ñoñoso)

FLUENCY BUILDER Use *Intervention Practice Book* page 71. Explain that today children will practice the sentences on the bottom half of the page by reading them aloud on tape. Assign new partners. Have children take turns reading the sentences aloud to each other and then reading them on tape.

INTERVENTION PRACTICE BOOK
page 71

BEFORE

Drafting a Letter of Invitation
page 93A

Writing Process: Letter of Invitation

Build on prior knowledge. Tell children that they are going to talk about and write about letters of invitation. Explain that people write letters of invitation to invite people to something. Talk about the reasons why people write letters of invitation and the people they write these letters to. Ask children to discuss letters of invitation they have written or received.

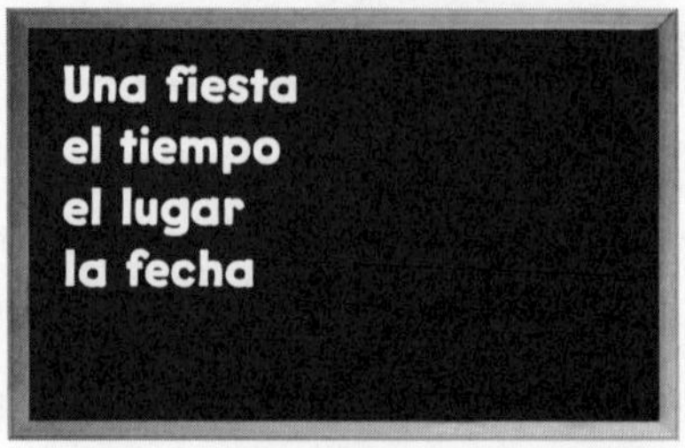

Construct the text. "Share the pen" with children. Tell them that the list names a purpose for writing a letter of invitation and some of the things to be included in the letter. Then help them construct a letter of invitation. For example:

Querida Andy:

Voy a hacer una fiesta. La fiesta es en mi casa. La fiesta será el domingo 27 de mayo. La fiesta empieza a las 4 de la tarde.

Tu amiga,

Jennifer

Revisit the text. Go back and read the letter of invitation together. Ask: **¿De qué trata esta carta?** (*De invitar a un amigo a una fiesta.*)

- Guide children to make the letter read more smoothly. Ask: **¿Cómo puedo combinar las frases para que sean más fáciles de leer.?** (*Por ejemplo: Voy a hacer una fiesta. La fiesta es el domingo 27 de mayo a las 4 de la tarde.*) **¿Qué más podrías incluir en la carta?** (*Por qué hay una fiesta, para quién es, direcciones para llegar a la fiesta*)
- Have children read the completed letter of invitation aloud and then copy it on their papers.

On Your Own

Have children list four things to include in a different letter of invitation. Then have them use their list to write a letter of invitation.

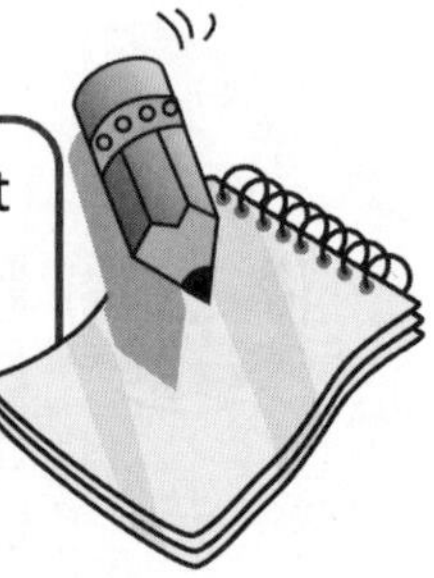

AFTER

Spelling Lesson
page 89I

Connect Spelling and Phonics

RETEACH words with *ll* and *ñ*. Tell children to number their papers 1–8. Write the word *cañón* on the board, and tell children that in the words you say, the long /ñ/ sound will be spelled *ñ* as in *cañón*. Words with the /y/ sound as in *llamar* will be spelled *ll* as in *llamar*. Dictate the following words, and have children write them. After each word is written, write it on the board so children can proofread their work. They should draw a line through a misspelled word and write the correct spelling below it.

1. señor*	**2. ballenas***	**3. baño**	**4. lloroso**
5. llamo*	**6. caña**	**7. pequeño***	**8. cariño***

*** Word appears in *Sr. Bigotes*.**

Dictate the sentence and have children write it: *Yo sueño que las ballenas en el océano, bañan a las ballenitas y las tratan con mucho cariño.*

Build and Read Longer Words

Remind children that they have learned how to decode words with the long /y/ and the /ñ/ sounds. Explain that now they will use what they have learned to help them read some longer words.

INTERVENTION ASSESSMENT BOOK

Write the word *bañarme* on the board. Remind children that they can often figure out longer words by looking for smaller words in them. Cover *me,* and have children read the smaller word. Follow a similar procedure to have them read the smaller word *me*. Model how to blend the two smaller words to read aloud the longer word *bañarme*. Do the same to have children blend word parts to read these longer words: *llamamiento, lloriquear, enseñar.*

FLUENCY BUILDER Have children choose a passage from *Sr. Bigotes* to read aloud to a partner. You may have children choose passages that they found particularly interesting, or have them choose one of the following options:

- Read pages 142–143. (From *¡Hola! Me llamo Pablo*... through ...*¡saludar a tantos amigos!* Total: 101 words.)
- Read page 147. (From *El Sr. Bigotes es*... through ...*¡Fue el ganador!* Total: 118 words.)

Children should read the selected passage aloud to their partners three times. Have the child rate his or her own reading on a scale of 1 to 4.

BEFORE
Weekly Assessments

Review Vocabulary

To revisit Vocabulary Words prior to the weekly assessment, use these sentence frames. Have volunteers take turns reading aloud the sentence stem and choices. Children should identify the correct choice and explain why that choice makes sense in the sentence.

1. Cuando visitas el **océano**, puedes ver
   a. leones y tigres.
   b. ballenas y otros peces.
2. Si das una **información**, tienes
   a. datos sobre un tema.
   b. no tienes datos.
3. Ella nadó en el **estanque** porque
   a. es como una calle.
   b. es como una piscina.
4. Un animal **migratorio**
   a. viaja una vez al año.
   b. nunca viaja.
5. Yo **acaricio** a mi gato por que a él le gusta
   a. que le hagan daño.
   b. que le toquen con suavidad.
6. No quiero **decepcionarte** porque vas a estar
   a. muy triste.
   b. muy alegre.

Correct responses: 1.b, 2.a, 3.b, 4.a, 5.b, 6.a.

You may want to display the vocabulary words and definitions on page 179 and have children copy them to use when they study for the vocabulary test.

Días maravillosos
pages 68–88

Focus Skill

Make Inferences

INTERVENTION PRACTICE BOOK
page 74

To review before the weekly assessment, distribute *Intervention Practice Book* page 74. Have volunteers read aloud the direction line and the story. Remind children to use their own personal experience when making inferences.

Review Test Prep

INTERVENTION ASSESSMENT BOOK

Ask children to turn to page 95 of the *Pupil Edition*. Call attention to the tips for answering the test questions. Tell children that paying attention to these tips can help them answer not only the questions on this page, but also other test questions like them.

Have children follow along as you read each test question and the tip that goes with it. Remind children to reread each choice before making their final decision.

Self-Selected Reading

Have children select their own books to read independently. They might choose books from the classroom library, or you may wish to offer appropriate books from which children can choose, such as these:

- *La ballena Berta* See page 950 in the *Teacher's Edition* for a plan.
- *El perro cantor* por Mary Blocksma. Children's Press, 1990.
- *Me gustaría tener* por Alma Flor Ada. Santillana, USA, 1969.

After children have chosen their books, give each child a copy of *Mi diario de lectura,* which can be found on page R35 in the back of the *Teacher's Edition*. Have children fill in the information at the top of the form. Then have them use the log to keep track of their reading and to record their responses to the literature.

Conduct student-teacher conferences. Arrange time for each child to meet with you individually to discuss his or her self-selected reading. Have children bring their *Reading Logs* to share with you at the conference. Children might also like to choose a favorite passage to read aloud to you. Ask questions designed to stimulate discussion of the book. For example, you might ask what sea animals live in the ocean.

FLUENCY PERFORMANCE Have children read aloud to you the passage from *El Sr. Bigotes* that they selected and practiced with their partners. Keep track of the number of words each child reads correctly. Have children use the 1–4 scale to rate their performance. Give then a second chance to read if they are not satisfied with their performance.

See *Oral Reading Fluency Assessment* for monitoring progress.

LESSON 19

Use with

"La frescura de Ali"

BEFORE

Building Background and Vocabulary

Review Phonics: Syllables *güe/güi*

Identify the sound. Have children repeat the following sentence three times: *Nunca queremos argüir sobre la güira ¡qué vergüenza!* Ask them which words in the sentence have the /güe/güi/ sound. (*argüir, güira, vergüenza*)

Associate letters to sound. On the board, write: *Nunca queremos argüir sobre la güira ¡qué vergüenza!* Circle the words *argüir* and *güira.* Ask children to tell how the words are alike. (*all have the /güi/ sound.*) Then underline the letters *güi* in both words. Tell children that the letters *güi* stand for the /güi/ sound. Repeat for *güe* in *vergüenza* where *güe* stands for /güe/ sounds.

INTERVENTION PRACTICE BOOK

page 76

Word blending. Model how to blend and read the word *yegüita.* Slide your hand under the letters as you slowly elongate the sounds /yeegguuiiita/. Then read *yegüita* naturally. Follow a similar procedure for *pingüino* and *desagüe.*

Apply the skill. *Vowel/Consonant Substitution* Write the following words on the board, and have children read them aloud. Make the changes necessary to form the words in parentheses. Have children read each new word.

quiero (güero)	**gira** (güira)	**golfo** (güelfo)
genuino (pingüino)	**pinche** (pingüe)	**trigueña** (cigüeña)

Introduce Vocabulary

PRETEACH lesson vocabulary. Tell children that they are going to learn six new words that they will see again when they read a story called *La frecura de Ali.* Teach every vocabulary word using the following process.

Write the word.

Say the word.

Track the word and have children repeat it.

Give the meaning or context.

Use the following suggestions or similar ideas to give the meaning or context.

arremolinada Point out the *-ada* ending. Role play this with 3 or 4 volunteers all trying to get out of the door.

refrescante Relate fanning yourself and taking a cool glass of water.

bruma Relate by spraying a bit of water in the air and pointing to the tiny drops of water in the air.

carámbanos Draw a house on the blackboard in the dead winter. Show the *carámbanos* forming off of the gutters and rooftop.

pálido Relate by showing different colored crayons, some pale and some dark.

For vocabulary activities, see Vocabulary Games on pages 2–7.

Vocabulary Words

copos pequeña masa que cae al nevar

refrescante que refresca; reducir la temperatura

bruma niebla, neblina

carámbanos hielo que cuelga al helarse el agua

arremolinada agrupada, amontonada

pálido de color suave

Apply Vocabulary Strategies

AFTER
Building Background and Vocabulary

Use familiar patterns. Write the word *arremolinada* on chart paper and underline the letters *ada.* Tell children that they can sometimes figure out the meaning of a new word by looking for letter patterns that they know.

MODEL **La combinación *ada* me suena porque la he visto en otras palabras como *mojada.* Yo sé que este sufijo significa la condición de algo o alguien. Si lo combino con *arremolin-,* yo leo *arremolinada.***

Guide children in using a similar procedure to decode the words *refrescante* and *carámbanos.*

Vocabulary Activity

RETEACH **lesson vocabulary.** Have children write each Vocabulary Word on a word card and then listen to each of the following groups of words. Tell them to hold up the word that matches each group of words

1. ligero / color / no oscuro (*pálido*)
2. niebla / agua / nebuloso (*bruma*)
3. porción / nieve / blanco (*copos*)
4. hielo / puntiagudo / pieza (*carámbanos*)
5. fresca / frío / bebida (*refrescante*)
6. atestado / mucha gente / sin orden (*arremolinada*)

FLUENCY BUILDER Use *Intervention Practice Book* page 75. Read each word in the first column aloud and have children repeat it. Then have partners read the words in the first column aloud to each other. Tell children to follow the same procedure with each of the remaining columns. After partners have practiced reading aloud the words in each column, have them practice the entire list. Save *Intervention Practice Book* page 75 to use on pages 191 and 193.

BEFORE

Reading
La frescura de Ali
pages 98–112

USE SKILL CARD 18A

Focus Skill Antonyms

PRETEACH the skill. Point out to children that antonyms are words that have opposite meanings. Help children see that good readers use clues in what they read to help them find the meanings of antonyms. Discuss how children feel on a hot day, and how they feel on a very cold day. Guide children to notice antonyms in their discussion.

Have children look at **side A** of ***Tarjeta de destrezas 19: Antónimos*/Skill Card 19: Antonyms.** Read the definition of *antonyms.* Next read the story, and, then have children read it with you. Have volunteers take turns reading the information in the chart aloud. Ask:

- **¿Cuál es el opuesto de la palabra *terrible*?** (*Possible response: fenomenal*)
- **¿Cuál es el opuesto de la palabra *feo*?** (*Possible response: hermoso*)

Prepare to Read: *La frescura de Ali*

Dias maravillosos
pp. 98–112

Preview. Tell children that they are going to read a selection entitled *La frescura de Ali.* Explain that this is a realistic fiction about a girl who uses her creativity to solve a problem. Then preview the selection.

Pages 98–99: Yo veo el título, *La frescura de Ali,* y el nombre de la autora en las páginas 98–99. Veo un dibujo de una chica que está dibujando en la acera. Creo que la chica es Ali.

Pages 100–101: En estas páginas, veo un dibujo y leo sobre la gente que vive en el mismo edificio. Leo sobre una chica llamada Ali; a ella le encanta dibujar. Creo que leeré más sobre lo que la gente en el edificio piensa sobre sus dibujos.

Pages 102–103: En estas páginas, veo unos dibujos y leo sobre las cosas que Ali dibuja. Creo que Ali intenta ayudar a sus vecinos creando dibujos de cosas refrescantes que están en sus mentes, a fin de que se olviden cuán acalorados están.

Set purpose. Model setting a purpose for reading *La frescura de Ali.*

> MODEL **Por lo que he visto hasta ahora, creo que leeré más sobre los dibujos de Ali y de cómo éstos ayudan a sus vecinos a mantenerse frescos en el calor. También leeré para entretenerme con los dibujos imaginativos de Ali.**

AFTER

Reading
La frescura de Ali
pages 98–112

Reread and Summarize

Have children reread and summarize *La frescura de Ali* in sections.

Pages 98–101
Vamos a releer las páginas 98–101 para recordar quién es Ali y lo qué está ocurriendo fuera de su edificio.

Summary: Ali es una chica que le encanta dibujar. Ella está dibujando en la acera mientras sus vecinos se quejan del calor.

Pages 102–105
Releyendo las páginas 102–105, recordamos las cosas que Ali dibujó y porqué las dibujó.

Summary: Ali dibujó un lago, un paraguas de playa, el viento del norte, y un oso blanco. Los dibujó porque éstos harían que las gentes pensaran en cosas frías y les ayudarían a olvidarse del calor.

Pages 106–107
Al releer las páginas 106–107 vemos la idea más refrescante de Ali y cómo reaccionaron sus vecinos.

Summary: Ali dibujó copos de nieve, huellas de osos polares y los carámbanos para que pareciera invierno. Sus vecinos estaban alegres y se sentían más frescos.

Pages 108–112
Vamos a releer las páginas 108–112 para recordar qué pasó con los dibujos de Ali y cómo se sintió ella por esto.

Summary: Una tormenta sorprendió a todos. La lluvia destruyó los dibujos de Ali. Al principio ella estaba disgustada, luego estaba feliz cuando sus vecinos la aclamaron por haberles ayudado a vencer el calor.

FLUENCY BUILDER Use *Intervention Practice Book* page 75. Call attention to the sentences on the bottom half of the page. The slashes break the sentences into phrases to allow you to work on natural phrasing. Tell children that their goal is to read each phrase or sentence smoothly. Model appropriate pacing, expression and phrasing as you read each sentence and have children read it after you. Then have children practice by reading the sentences aloud three times to a partner.

BEFORE

Making Connections
pages 118–119

Directed Reading of *Sonidos por todas partes* *pp. 150–156*

Sonidos alegres
pp. 150–156

Ask a volunteer to read aloud the title. Ask children what they might hear all around. Have children read page 158 to see if Julio, the boy in the story, hears some sounds. Ask: **¿Julio oye sonidos mientras se dirige a casa?** (*Possible response: Todavía no.*) **INTERPRET STORY EVENTS** **¿Por qué está triste Julio?** (*Possible response: Extraña a la Sra Li.*) **IDENTIFY CHARACTERS' FEELINGS** **¿Cuál es un antónimo para la palabra alegre?** (*Possible response: triste*) Focus Skill **ANTONYMS**

Page 159 Have children read to find out what sounds Julio hears. Ask: **¿Qué oye Julio mientras camina?** (*Possible response: Oye la tiza del Sr. Jones por la acera; los niños jugando; la Sra. Gómez vendiendo fruta; la melodía de la flauta de Susana; un camión de basura, la lluvia.*) **¿Qué crees que Julio está planeando?** (*Possible response: Acepta respuestas razonables.*) **MAKE PREDICTIONS**

Page 160 Have children read page 160 to find out what Julio does the next day. Ask: **¿Qué hace Julio la mañana siguiente?** (*Possible response: Visita a la Sra. Li en el hospital.*) **NOTE DETAILS** **¿Qué crees que hay en la bolsa?** (*Possible response: Acepta respuestas razonables.*) **MAKE PREDICTIONS**

Page 161 Have children read page 161 to find out what is in Julios's bag. Ask: **¿Qué hay en la bolsa?** (*Possible response: fruta para la Sra. Gómez, dibujos de los niños, tiza del Sr. Jones*) **NOTE DETAILS** **¿Cuál crees que es el regalo más interesante?** (*Possible response: Acepta respuestas razonables pero anime a los niños a considerar el título en sus respuestas.*) **MAKE PREDICTIONS**

Pages 162–163 Read aloud pages 162–163 to children. Model using the Create Mental Images strategy in order for children to understand why the tape recorder helped *Sra. Li* feel as if she were right there in the crowd.

MODEL **Creo imágenes mentales para entender lo que estoy leyendo. Utilizo los detalles sobre los personajes, el ambiente y los hechos para imaginar lo que la autora está describiendo. Podría dibujar un dibujo sobre una imagen en mi mente. Creo que la Sra. Li estaba creando imágenes mentales basadas en los sonidos que oía y los recuerdos de su barrio. Por eso es que se sentía como si estuviera en medio de la gente.** Focus Strategy **CREATE MENTAL IMAGES**

Page 164

INTERVENTION PRACTICE BOOK page 77

Read aloud the first sentence on page 164. Then have children read the page 156 to find out about the last sound on the tape. Ask: **¿Cuál es el último sonido en la cinta?** (*Possible response: la lluvia.*) **NOTE DETAILS** **¿Por qué la Sra. Li dibuja un arco iris?** (*Possible response: Acepte respuestas razonables.*) **SPECULATE** **¿El plan de Julio funciona?** (*Possible response: Sí, él planificó alegrar a la Sra. Lee y lo logró.*) **DRAW CONCLUSION**

Summarize the selection. Ask children to tell how the sounds of Julio's neighborhood tell what the place is like. Then have yhem complete *Intervention Practice Book* page 77.

Answers to *Think About It* Questions

1. Le llevó regalos de todos. Pero el mejor fue la casetera con los sonidos grabados de la calle, el ruido de la lluvia cayendo, los niños saltando en la cuerda, la música de Susana. **SUMMARIZE**
2. Las respuestas pueden variar. **DRAW CONCLUSIONS**
3. Las respuestas pueden variar. Anime a los niños a imaginare en sus mentes el barrio de Julio para ayudarlos a hacer sus dibujos. **GENERALIZE**

AFTER

Skill Review
pages 119I–121

USE SKILL CARD 19B

Focus Skill Antonyms

RETEACH the skill. Have children look at **side B** of ***Tarjeta de destreza 19: Antónimos*/Skill Card 19: Antonyms.** Read the skill reminder with them, and have a volunteer read the story aloud.

Read aloud the set of directions. Explain that partners will create their own charts. Remind them to look for words that have opposite meanings as they read the story. After children have completed their antonym charts, have them explain their work. Ask volunteers to name some words and their antonyms from *Sonidos por todas partes.*

Focus Skill Review Phonics Skill *La frescura de Ali*

RETEACH Syllables güe, güi. Read aloud the following sentence: *La cigüeña tenía vergüenza porque el pingüino lo supo todo.* Have children listen for the /güe/ sound. Then read this list aloud and have children raise their hands when they hear the /güe/ sound: *cigüeña, vergüenza.* Repeat the procedure for the /güi/ sound. (*pingüino*)

FLUENCY BUILDER Use *Intervention Practice Book* page 75. Explain that today children will practice the sentences on the bottom half of the page by reading them aloud on tape. Assign new partners. Have children take turns reading the sentences aloud to each other and then reading them on tape. Have children listen to the tape and tell how they think their reading has improved. Then have them record the sentences one more time.

INTERVENTION PRACTICE BOOK page 75

BEFORE

Drafting a Personal Story
page 119A

Writing Process: Personal Story

Build on prior knowledge. Tell children that they are going to talk about and write personal stories. Explain that sometimes people write personal stories to tell about events that have happened to them. Tell children that it is important to have a good beginning in a personal story, so that readers can understand what the story will be about, or to tell about something surprising that will make the reader interested or curious about the story. Have children share ideas for a good beginning of a personal story. They might write as if they lived in the neighborhood in *La frescura de Ali.*

el barrio
hace calor
muchos buenos vecinos
dibujos de tiza

Construct the text. "Share the pen" with children. Help children to organize some or all of the items on the list into a good beginning for a personal story. For example:

> **Era un día muy caluroso en mi barrio. Mis vecinos estaban en mi barrio y se estaban quejando del calor. Dibujé con la tiza, dibujos de la nieve para mantener a mis vecinos frescos.**

Revisit the text. Read the personal story beginning together. Ask: **¿De qué trata este cuento?** (*Trata de alguien que dibuja unos dibujos de la nieve y el invierno para ayudar a los vecinos a olvidarse del calor.*)

- Guide children to make the beginning read more smoothly. Ask: **¿Qué palabras puedo sacar de la segunda frase para que se lea mejor el principio de este cuento?** (*en mi barrio y estaban*) Make appropriate changes.
- Ask: **¿Qué palabras puedo eliminar de la segunda oración para mejorar el inicio del cuento?** (*Possible response: detalles sobre los dibujos y cómo reaccionan los vecinos*) Make appropriate changes.
- Have children read the completed personal story beginning aloud and then copy it on their papers.

On Your Own

Have children write three sentences that could be the beginning of their personal story about something they did. Invite them to read their story beginnings aloud.

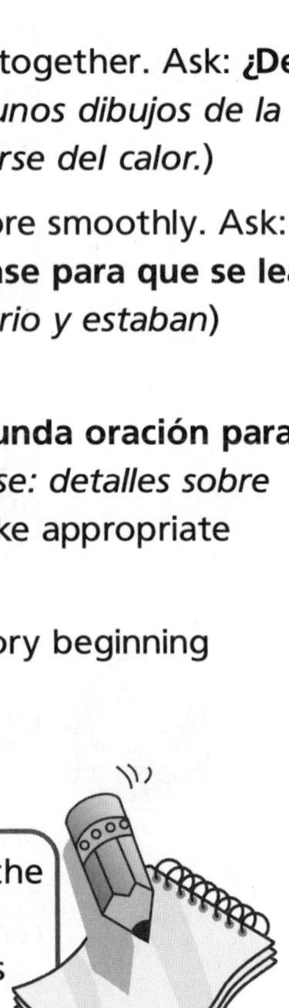

AFTER

Spelling Lesson
page 119G

Connect Spelling and Phonics

RETEACH Syllables *güe/güi.* Tell children to number their papers 1–8. Write the letters *güe* on the board, and tell children that in the words you say, the /güe/ sound will be spelled *güe.* Repeat for the letters *güi* which stand for the sound /güi/. Dictate the following words, and have children write them. After children write each word, write it on the board so that they can proofread their work. They should draw a line through a misspelled word and write the correct spelling beside it.

1. argüir	**2. agüita**	**3. desagüe**	**4. yegüita**
5. güero	**6. pingüino**	**7. vergüenza**	**8. cigüeña**

Tell children that in the following sentence, the /güe/ sound will be spelled *güe* and the /güi/ sound will be spelled *güi.* Dictate the sentence and have children write it: *No quiero argüir porque me da vergüenza.*

Build and Read Longer Words

Remind children that they have learned how to decode words with the /güe/ and /güi/ sounds. Explain that now they will use what they have learned to help them read some longer words.

INTERVENTION ASSESSMENT BOOK ✓

Write the word *pingüino* on the board. Remind children that they can often figure out longer words by looking for smaller words in them. Cover *ino,* and have children read the remaining word. Follow a similar procedure to have them read the smaller word *ino.* Model how to blend the two smaller words to read aloud the longer word *pingüino.* Do the same to have children blend word parts to read the word: *argüir.*

FLUENCY BUILDER Have children choose a passage from *Sonidos por todas partes* to read aloud to a partner. You may have children choose passages that they found particularly interesting, or have them choose one of the following options:

- Read pages 158–160. (From *Julio fue el...* through ...*Un camión pasó veloz.* Total: 94 words.)
- Read pages 162–163. (From *Cuando Julio se levantó...* through ...*todos los regalos.* Total: 121 words.)

Children should read the selected passage aloud to their partners three times. Have the child rate each reading on a scale of 1 to 4.

SCALE	
1	Not good
2	Pretty good
3	Good
4	Great!

BEFORE
Weekly Assessments

Review Vocabulary

To review the Vocabulary Words prior to the assessment, use these sentences. Read aloud the sentence items and answer choices. Children identify the correct answer and explain why it makes sense.

1. Si estás en una **bruma**, las cosas
   a. son difíciles de ver.
   b. están claras.

2. Si tienes **copos** de algodón, los tienes
   a. para comer.
   b. para hilar.

3. Si quieres algo **refrescante**, quieres
   a. algo frío.
   b. algo cálido.

4. Los **carámbanos** se forman en
   a. el invierno.
   b. el verano.

5. Si mi cara es **pálida**,
   a. tiene mucho color.
   b. no tiene color.

6. Si la clase estaba **arremolinada**, estaba
   a. sin orden.
   b. muy organizada.

Correct responses: 1.a, 2.b, 3.a, 4.a, 5.b, 6.a.

You may want to display the Vocabulary Words and definitions from page 189 and have children copy them to use when they study.

Focus Skill Review Antonyms

To review antonyms before the weekly assessment, distribute *Intervention Practice Book* page 78. Have volunteers read aloud the direction line and the story. Guide children to remember to write words that mean the opposite of the words in the story.

Review Test Prep

Ask children to turn to page 121 of the *Pupil Edition.* Call attention to the Tips for answering the test items. Tell children that paying attention to these tips can help them answer not only the items on this page but also other items like them.

Have children follow along as you read each test item and the tips. Tell children to choose the antonym and then reread the item with the answer to check whether it is correct.

Self-Selected Reading

Have children select their own books to read independently. They might choose books from the classroom library shelf, or you may wish to offer a group of appropriate books from which children can choose.

- *El jardín de flores* See Teacher's Edition page 210 for an Independent Reading Plan.
- *Cuando Lía dibujó el mundo* por Vivi Escrivá. Espase-Calpe, 1991.
- *Gilberto y el viento* por Marie Hall Ets. Lectorum, 1995.

After children have chosen their books, give each child a copy of *Mi diarios de lectura* which can be found on page R35 in the back of the *Teacher's Edition.* Have children fill in the information at the top of the form. Then have them use the log to keep track of their reading and to record their responses to the literature.

Conduct student-teacher conferences. Arrange time for each child to confer with you individually about his or her self-selected reading. Have children bring their *Reading Logs* to share with you at the conference. Children might also like to choose a favorite passage to read aloud to you. Ask questions designed to stimulate discussion about the book. For example, ask why children chose the books, whether they would like to do any the activities they read about or what was the funniest/saddest/most interesting part.

FLUENCY PERFORMANCE Have children read aloud to you the passage from *Sonidos por todas partes* that they practiced. Observe children's pronunciation, intonation, phrasing, and the amount of words, in general, that they read correctly. Ask each child to rate his or her own performance on the 1–4 scale. If children are not happy with their oral reading, give them an opportunity to continue practicing and then to reread the passage to you.

***See Oral Reading Fluency Assessment* for monitoring progress.**

LESSON 20

BEFORE

Building Background and Vocabulary

Use with

"La paciencia del emperador"

Review Phonics: Combinación de consonantes *bl, br*

Identify the sound. Have children repeat the following sentence three times: *Sobre el establo soplaba una brisa.* Ask them which words in the sentence have the consonant blends *br* or *bl*. (*br-sobre, brisa/bl-establo*)

Associate letters to sound. On the board, write: *Sobre el establo soplaba una brisa.* Circle the words *sobre, brisa* and *establo.* Ask children to tell how the words are alike. Then underline the letters *br* in *sobre* and *brisa* and the letters *bl* in *establo*. Tell children that the letters *br* and *bl* are consonant blends.

Word blending. Model how to blend and read the word *pueblo*. Slide your hand under the letters as you slowly elongate the sounds /pueeblo/. Then read *pueblo* naturally. Follow a similar procedure for *blusa*, *tabla*, *libro*, and *brazo*.

INTERVENTION PRACTICE BOOK
page 80

Apply the skill. *Consonant Substitution* Write the following words on the board, and have children read them aloud. Make the changes necessary to form the words in parentheses. Have children read each new word aloud.

misa (brisa) **pedazo** (brazo) **flanco** (blanco) **sable** (cable)

Introduce Vocabulary

PRETEACH lesson vocabulary. Tell children that they are going to learn six new words that they will see again when they read a story called *La paciencia del emperador* Teach every vocabulary word using the following process.

Write the word.
Say the word.
Track the word and have students repeat it.
Give the meaning or context.

Use the following suggestions or similar ideas to give the meaning or context.

aletas Relate by showing pictures of penguin or rubber flippers and using your hands to show how they move.

empollar Relate to what a hen does before the chick breaks out of eggs.

desdichado Related words: *triste, miserio, desanimado.* Role-play the facial expression of a person who feels miserable.

resbalosa Relate by role-playing a person walking on a floor that is slippery.

graznido Relate by having children role-play quacking like ducks.

horizonte Relate by drawing a picture of a simple landscape and the sun setting or rising on the horizon.

For vocabulary activities, see Vocabulary Games on pages 2–7.

Vocabulary Words

aletas pequeñas palas usadas como manos o pies

empollar incubar, calentar los huevos para que nazcan los pollos

desdichado muy infeliz

resbalosa que no se pega, que hace resbalar

graznido sonido que emite el pato

horizonte donde parece que se encontraran el cielo y la tierra

AFTER

Building Background and Vocabulary

Apply Vocabulary Strategies

Use familiar patterns. Write the word *empollar* on chart paper and underline the letters *em*. Tell children that they can sometimes figure out the meaning of the word by looking for letter patterns that they know.

> MODEL **Reconozco la combinación de letras *em* porque la he visto en palabras como *empacar.* He visto la combinación *po* en palabras como *poder.* He visto la letra *ll* y la combinación *ar* en palabras como *llegar.* Cuando lo leo todo junto, leo *empollar.***

Guide children in using a similar procedure to decode the words *desdichado* and *resbalosa.*

RETEACH **lesson vocabulary.** Have children write each Vocabulary Word on a word card and then listen to each of the following definitions. Tell them to hold up the word card that names each definition. Reread the sentences aloud with the correct answer. Then discuss how children made their choices.

1. Así es como se siente la clara de un huevo crudo. (*resbalosa*)
2. Esta palabra es donde el cielo y la tierra parecen encontrarse. (*horizonte*)
3. Esta palabra dice lo que hace el ave para calentar sus huevos. (*empollar*)
4. Tú tienes manos, pero las focas y los pingüinos tienen ésto. (*aletas*)
5. ¿Cómo te sentirías si tuvieras frío y te hallaras solo? (*desdichado*)
6. Algunas aves, emiten este sonido cuando se asustan. (*graznido*)

FLUENCY BUILDER Use *Intervention Practice Book page 79.* Read each word in the first column aloud and have children repeat it. Then have partners read the words in the first column aloud to each other. Tell children to follow the same procedure with each of the remaining columns. After partners have practiced reading aloud the words in each column, have them practice the entire list. Save *Intervention Practice Book* page 79 to use on pages 201 and 203.

BEFORE

Reading
La paciencia del emperador
pages 124–145

USE SKILL CARD 20A

Focus Skill Fact and Fiction

PRETEACH the skill. Point out to children that a fact is information that is real and can be proved and that fiction is information that is made up and cannot happen in real life. Discuss the difference between real and make-believe things. Guide children to see that facts can be proved by methods such as observation, looking them up in books, or by asking experts.

Have children look at **side A** of ***Tarjeta de destreza 20: Hecho y ficción/*** **Skill Card 20: Fact and Fiction.** Read the definitions of fact and fiction. Next read the story, and then have children reread it with you. Then have volunteers take turns reading the information in the chart aloud. Ask:

- **¿Cómo pruebas que a los gatos les gusta comer peces?** (*Possible response: Lo puedo buscar en un libro.*)
- **¿Por qué es el detalle "—Tengo un plan —*dijo* Alberto" ficticio?** (*Possible response: Los peces no pueden hablar.*)

Prepare to Read *La paciencia del emperador*

Días maravillosos pages 124–144

Preview. Tell children that they are going to read a selection entitled *La paciencia del emperador.* Explain that this is an informational story. Tell children that *La paciencia del emperador* explains about a certain kind of penguin called the Emperor penguin. Then preview the selection.

- **Pages 124–125:** Veo el título, *La paciencia del emperador,* y el nombre del autor en las páginas 124–125. Veo un dibujo de unos pingüinos grandes y un pingüinito. Creo que esta selección tratará sobre el pingüinito.
- **Pages 126–127:** En estas páginas, veo dibujos y leo sobre un lugar que se llama Antártida. Creo que la forma del dibujo es un pingüino.
- **Pages 128–129:** En estas páginas, veo dibujos y leo sobre el pingüino Emperador, su hembra y su huevo. Creo que voy a leer más hechos sobre el pingüino Emperador y su huevo.

Set purpose. Model setting a purpose for reading *La paciencia del emperador.*

MODEL **Por lo que he visto en estas páginas, creo que voy a leer sobre la vida del pingüino Emperador durante el período en que empolla su huevo. Voy a leer sobre cómo él cuida del huevo mientras empolla y del pingüinito cuando nace.**

AFTER

Reading
La paciencia del emperador
pages 124–144

Reread and Summarize

Have children reread and summarize *La paciencia del emperador* in sections, as described below.

Pages 124–129
Leamos las páginas 124–129 para recordar cómo es la Antártida y quién vive allí.

Summary: La Antártida es el lugar más frío de toda la Tierra. El pingüino Emperador vive allí.

Pages 130–137
Leamos las páginas 130–137 para recordar qué hacen los pingüinos después de poner un huevo.

Summary: Por dos meses, la hembra nada y come mucho. El macho empolla el huevo durante ese tiempo entre sus patas y debajo de su estómago para mantenerlo caliente. Él tiene mucha grasa y muchas plumas para mantener la temperatura. Todos los pingüinos papás se reúnen y se mueven lentamente por el hielo.

Pages 138–140
Leamos las páginas 138–140 para recordar qué pasa cuando el huevo se empieza a romper.

Summary: Cuando el pingüinito nace, el padre le calienta y le da de beber un tipo de leche que produce.

Pages 141–144
Leamos las páginas 141–144 para recordar qué pasa cuando se acaba la leche del padre.

Summary: Ahora la madre le da de comer al pingüinito. Ella le cuida mientras el padre va a comer.

FLUENCY BUILDER Use *Intervention Practice Book* page 79. Call attention to the sentences on the bottom half of the page. The slashes break the sentences into phrases to allow you to work on natural phrasing. Tell children that their goal is to read each phrase or sentence smoothly. Model appropriate pace, expression and phrasing as you read each sentence, and have children read it after you. Then have children practice by reading the sentences aloud three times to a partner.

BEFORE

Making Connections
pages 146–147

Directed Reading of *Los pequeños pingüinos azules*, pp. 158–163

Sonidos alegres
pages 158–163

Ask a volunteer to read aloud the title. Ask children what they might find out about little blue penguins. Have children read pages 158–159 to find out if the story tells facts or fiction about little blue penguins. Ask: **¿Son los pingüinos de este cuento reales? ¿Cómo sabes?** (*Possible response: Sí, leo hechos sobre ellos que se pueden comprobar en libros.*) Focus Skill **FACT AND FICTION**

Reread page 159 aloud. Model using the Look at Word Bits and Parts strategy to help children understand how to read and figure out the meanings of long or unfamiliar words.

> MODEL **No conozco todas las palabras que leo. Si me parece difícil una palabra más larga, busco partes que reconozco. Reconozco las parte *a, le,* y *ta* de las palabras *ave, leer* y *tarde.* Ahora, si pongo todas las partes juntas, leo *aleta.*** Focus Strategy **LOOK AT WORD BITS AND PARTS**

Page 160

Have children read page 160 to compare and contrast little blue penguins and emperor penguins. Ask: **¿Cuáles son las semejanzas y las diferencias entre los pequeños pingüinos azules y los emperadores?** (*Possible response: Los dos son pingüinos; el azul es el más pequeño y el emperador el más grande.*) **COMPARE AND CONTRAST**

Page 161

Have children read page 161 to find out why the little blue penguin would be miserable in Antarctica. Ask: **¿Por qué serían desdichados los pequeños pingüinos azules en Antártida?** (*Possible response: Siempre hace frío en la Antártica, y los pequeños pingüinos azules prefieren el clima caliente de Australia y Nueva Zelanda.*) **CAUSE AND EFFECT**

Page 162

Have children read page 162 to find out what happens after the little blue penguins lay their eggs. Ask: **¿Qué ocurre después que los pequeños pingüinos azules ponen los huevos? ¿y después?** (*Possible response: Papá y mamá se turnan en el nido, uno se queda en el nido mientras el otro sale a comer; los huevos se rompen, y, un mes después, los pingüinitos ya pueden salir de sus nidos.*) **SEQUENCE OF EVENTS**

Page 163

INTERVENTION PRACTICE BOOK
page 81

Have children read page 163 to find out what happens to the chicks. Ask: **¿Qué cambia en los pingüinitos después de nacer?** (*Possible response: Al principio tienen plumas oscuras, pero después se vuelven como sus padres.*) **NOTE DETAILS**

Summarize the selection. Ask children to summarize the selection by telling about the stages in a little blue penguin life, beginning with the egg. Then have them complete *Intervention Practice Book* page 81.

Page 164

Answers to *Think About It* Questions

1. Los pingüinos azules viven en un nido subterráneo en las dunas de arena. Se alimentan de *krills* y también comen peces. **SUMMARY**
2. Possible response: No, porque estarían lejos del océano donde encuentran su alimento. **INTERPRETATION**
3. Accept reasonable responses. Encourage children to add details to the picture and the words on their posters. **IMPORTANT DETAILS**

AFTER

Skill Review
page 149C–149D

USE SKILL CARD 20B

Focus Skill Fact and Fiction

RETEACH the skill. Have children look at **side B** of ***Tarjeta de destreza 20: Hecho y ficción*/Skill Card 20: Fact and Fiction.** Read the skill reminder with them, and have a volunteer read the story aloud.

Read aloud the set of directions. Explain that children will work with partners to create their own charts. Remind them to think about what is real and what is make-believe, or facts, or fiction, as they read the story.

After children have completed their fact and fiction charts, have them display and explain their work. Point out that there are many facts in the selection *Los pequeños pingüinos azules.* Ask volunteers to name some facts that they have learned about little blue penguins.

Review Phonics from *La paciencia del emperador*

RETEACH combinación de consonantes *bl, br.* Read aloud the following sentence: *El hombre usa la brújula para encontrar el pueblo de Tabla Grande.* Have children listen for the consonant blends *bl* and *br.* Then read this list aloud and have children raise their hands when they hear the consonant blend *bl: abuela, amigo, cable, blando, blinda, barba, bloque.* Now repeat the process for the consonant blend *br: veinte, pobre, poder, brisa, bronce, bruja, broma.*

FLUENCY BUILDER Use *Intervention Practice Book* page 79. Explain that children will practice the sentences on the bottom half of the page by reading them aloud on tape. Assign new partners. Have children take turns reading the sentences aloud to each other and then reading them on tape. Have children listen to the tape and tell how they think their reading has improved. Then have them record the sentences one more time.

BEFORE

Drafting a Fantasy Story Beginning
page 147A

Daily Writing: Fantasy Story Beginning

Build on prior knowledge. Tell children that they are going to talk about and write the beginning of a fantasy story. Explain that fantasy stories tell about things that are make-believe. Tell children that fantasy stories can take place in made-up places or settings. Have children share ideas for character and settings for a fantasy story.

pequeño pingüino rojo
cielo rosado
nubes verdes
nieve

Construct the text. "Share the pen" with children. Tell them that the list names things that are in a fantasy story. Help children organize the items on the list into the beginning of a fantasy story. Guide them to focus on the setting of their story. For example:

> Érase una vez un pequeño pingüino rojo. El pequeño pingüino rojo vivía en un lugar hermoso. Él podía ver un cielo rosado y nubes de color verde. Había nieve por todas partes.

Revisit the text. Reread the fantasy story beginning together. Ask: **¿Cuál es el escenario del cuento?** (*un lugar hermoso con un cielo rosado, nubes verdes y nieve*) **¿Quién es el personaje del cuento?** (*un pequeño pingüino rojo*)

- Guide children to add details to the story. Ask: **¿Cómo es la nieve?** (*Possible response: Es anaranjada y brillosa.*) Make appropriate changes.
- Ask: **¿Qué más puedo decir del escenario?** (*Podemos decir cuando ocurre el cuento.*) Make appropriate changes.
- Have children read aloud the completed fantasy story beginning and then copy it onto their papers.

On Your Own

Have children draw a picture and then write a list of details that tell about the setting of a fantasy story they would like to write.

AFTER

Spelling Lesson
page 149A

Connect Spelling and Phonics

RETEACH **combinación de consonantes *bl, br.*** Tell children to number their papers 1–8. Write say on the board, and tell children that in the words you say will have the consonant blends *bl* or *br* as in the words *blanco* or *brisa.* Dictate the following words, and have children write them. After children write each word, write it on the board so that they can proofread their work. They should draw a line through a misspelled word and write the correct spelling beside it.

1. hembra*	**2. abre**	**3. blancos***	**4. establo**
5. sobre*	**6. pueblo**	**7. cable**	**8. insoportable**

*** Word appears in *Los pequeños pingüinos azules.***

Tell children that in the following sentence, there are the consonant blends *bl* and *br*. Dictate the sentence and have children write it: *La blusa de Briana es blanca.*

Build and Read Longer Words

Remind children that they have learned how to decode words with the consonant blends *bl* and *br*. Explain that now they will use what they have learned to help them read some longer words.

INTERVENTION ASSESSMENT BOOK

Write the word *bronceado* on the board. Remind children that they can often figure out longer words by looking for smaller parts in them. Cover the letters *ado*, and have children read the word part that is left. Then cover *bronce* and have them read the word part *ado*. Model how to blend the two word parts to read aloud the longer word *bronceado.* Follow a similar procedure to have children blend word parts to read these longer words: *blanqueo, bloqueador,* and *brazado.*

FLUENCY BUILDER Have children choose a passage from *Los pequeños pingüinos azules* to read aloud to a partner. You may have children choose passages that they found particularly interesting, or have them choose one of the following options:

- Read pages 158–159. (From the title... through ...*bajo la tierra.* Total: 87 words.)
- Read pages 162–163. (From *En verano*... through ...*como sus padres.* Total: 70 words.)

Children should read the selected passage aloud to their partners three times. Have children rate each of their own readings on a scale from 1 to 4.

BEFORE
Weekly Assessments

Review Vocabulary

To review the Vocabulary Words prior to the weekly assessment, use these sentences. Read aloud the sentence items and answer choices. Invite children to identify the correct answer and explain why it makes sense.

1. Esta palabra rima con amorosa.
   a. resbalosa b. aletas
2. Esta palabra comienza con el prefijo *des.*
   a. graznido b. desdichado
3. Esta palabra tiene tres sílabas.
   a. resbalosa b. aletas
4. Esta palabra tiene la palabra *nido.*
   a. graznido b. empollar
5. Esta palabra viene de la palabra *pollo.*
   a. graznido b. empollar
6. Esta palabra rima con *monte.*
   a. hielo b. horizonte

Correct responses: 1.a, 2.b, 3.b, 4.a, 5.b, 6.b.

You may want to display the Vocabulary Words and definitions on page 199, and have children copy them to use when they study for the vocabulary test.

INTERVENTION PRACTICE BOOK page 82

Focus Skill Review Fact and Fiction

To review Fact and Fiction before the weekly assessment, distribute Intervention Practice Book page 82. Have volunteers read aloud the direction line and the story. Remind children to think about wich details are make-believe or fiction, and which are real, or fact.

Review Test Prep

Días maravillosos pages 148–149

Ask children to turn to page 149 of the *Pupil Edition.* Call attention to the Tips for answering the test questions. Tell children that paying attention to these tips can help them answer not only the items on this page but also other test items like them.

INTERVENTION ASSESSMENT BOOK

Have children follow along as you read each test item and the Tips. Tell children to take their time as they think about the choice answer for each item.

AFTER

Weekly Assessments

Self-Selected Reading

Have children select their own books to read independently. They might choose books from the classroom library, or you may wish to offer appropriate books from which children can choose, such as these:

- *El camino de las mariposas monarca.* See page 149Q of the *Teacher's Edition* for an Independent Reading Plan.
- *Un bebé ¡qué aventura!* por Marie-Agnes Guadrat. Juventud, 1997.
- *Alfa y el bebé sucio* por Brock Cole. Farrar, Straus & Giroux, 1991.

After children have chosen their books, give them a copy of *Mi diario de lectura,* which can be found on page R35 in the back of the *Teacher's Edition.* Have children fill in the information at the top of the form. Then have them use the log to keep track of their reading and to record their responses to the literature.

Conduct student-teacher conferences. Arrange time for each child to confer with you individually about his or her self-selected reading. Have children bring their *Diarios de lectura* to share with you at the conference. Children might also like to choose a favorite passage to read aloud to you. Ask questions designed to stimulate discussion about the book. For example, ask what children find especially interesting.

FLUENCY PERFORMANCE Have children read aloud to you the passage from *Los pequeños pingüinos azules* that they practiced. Observe children's pronunciation, intonation, phrasing, and the amount of words, in general, that they read correctly. Ask each child to rate his or her own performance on the 1–4 scale. If children are not happy with their oral reading, give them an opportunity to continue practicing and then to reread the passage to you.

See *Oral Reading Fluency Assessment* for monitoring progress.

LESSON 21

BEFORE
Building Background and Vocabulary

Use with

"El misterio del Parque del Pino"

Review: Words with /k/c, /s/c

Identify the sound. Ask children to listen for the /k/ and /s/ sounds as you say the words *curioso* and *cerca.* Then have children repeat the following sentence twice: *Hace calor en la ciudad.* Ask them to identify the three words that have the /k/ and/or /s/ sounds.

Associate letters to sound. Write on the board: *Hace calor en la ciudad.* Underline the *c*'s in *hace, calor* and *ciudad.* Explain that the *c*'s in *hace* and *ciudad* make the sound /s/ and the *c* in *calor* makes the sound /k/.

Word blending. Write on the board the spelling words that have the /k/ *c* (*curioso, cerca, calor, banca, cobija, cuarto*). Read each word aloud and ask children how many syllables each word has. Invite volunteers to underline the syllables which contain /k/ *c.* Then repeat the process with the /s/ words.

INTERVENTION PRACTICE BOOK
page 84

Apply the skill. Write the spelling words on the board in random order. Form two columns with the heads *c fuerte* and *c débil.* Ask children to come to the board and write the words in the correct column.

Introduce Vocabulary

PRETEACH lesson vocabulary. Tell children that they are going to learn seven new words that they will see again when they read a story called *El misterio del Parque del Pino.* Teach every vocabulary word using the following process.

> Write the word.
> Say the word.
> Track the word and have children repeat it.
> Give the meaning or context.

Use the following suggestions or similar ideas to give the meaning or context.

acorralada Point out the base word *corral. Acorralada* is to be in a *corral.*

broche Explain that *broche* is a clasp or a brooch. Pass around a sample so all children can see one.

detectives Show the base word *detectar.* Explain that detectives are the people who detect.

extrañada Ask children to think of other words that sound similar and define them (*extrañar, extraño...*) If these mean strange, then it is easy to see how *extrañada* means surprising.

objetos Contrast between objects and people. Name some objects around the room or persons and ask children to identify them as *objetos* o *personas.*

prendedor Bring in some examples of pins or brooches. Name the word as you show the brooches.

silbato Show children how to whistle as you say the word.

For vocabulary activities, see Vocabulary Games on pages 2–7.

Vocabulary Words

acorralada estar una persona o animal en una situación sin salida

broche conjunto de dos piezas que encajan para sujetar algo

detectives personas dedicadas a investigar

extrañada sorprendida

objetos cosas que puedes ver y tocar, pero que no están vivas

prendedor un pendiente que se puede usar para sujetar algo

silbato instrumento que produce un sonido agudo

AFTER
Building Background and Vocabulary

Apply Vocabulary Strategies

Use synonyms/antonyms. Ask children to look at the words *broche* and *prendedor.* Have volunteers define each word. Explain that the words have similar meanings and are therefore, synonyms. Challenge children to name synonyms for the words *extrañada* (sorprendida) and *objetos* (cosas).

MODEL **Sé que broche significa un conjunto de dos piezas que encajan para sujetar algo pero veo también que es un sinónimo de prendedor. Así que cuándo veo una palabra, recuerdo la otra.**

RETEACH lesson vocabulary. Have children listen to each of the following questions. Tell them to hold up the word card that answers each question. You may want to write the questions on the board to help visual learners.

1. ¿Qué palabra significa *sorprendida*? (*extrañada*)
2. ¿Qué palabra explica cómo podría sentirse una niña si no pudiera escapar de algo? (*acorralada*)
3. ¿Qué palabra se refiere a las personas que investigan? (*detectives*)
4. ¿Cómo se llama lo que sujeta un brazalete o un collar? (*broche*)
5. ¿Qué son los libros, juguetes y muebles? (*objetos*)
6. ¿Qué palabra nombra un gancho que une dos partes? (*prendedor*)
7. ¿Qué palabra nombra un instrumento con sonido agudo? (*silbato*)

FLUENCY BUILDER Using *Intervention Practice Book* page 83, read each word in the first column aloud and have children repeat it. Then have children work in pairs to read the words in the first column aloud to each other. Follow the same procedure with each of the remaining columns. (Save *Intervention Practice Book* page 83 to use on pages 211 and 213.)

INTERVENTION PRACTICE BOOK
page 83

BEFORE

Reading *El misterio del Parque del Pino* pages *154–169*

USE SKILL CARD 21A

Focus Skill Narrative Elements

PRETEACH the skill. Have children recall the elements of a story. (setting, characters, and plot) Ask a volunteer to tell a story that is familiar to the class. Guide children to identify the story's setting and characters.

Have children look at **side A** of ***Tarjeta de destreza 21: Elementos narrativos*/Skill Card 21: Narrative Elements.** Read the definition of narrative elements. Then have children look at the picture on the skill card and determine which parts represent each element.

Remind children that as they read *El misterio del Parque del Pino,* they should look for the narrative elements. Explain that in plays, the narrative elements of character and setting are often listed at the beginning. Have children turn to page 154 and ask:

- **¿Cuál es el escenario?** (*Possible response: El Parque del Pino, un parque público*)
- **¿Quiénes son los personajes?** (*Possible response: Lin, Jorge, la alcaldesa Paz, el jefe de policía Wilson, el entrenador León y la señorita Rosa*)

Prepare to Read *El misterio del Parque del Pino*

Días maravillosos
pages
154–169

Preview. Tell children that they are going to read a selection entitled *El misterio del Parque del Pino.* Explain that this is a play written for seven characters. The play is about a mystery and how the mystery is solved. Then preview the selection.

- **Pages 156–160:** En éstos dibujos veo que las personas buscan algo. Mira a cada persona, ¿Qué busca cada uno? ¿Cómo lo sabes?
- **Pages 162–163:** Ahora veo que Lin y Jorge empiezan a buscar los objetos. ¿Cómo van a descubrir al ladrón?
- **Pages 164–168:** Veo en los dibujos que al principio la gente se siente ansiosa y después veo que se siente contenta. ¿Qué debería pasar? ¿Qué hicieron Lin y Jorge para ayudar a la gente?

Set purpose. Model setting a purpose for reading *El misterio del Parque del Pino.*

> MODEL **De lo que he visto en éstos dibujos, veo que *El misterio del Parque del Pino* debería tratar de objetos desaparecidos. Un propósito de lectura será descubrir quién es el ladrón. Voy a leer para resolver el misterio.**

AFTER

Reading *El misterio del Parque del Pino* pages 154–169

Reread and Summarize

Have children work in pairs to reread and summarize *El misterio del Parque del Pino* in sections, as described below.

Pages 156–161

Leamos las páginas 156–161 para identificar todos los objetos que están desaparecidos. ¿Cuáles son? ¿De quién es cada uno?

Summary: Los objetos desaparecidos son el prendedor de la alcaldesa Paz; el broche de Lin; la placa del jefe Wilson y el silbato del entrenador León.

Pages 162–163

Leamos las páginas 162–163 para descubrir las claves al misterio. ¿Cuáles son? Leamos para identificar las claves del misterio.

Summary: Los objetos perdidos son todos pequeños y brillantes. La ladrona trabaja rápidamente. La ladrona está en un árbol.

Pages 164–168

Leamos las páginas 164–168 para ver cómo se sienten todos los personajes al final de la obra.

Summary: La señorita Rosa lamenta que Dynah haya causado tantos problemas. Lin y Jorge se sienten orgullosos de haber resuelto un crimen. El jefe Wilson, el entrenador León y la alcaldesa Paz están contentos de tener sus objetos de nuevo.

FLUENCY BUILDER Be sure children have copies of *Intervention Practice Book* page 83, which you used for the previous Fluency Builder activity. Call attention to the sentences on the bottom half of the page. The slashes break the sentences into phrases to allow to work on natural phrasing. Tell children that their goal is to read each phrase or sentence smoothly. Model appropriate pacing, expression and phrasing as you read each sentence and have children read it after you. Then have children practice by reading the sentences aloud three times to a partner.

BEFORE
Making Connections
pages 172–173

Directed Reading of *Un lugar secreto* pp. 166–172

Sonidos alegres
pages 166–173

Read the title of the play aloud. Remind them that this is a play and ask how it is different from a regular story. Read aloud the names of the characters and ask a volunteer to explain what a narrator is. Encourage them to use what they learned from reading *El misterio del Parque del Pino.* Ask: **¿Quién sabe qué es un narrador? ¿Qué hizo el narrador en *El misterio del Parque del Pino*?** (*Possible response: El narrador es la persona que cuenta la obra, la que describe el escenario.*) **NARRATIVE ELEMENTS**

Page 167

Point out the word *escondite.* Ask: **¿Qué significa esta palabra? ¿Qué partes de la palabra reconoces? ¿Te ayuda esto a descubrir el significado de *escondite*? WORD BITS AND PARTS**

Page 168

Ask a volunteer to read aloud the "Mamá" part on page 168 while children listen to find out what the word *objetos* means. Model using the Use Context to Confirm Meaning strategy:

> MODEL **Cuando escuché esta sección, puse atención a la frase que sigue a la que mencionó la palabra *objetos.* Mencionó un coche y unos cubos. Estas cosas deben ser los objetos. Objetos deben ser cosas que se pueden tocar como los juguetes.** Focus Strategy **USE CONTEXT TO CONFIRM MEANING**

Discuss whether children agree with your thinking.

Page 171

Ask three volunteers to read and act out the dialogue on this page. Give them time to practice their parts and decide what setting they will use. After the children have acted the scene several times, ask: **¿Qué significa la frase "me rindo"? Usando el contexto del diálogo, ¿puedes entender su significado?** (*Possible response: "Me rindo" significa me doy por vencido.*) Remind students that whenever they find a word they are unfamiliar with, they can read the surrounding words or sentences to help figure out the meaning of the unfamiliar word. **USE CONTEXT TO CONFIRM MEANING**

At the end of the reading, help children review what they know, ask: **¿Quién es Manchas?** (*Possible response: el perro*) **¿Qué son los bultos en la cama de Manchas?** (*Possible response: los objetos perdidos*) **SUMMARIZE**

INTERVENTION PRACTICE BOOK
page 85

AFTER
Skill Review
page 173I

USE SKILL CARD 21B

Summarize the selection. Encourage children to explain what happened to the missing toys.

Answers to *Think About It* Questions

1. Estaban en la cama de Manchas. **SUMMARIZE**
2. Estaban sorprendidos porque encontraron sus objetos en un lugar gracioso después de una búsqueda larga. Muestran su sorpresa con el uso de exclamaciones como ¡Vaya! y ¡Qué vergüenza! **INTERPRET STORY EVENTS**
3. Responses wil vary. **TASK**

Focus Skill Narrative Elements

RETEACH the skill. Have children look at **side B** of ***Tarjeta de destreza 21: Elementos narrativos/* Skill Card 21: Narrative Elements.** Read the skill reminder with them, and have a volunteer read the writing instructions aloud.

Explain that students will be writing a scene or mini play from the point of view of Manchas. Ask them to turn to the first pages of *El misterio del Parque del Pino* and *El lugar secreto* to see how characters and setting are listed. Encourage them to share in pairs ideas for problems and resolutions in their scenes.

After children have completed their scenes, they can form groups to read them. They can then choose the best scene and practice it to perform for the class. Encourage them to use simple props and costumes.

Review Phonics Skill: hard and soft c.

RETEACH the skill. Write the word *cometa* on the board. Explain that you will say four more words in which the /k/ sound is used. Have volunteers write each word on the board. Then write the word *ciruela* on he board, explain that you will say four words in which the /s/ sound is used, and repeat the process.

1. carretera	**2. culpa**	**3. correr**	**4. alcanzar**
5. centeno	**6. cine**	**7. precioso**	**8. racimo**

Dictate the following sentence and have children write it: *Las ciruelas crecen en la cima de la sierra.*

FLUENCY BUILDER Be sure that children have copies of *Intervention Practice Book* page 83. Explain that today children will practice the sentences on the bottom half of the page by reading them aloud on tape. Assign new partners. Have student take turns reading the sentences aloud to each other and then reading them on tape.

INTERVENTION PRACTICE BOOK
page 83

BEFORE

Drafting a Descriptive Paragraph
page 175C

Word Choice: Descriptive Paragraph

Build on prior knowledge. Explain that a descriptive paragraph has two parts. A **topic sentence** tells what the paragraph is about. **Describing words in detail sentences** help paint a picture for the reader by providing specific details about what the person, place, or thing is like. Tell children that they are going to write about popcorn.

ver—nubes blancas
escuchar—crujido
gustar—sal
oler—mantequilla
sentir—granos pequeños

Construct the text. "Share the pen" with children. Guide them in using the words to write descriptive sentences. For example:

- Veo las nubes blancas de las rositas de maiz.
- Escucho el crujido cuando las como.
- Saboreo la sal.
- Huelo la mantequilla.
- Siento los granos pequeños.

Revisit the text. Go back and read the sentences together. Ask: **¿Cómo podemos arreglar las frases de una manera que tenga más sentido?**

- Explain that they can also create descriptions by comparing how two things are alike. These are called *símiles,* and often use words such as *como.* Say: **Sus ojos son como estrellas.** Then ask: **¿De qué trata esta frase? ¿Cómo son sus ojos?** Encourage children to suggest similes for the class' paragraph.
- Explain that one part of revising is making sure that the appropriate word choice has been used. Remind them that descriptions should use colorful and precise words to help readers picture what they are writing about. Ask: **¿Hay palabras en nuestro párrafo que no son exactas o correctas? Cómo podemos encontrar otras?**

On Your Own

Remind children to think about what they see, hear, taste, smell, and feel when they think about this person, place, or thing. Have children set up a sheet of scrap paper in a similar format. Then have them fill in the details. Finally, they are ready to write their own paragraph.

AFTER

Spelling Lesson
page 169H

Connect Spelling and Phonics

RETEACH hard and soft c. Write the word *cometa* on the board. Explain that you will say five more words in which the /k/ sound is used. Have volunteers write each word on the board. Then write the word *ciruela* on the board, explain that you will say three words in which the /s/ sound is used, and repeat the process.

1. clase*	**2. cubos***	**3. corriendo***	**4. cebolla**
5. cera	**6. escondite***	**7. secreto***	**8. encima**

*** Word appears in *Un lugar secreto.***

Dictate the following sentence and have children write it: *Las ciruelas crecen en la cima de la sierra.*

Build and Read Longer Words

Remind students that they have learned how to decode words with the hard and soft c sound.

Write the word *encima* on the board. Tell children that they can sometimes figure out long words by looking for syllables, prefixes and suffixes. Cover *en* and have a volunteer read the word *cima.* Then cover *cima* and have a volunteer read the prefix *en.* Point out that *cima* uses the soft c /s/. Follow a similar procedure with these words: *encajar, entrecejo* and *encerrar.* Encourage children to build other long words like these.

FLUENCY BUILDER Have children choose a passage from *Un lugar secreto* to read aloud to a partner. You may have children choose passages that they found particularly interesting, or have them choose one of the following options:

- Read pages 166–167. (From *Hoy no es un día típico*... through ...*¡¡¡Mamá!!!* Total: 111 words)
- Read pages 171–172. (From *¡Me rindo!*... through ...*¡Manchas tiene su propio escondite secreto!* Total: 112 words)

Children should read the selected passage aloud to their partners three times. Have the child rate each reading on a scale of 1 to 4.

BEFORE
Weekly Assessments

Review Vocabulary

To revisit vocabulary words prior to the weekly assessment, use these true or false questions. Have volunteers take turns reading aloud the sentences. Children determine whether the definitions are true or false. Encourage them to then correct the false sentences.

1. Un **broche** es un conjunto de dos piezas usado para mantener sujeto un collar. (*verdadero*)
2. Si estás **extrañada**, también estás sorprendida. (*verdadero*)
3. Los **objetos** pueden respirar. (*falso*)
4. Puedes llevar un **prendedor** en la solapa de tu chaqueta. (*verdadero*)
5. Los **detectives** se ocupan de pintar murales. (*falso*)
6. Si estás **acorralada**, puedes escapar. (*falso*)
7. El entrenador de tu equipo usa un **silbato.** (*verdadero*)

You may want to display the Vocabulary Words and definitions on page 209 and have children copy them to use when they study for the vocabulary test.

INTERVENTION PRACTICE BOOK
page 86

Focus Skill Review Narrative Elements

To review narrative elements before the weekly assessment, distribute *Intervention Practice Book* page 86. Have volunteers read aloud the first direction line and the sentences. Guide children by having them read the first sentence together. Discuss whether this is the character's problem. Have children underline the problem.

Review Test Prep

Días maravillosos
page 175

Ask children to turn to page 175 of the *Pupil Edition.* Call attention to the tips for answering the test questions. Tell children that paying attention to these tips can help them answer not only the test questions but also other test questions like these.

INTERVENTION ASSESSMENT BOOK

Have children follow along as you read each test question and the tip that goes with it. Discuss why the beginning of the story is most important to reread. (*Possible response: The problem is usually found at the beginning.*) Discuss why it is important to read each answer choice carefully before choosing an answer to question 2. (*Some answers are very similar.*)

AFTER

Weekly Assessments

Self-Selected Reading

Have children select their own books to read independently. They might choose books from the classroom library shelf, or you may wish to offer a group of appropriate books from which children can choose.

- *Buscar animales.* See page 1750 of the *Teacher's Edition* for an Independent Reading Plan.
- *¡La señorita Nelson ha desaparecido!* por Harry Allard y James Marshall, 1998.
- *¿Sabes dónde está tu monstruo esta noche?* por Joanne y David Wylie. Children's Press, 1986.

You may also wish to choose additional books that are of the same genre or by the same author or that have the same kind of text structure as the selection.

After children have chosen their books, give each child a copy of *Mi diario de lectura,* which can be found on page R35 in the back of the *Teacher's Edition.* Have children fill in the information at the top of the form. Then have them use the log to keep track of their reading and to record their responses to the literature.

Conduct student-teacher conferences. Arrange time for each child to confer with you individually about his or her self-selected reading. Have children bring their Reading Logs to share with you at the conference. Children might also like to share a favorite passage to read aloud to you. Ask questions designed to stimulate discussion about the book. For example, you might ask children to compare the narrative elements found in a play with those in a story. Ask whether they saw similarities between their book and the plays they read in class.

FLUENCY PERFORMANCE Have children read aloud to you the passage from *Un lugar secreto* that they selected and practiced with their partners. Keep track of the number of words each child reads correctly. Ask the child to rate his or her own performance on the 1–4 scale. If children are not happy with their oral reading, give them an opportunity to continue practicing and then to reread the passage to you again.

See *Oral Reading Fluency Assessment* for monitoring progress.

LESSON 22

BEFORE

Building Background and Vocabulary

INTERVENTION PRACTICE BOOK

page 88

Use with

"Adiós, Curtis"

Introduce Phonics: *Diphthongs ai and ei*

Identify the sound. Say the words *bailarín* and *aceite.* Ask children to listen for the diphthongs. Say the sentence *El bailarín tiene veinte peines.* Encourage students to identify the three words with the diphthongs *ai* and *ei.*

Associate letters to sound. Write on the board: *El bailarín tiene veinte peines.* Underline the letters *ai* in *bailarín* and *ei* in *veinte* and *peines.* Explain to the children that these letters represent the diphthongs *ai* and *ei.*

Word blending. Read the word *bailarín* slowly. Exaggerate the pronunciation of the diphthong *ai.* Ask children to repeat the sound in *bailarín, veinte* and *peines.*

Apply the skill. In order for children to better recognize words with *ai* and *ei*, show them objects, illustrations or photographs of items such as:

bailarín (dancer)	**caimán** (alligator)	**naipe** (set of playing cards)
aceite (oil)	**aceituna** (olive)	**peine** (comb)

Introduce Vocabulary

PRETEACH lesson vocabulary. Tell children that they are going to learn six new words that they will see again when they read a story called *Adiós Curtis.* Teach each vocabulary word using the following process.

Write the word.

Say the word.

Track the word and have children repeat it.

Give the meaning or context.

Use the following suggestions or similar ideas to give the meaning or context.

direcciones Encourage children to name other meanings of the word besides *direcciones.* Knowing that *direcciones* means direction may help them understand its other meaning.

empleado Show children how to read the word according to syllables. Say *em-ple-a-do* slowly. Then invite children to repeat.

crecido Ask children to recognize the base word *crecer.*

honor Have children discuss honors that they have received or that they have heard of others receiving.

salen Act out leaving the classroom as you say the word *salen.* Then have volunteers repeat the process while the whole class repeats the word.

ruta Demonstrate a route on a map. Encourage children to find alternate routes as they name the vocabulary word *ruta.*

For vocabulary activities, see Vocabulary Games on pages 2–3.

Vocabulary Words

direcciones nombre y número de las calles, ciudades y estados donde se encuentran los negocios o las casas

empleado dependiente en un negocio

crecido se han hecho adultos

honor muestra de respeto y amor

salen se van del lugar donde estaban

ruta serie de lugares o clientes visitados regularmente por una persona que entrega o vende algo

AFTER
Building Background and Vocabulary

Apply Vocabulary Strategies

Use syllabication. Write the word *di-rec-cio-nes* on the board with hyphens separating the syllables. Explain that sometimes breaking a word into syllables will help with correct pronunciation which may help to identify the word.

> MODEL **Cuando leo ésta palabra lentamente, sílaba por sílaba, reconozco la palabra y entonces puedo dar la definición. Help children repeat the process for the words *cre-ci-do* and *sa-len.***

RETEACH lesson vocabulary. Ask children to listen to each of the following sentences. Tell them to hold up the word card that completes each sentence. Reread the sentence aloud with the correct word choice. Then discuss how the meaning of the vocabulary word fits the sentence.

1. Hicieron una fiesta en __________ a su mamá. (*honor*)
2. Con el tiempo, los niños habían __________. (*crecido*)
3. A la hora del recreo, los niños __________ a jugar. (*salen*)
4. Un __________ lo ayudó a escoger la ropa. (*empleado*)
5. Tenía todas las __________ escritas en su libreta. (*direcciones*)
6. El cartero sale en su __________ cada mañana. (*ruta*)

FLUENCY BUILDER Using *Intervention Practice Book* p. 87, read each word in the first column aloud and have children repeat it. Then have children work in pairs to read the words in the first column aloud to each other. Follow the same procedure with each of the remaining columns. After partners have practiced reading aloud the words in each column separately, have them practice the entire list.

BEFORE

Reading
Adiós, Curtis
pages 178–193

USE SKILL CARD 22A

Focus Skill Compare/Contrast

PRETEACH the skill. Point out to children that figuring out how characters, settings, and plots are the same and different can help them remember more about the characters and events in a story.

Have children look at **side A** of ***Tarjeta de destreza 22: Comparar y contrastar*/Skill Card 22: Compare/Contrast**. Read the definition of compare and contrast. Then have children compare and contrast the two pictures.

Encourage children to look at the details of each picture, noting the characters, settings and plots of the two. Ask:

- **¿Cuáles son las similitudes y las diferencias entre los dibujos?** (*Possible response: Uno muestra el principio de una fiesta, el otro muestra el fin, pero está la misma gente en la misma casa.*)

Prepare to Read *Adiós, Curtis*

Días maravillosos
pages 178–187

Preview. Tell children that they are going to read a selection entitled *Adiós, Curtis.* Explain that this is a story about a letter carrier. It is his last day on the job after forty-two years. Then preview the selection.

- **Pages 178–179:** Veo el título y pienso que alguien se vaya en un viaje. Pero cuando miro a los dibujos veo que el cuento trata de un cartero viejo. Quizás el cartero se vaya en un viaje o vaya a dejar de trabajar.
- **Pages 182–183:** Miro a todos los regalos y las personas queridas y determino que sí el cartero va a dejar de trabajar. Puede ser que hoy es su último día de trabajo. Veo que todo el mundo le quiere a él muchísimo.
- **Pages 184–187:** En éstas páginas veo que toda la gente querida tiene una fiesta para el cartero. Luego, el escribe. Supongo que escribe cartas a todos sus amigos para agradecerles por su fiesta.

Set purpose. Model setting a purpose for reading *Adiós, Curtis.*

MODEL **Desde lo que he visto en los dibujos, creo que voy a leer sobre el cartero y sus amigos. Un propósito de leer es para descubrir quiénes son sus amigos y cómo han cambiado durante su vida como cartero.**

AFTER

Reading
Adiós, Curtis
pages 178–193

Reread and Summarize

Have children reread and summarize *Adiós, Curtis* in sections, as described below.

Pages 180–185

Leemos las páginas 180–185 para recordar la gente querida de Curtis y los regalos que le dieron a él.

Summary: La gente querida de Curtis son la anciana de la colina, el bebé del 4-C, el empleado de la carnicería y el guardia que nos ayuda a cruzar la calle. Dieron a él un pastelillo de chocolate con chispas, un dibujo, una botella de loción, una cajita de nueces, tarjetas, dulces, galletas, abrazos, saludos, besos, un libro y un sacapuntas.

Pages 186–187

Leemos las páginas 186–187 para ver como han cambiado la gente querida.

Summary: Curtis fue cartero por tanto tiempo que la gente en su comunidad ha cambiado mucho. Los niños han crecido y son adultos. Tienen hijos y algunos tienen nietos. Los perros han tenido cachorros y los gatos han tenido gatitos.

Pages 188–192

Leemos las páginas 188–192 para descubrir lo que hace la gente de la comunidad de Curtis y lo que hace Curtis para ellos.

Summary: Al llegar a la última casa en su ruta, Curtis descubrió una fiesta en su honor. Toda la gente querida estaba. Festejaban a Curtis y su vida. En el día próximo, Curtis les escribió unas tarjetas a todos sus amigos para agradecerles por su fiesta.

FLUENCY BUILDER Use *Intervention Practice Book* p. 87, which you used for the previous Fluency Builder activity. Call attention to the sentences on the bottom half of the page. The slashes break the sentences into phrases to allow you to work on natural phrasing. Tell children that their goal is to read each phrase or sentence smoothly. Model appropriate pace, expression and phrasing as you read each sentence and have children read each sentence after you. Then have children practice by reading the sentences aloud three times to a partner.

BEFORE

Making Connections
pages 196–197

Directed Reading of *Hola, desde aquí* pp. 174–180

Sonidos alegres
pp. 174–180

Ask the children to look at the title and illustrations of the selection. Help them identify the significance of the postcards on pages 175 and 176. Ask: **¿Cómo es el barrio del niño?** (*Possible response: Es un barrio típico con casas junto a otras y patios donde juegan los niños.*) **IMPORTANT DETAILS**

Pages 175–176

Have children read pages 175 and 176 to predict who is writing these postcards. Ask: **¿Quién escribe las tarjetas? ¿Qué pista leíste en la página 174?** (*Possible response: En la página 174 leí que hay dos hombres en la calle, Alberto Pérez y el señor Suárez. A lo mejor uno de ellos ha escrito las tarjetas.*) **IMPORTANT DETAILS/DRAW CONCLUSIONS**

Page 179

Ask children to read page 179 to find out about this postcard. **¿Quién escribe esta postal?** (*Possible response: El niño*) **NOTE DETAILS ¿Por qué manda esta postal?** (*Possible response: para invitar a todos los niños al cumpleaños del señor Suárez*) **NOTE DETAILS ¿Por qué tienen una fiesta para el señor Suárez?** (*Possible response: Quería hacer algo bueno para el señor Suárez.*) **INTERPRET CHARACTERS' MOTIVATIONS**

Pages 178–179

Read aloud pages 178–179. Ask students to describe the party and discern the feelings of señor Suárez. Ask: **¿Qué siente el señor Suárez por los niños del barrio? ¿Cómo sabes?** (*Possible response: El señor Suárez siente cariño por los niños porque es muy buen hombre.*)

Ask a volunteer to briefly restate the events of the story by looking at the pictures and briefly describing what is happening in each.

MODEL **Cuando escuché al cuento, trataba de verificar que comprendía todo. Necesito que el cuento tenga sentido para mí.**

Focus Strategy **SEQUENCE EVENTS/SUMMARIZE** Discuss whether children agree with your thinking.

Summarize the selection. Ask children to think about Myles's mystery, his clues, and his solution. Then help them summarize the story.

Answers to *Think About It* Questions

INTERVENTION PRACTICE BOOK page 89

1. Al señor Suárez le gustan todos los niños. Se siente como si fueran sus nietos. Les manda postales. **SUMMARIZE**
2. Al niño le gusta el señor Suárez, pero también siente pena por él porque el señor Suárez está solo. El niño decide tener un cumpleaños para él. **INTERPRET STORY DETAILS**
3. Las respuestas variarán. **TASK**

AFTER

Skill Review
page 199C

USE SKILL CARD 22B

Focus Skill Compare/Contrast

RETEACH **the skill.** Have children look at **side B** of ***Tarjeta de destreza 22: Comparar y contrastar*/Skill Card 22: Compare/Contrast.** Read the skill reminder with them, and have a volunteer read the directions for the compare and contrast activity.

Explain that children will work with partners to write stories and make charts for their stories. Remind them to include characters, setting, and plot. After children have completed their Venn diagrams, have them display and explain their work. Point out that you could also compare the mystery *Hola desde aquí* to *El misterio del Parque del Pino* to learn more about what makes a story a mystery.

Review Phonics Skill: Diphthongs *ai* and *ei*.

RETEACH **the skill.** Read the following words and ask children to hold up their diphthong cards showing either the *ai* side or the *ei* side depending on the diphthong they hear.

vaina	reino	bailan	aceite	reina
aire	peine	afeitarse	vainilla	aislar

FLUENCY BUILDER Use *Intervention Practice Book* page 87. Explain that today children will practice the sentences on the bottom half of the page by reading them aloud on tape. Assign new partners. Have children take turns reading the sentences aloud to each other and then reading them on tape.

INTERVENTION PRACTICE BOOK page 87

BEFORE

Drafting a Poem
page 199G

Using Rhythm and Rhyme: Poems

Build on prior knowledge. Tell children that they are going to talk and write about things they like using words that rhyme. On a chart, create rhyming pairs of words representing things they like, for example: *bikes/hikes; cats/hats*.

Construct the text. "Share the pen" with children. Guide them in using the words generated above to fill in the second blank only of the following couplets. Add as many "I like" lines as needed.

Me gusta __________ y me gusta __________ .

Me gusta __________ y me gusta __________ .

Me gusta __________ y me gusta __________ .

Pero de todo, más me gusta __________ .

Revisit the text. Go back and read the sentences together. Ask: **¿Qué palabras ponemos en los primeros espacios?**

- Guide children to put words in similar categories in the first blank of each couplet.
- Ask: **¿Cambiamos algunas palabras para hacer rimas?** Make the appropriate changes.
- Have children read the completed poem aloud and then copy it on their papers.

On Your Own

Have children write a similar poem using the frame "I don't like." Suggest that they use a rhyming dictionary to help them find words or brainstorm a list of rhyming words to use in their poems.

AFTER

Spelling Lesson
page 195I

Connect Spelling and Phonics

RETEACH phonics: Diphthongs *ai* and *ei*. Write the word *peine* on the board. Explain that you will say more words which have diphthong *ai* or *ei*. Have volunteers write each word on the board.

1. paracaidismo*	**2. reino**	**3. bailan**	**4. aceite**
5. reina	**6. aire**	**7. vainilla**	**8. afeitarse**

*** Word appears in *Hola, desde aquí*.**

Dictate the following sentence, and have children write it: *El reino y la reina bailan en el aire.*

Build and Read Longer Words

Write the words *aireación* and *airear* on the board. Tell children that they can sometimes figure out long words by looking for syllables, prefixes and suffixes. Cover *ción* and have a volunteer read the word *aire*. Then cover *aire* and have a volunteer read the suffix *ción*. Point out that *aire* uses the diphthong *ai*. Repeat the process with the word *airear*.

FLUENCY BUILDER Have children choose a passage from *Hola, desde aquí* to read aloud to a partner. You may have children choose passages that they found particularly interesting, or have them choose one of the following options:

- Read page 174. (From *Mi calle es como la mayoría de las calles...* through *...Creo que simplemente es tímido.* Total: 79 words)
- Read page 176. (From *¿Quién nos enviaría estas tarjetas y por qué?...* through *...¡Ojalá estuvieras aquí!* Total: 57 words)

Children should read the selected passage aloud to their partners three times. Have the child rate each reading on a scale of 1 to 4.

BEFORE

Weekly Assessments

Review Vocabulary

To revisit vocabulary prior to the weekly assessment, encourage children to answer these questions about the vocabulary words.

1. ¿Qué palabra habla de una persona que vende cosas? (*empleado*)
2. ¿Qué palabra dice donde vive la gente o donde se puede hallar una empresa? (*direcciones*)
3. ¿Qué palabra dice que las personas van de adentro hacia afuera? (*salen*)
4. ¿Qué palabra dice el camino que un cartero recorre todos los días? (*ruta*)
5. ¿Qué palabra significa una muestra de amor y respeto? (*honor*)
6. ¿Qué palabra significa que alguien tiene más años que un adolescente? (*crecido*)

You may want to display the Vocabulary Words and definitions on page 219 and have children copy them to use when they study for the vocabulary test.

Focus Skill

Compare/Contrast

INTERVENTION PRACTICE BOOK
page 90

To review compare/contrast before the weekly assessment, distribute *Intervention Practice Book* page 90. Have volunteers read aloud the first direction line and the sentences. Guide children to turn back to the stories to make their comparisons. Discuss whether these characters are the same or different in each story. Have them put them in the appropriate places on the Venn diagram.

Review Test Prep

Días maravillosos
page 199

Ask children to turn to page 199 of the *Pupil Edition.* Call attention to the Tips for answering the test questions. Tell children that paying attention to these tips can help them answer not only the test questions but also other test questions like these.

INTERVENTION ASSESSMENT BOOK

Have children follow along as you read each test question and the tip that goes with it. Discuss why it is important to disregard answers that you know are not correct. (Possible response: It helps you focus on the correct answer.)

Self-Selected Reading

Have children select their own books to read independently. They might choose books from the classroom library shelf, or you may wish to offer a group of appropriate books from which children can choose.

- *Bizcochitos de cumpleaños.* (See page 199S of the *Teacher's Edition* for an Independent Reading Plan.)
- *Bomberos y bomberas* por Dee Ready. Bridgestone, 1999.
- *Dentistas.* por Dee Ready. Bridgestone, 1999.

You may also wish to choose additional books that are the same genre or by the same author, or that have the same kind of text structure as the selection.

After children have chosen their books, give each child a copy of *Mi diario de lectura*, which can be found on page R35 in the back of the *Teacher's Edition.* Have children fill in the information at the top of the form. Then have them use the log to keep track of their reading and to record their responses to the literature.

Conduct student-teacher conferences. Arrange time for each child to confer with you individually about his or her self-selected reading. Have children bring their Reading Logs to share with you at the conference. Children might also like to share a favorite passage to read aloud to you. Ask questions about the book to stimulate discussion. For example, you might want to ask what the problem and the solution were in a fiction text or how the meaning of a new vocabulary word was determined in a nonfiction text.

FLUENCY PERFORMANCE Have children read aloud to you the passage from *Hola, desde aquí* that they selected and practiced with their partners. Keep track of the number of words each child reads correctly. Ask the child to rate his or her own performance on the 1–4 scale. If children are not happy with their oral reading, give them an opportunity to continue practicing and then to reread the passage to you.

See *Oral Reading Fluency Assessment* for monitoring progress.

LESSON 23

Use with

"El ritmo de Max"

BEFORE

Building Background and Vocabulary

INTERVENTION PRACTICE BOOK

page 92

Introduce: Reconocer los hiatos *ae, ea, ee, eo*

Identify the sound. Explain to the children that in some words we find two vowels next to each other but they are part of two separate syllables. This is called a hiatus (hiatos). Ask children to listen for the hiatuses *ae, ea, ee* and *eo* in the words: *aldea*, *maestra*, *león* and *leer*. Encourage them to repeat the following sentence and identify the words with a hiatus. *No dejes caer el libro para leer*.

Associate letters to sound. Write the word *pasear* on the board and read it pronouncing each syllable. Point out that although the vowels *e* and *a* are together, they belong to different syllables *pa-se-ar*. Write these syllables and indicate the hiatus. Model how to blend them into the word *pasear*. Repeat this procedure for the words *aéreo* (*a-e-re-o*) and *leer* (*le-er*).

Word blending. Indicate the word *leer* (*le-er*) and read it aloud. Show children how it can be separated into syllables and have them read the word at a normal speed. Repeat this procedure for the rest of the two-syllable words. Later, point out words at random and ask volunteers to read them.

Apply the skill. *Syllabication*. Brainstorm with children action words which contain hiatuses (*traer, caer, leer, olear, saborear, golear*). Invite them to write these words, and then divide the syllables within the word by a line.

Introduce Vocabulary

PRETEACH lesson vocabulary. Tell children that they are going to learn six new words that they will see again when they read a story called *El ritmo de Max*. Teach each vocabulary word using the following process.

Write the word.
Say the word.
Track the word and have children repeat it.
Give the meaning or context.

Use the following suggestions or similar ideas to give the meaning or context.

apareció Explain that something that appeared became visible. For example, *El gato apareció de detrás del sillón.*

conduce Relate to the two kinds of *conduce*—the one who makes things run smoothly on a train and the one who leads a band or orchestra

creó Explain that *creó* means something was made that did not exist before.

imitaba Perform an action and have children repeat the action. Explain that they have just imitated you.

ritmo Bring in samples of music with different rhythms and encourage children to tap or clap the different beats.

asustan Use syllabication to help children pronounce this longer word. Say: *a-sus-tan* and have children repeat it three times. Challenge them to act out being frightened or surprised as they say the word.

For vocabulary activities, see Vocabulary Games on pages 2–7.

Vocabulary Words

apareció se mostró, surgió

conduce alguien que dirige

creó hizo o diseñó algo

imitaba copiaba algo o a alguien

ritmo una sucesión regular de sonidos, sílabas o imágenes

asustan sorprenden

AFTER

Building Background and Vocabulary

Apply Vocabulary Strategies

Use syllabication. Write the word *apareció* on the board. Demonstrate splitting it into syllables. Model figuring out the meaning by pronouncing the syllables.

MODEL **Algunas veces me ayuda entender una palabra si puedo pronunciarla correctamente. Si leo la palabra *apareció* en sílabas, *a-pa-re-ció*, veo que reconozco la palabra; ahora sé que significa se mostró o surgió.**

RETEACH **lesson vocabulary.** Have children listen to the following sentences. Tell them to hold up the word card that best answers the question or defines the phrase. Reread the sentence with the correct response.

1. ¿Qué palabra está relacionada con los sonidos que produce un tambor? (*ritmo*)
2. ¿Qué palabra quiere decir hizo? (*creó*)
3. ¿Qué palabra significa sorprenden? (*asustan*)
4. ¿Qué palabra dice lo que alguien hacía si copiaba a alguien? (*imitaba*)
5. ¿Qué palabra significa que se mostró? (*apareció*)
6. Esta palabra dice lo que hace alguien que maneja un tren. (*conduce*)

FLUENCY BUILDER Using *Intervention Practice Book* page 91, read each word in the first column aloud and have children repeat it. Then have children work in pairs to read the words in the first column aloud to each other. Follow the same procedure with each of the remaining columns. After partners have practiced reading aloud the words in each column separately, have them practice the entire list.

INTERVENTION PRACTICE BOOK

page 91

BEFORE

Reading
El ritmo de Max
pages 202–221

Focus Skill Multiple Meaning Words

PRETEACH the skill. Discuss with children how some words, such as *río*, have more than one meaning. (*river* of water; I *laugh*) Sometimes they may see a word they know but it does not make sense in the sentence. When that happens, they can use the words around it to figure out the meaning.

USE SKILL CARD 23A

Have children look at **side A** of ***Tarjeta de destreza 23: Palabras de significados múltiples*/Skill Card 23: Multiple Meaning Words.** Read the definition of Multiple Meaning Words. Next, have children read through the sentences. Explain that each boldface word can have at least two different meanings. Now call attention to the sentences. Ask:

- **¿Cuántos significados tiene la palabra *tapas y bote?*** (*Possible responses: dos y tres*).
- **¿Sabes algunos significados más para la palabra *banda y bote?*** (*Possible responses: cinta, lado, partido, bandada; pote, brinco, barco, lancha*)

Review how children used context clues to decide which meaning of the word made sense in each sentence.

Prepare to Read *El ritmo de Max*

Días maravillosos
pages 202–220

Preview. Tell children that they are going to read a selection entitled *El ritmo de Max.* Explain that this is a realistic fiction selection that includes characters, settings and a plot that could be real but aren't. Tell children that *El ritmo de Max* describes the different noises that a budding drummer can make on his city block. Then preview the selection.

- **Pages 204–208:** Veo las ilustraciones hermosas y sé que es un día de viento. Veo también que Max agarra dos varas en el viento. Pienso que el va a usarlas para hacer ritmo como dice el título.
- **Pages 209–215:** En estas páginas, compruebo que Max usa las varas para hacer ritmo en muchos objetos diferentes. Veo también a algunas personas, pienso que son la familia y los amigos de Max. Me gustaría saber quién más escucha a Max.
- **Pages 216–219:** Ahora sé que una banda pasa por la casa de Max y que un músico de la banda mira a Max. En la última página veo que Max también sueña con tocar un tambor en una banda.

Set purpose. Model setting a purpose for reading "El ritmo de Max."

MODEL **Por lo que he visto en estas páginas, creo que voy a leer sobre un día en que Max descubrió el ritmo usando varas y objetos comunes. Quiero saber cómo suenan estos "tambores" y como los toca Max.**

AFTER

Reading
El ritmo de Max
pages 202–220

Reread and Summarize

Have children reread and summarize *El ritmo de Max* in sections, as described below.

Pages 203–206

Leamos las páginas 203–206 para descubrir cómo encontró las varas.

Summary: En un día con muchas nubes y viento, se cayeron unas varas de un árbol.

Pages 207–215

Leamos las páginas 207–215 para ver en qué objetos toca Max y qué sonidos hace.

Summary: Max toca en sus muslos, imitando al sonido de los pichones que vuelan; toca en el balde, éste suena como la lluvia chocando contra la ventana; toca en unas cajas de sombrero, imitando el ritmo de los tambores; toca en unas botellas de refresco que suenan como las campanas de la iglesia; toca en los botes de basura, que imitan el sonido de las ruedas del tren sobre los rieles.

Pages 216–219

Leamos las páginas 216–219 para saber quiénes escuchan a Max y qué recibe de regalo para empezar a realizar sus sueños.

Summary: El abuelo, la madre, las hermanas y los amigos de Max lo escuchan. También una banda pasa por su casa y un baterista escucha y mira a Max. Él le da a Max unas baquetas. Ahora Max sueña con ser un baterista también.

FLUENCY BUILDER Be sure children have copies of *Intervention Practice Book* page 91, which you used for the previous Fluency Builder activity. Call attention to the sentences on the bottom half of the page. The slashes break the sentences into phrases to allow you to work on natural phrasing. Tell children that their goal is to read each phrase or sentence smoothly. Model appropriate pacing, expression and phrasing as you read each sentence and have children read it after you. Then have children practice by reading the sentences aloud three times to a partner.

BEFORE

Making Connections
pages 224–225

Directed Reading of *El compositor de música*

Sonidos alegres
pp. 182–188

p. 182

Ask a volunteer to read aloud the title. Help children predict what this story will be about. Ask: **¿Qué es un compositor? ¿Cómo puede ser un niño tan joven un compositor? ¿De qué debería tratar este cuento?** (*Possible responses: Un compositor es una persona que escribe música. Quizás el niño inventa una canción o una manera nueva de tocar una canción. Debería tratar de la composición de este niño.*) **MAKE AND CONFIRM PREDICTIONS**

pp. 183–185

Have students read pages 183–185 to find out what objects David tries to play in order to find the right sound for his song. Ask: **¿Qué tipos de objetos toca David?** (*Possible response: David toca en unas cajas, un cubo plástico y un cubo de basura.*) **SUMMARIZE**

pp. 186–187

Ask volunteers to read pages 186–187 to discover who helps David find the right drum for his song. Ask: **¿Quién ayuda a David a encontrar su tambor perfecto?** (*Possible response: Unos amigos, Jon y Linda, ayudan a David a descubrir el tambor de acero.*) **SUMMARIZE**

Model using the self-correct focus strategy by re-reading page 187. Focus on the word *cubo*. Remind children that they have seen this word throughout the story.

> **MODEL** **Cuando leí la palabra *cubo* en la página 184 pensé que se refería a una caja cuadrada con sus tres lados iguales. Y al comenzar a leer la página 187, pensé que tenía el mismo significado, pero cuando leo la palabra otra vez, veo que no. Sé que una palabra puede tener más de un significado. La palabra *cubo* debe significar algo distinto. Me autocorrijo y miro al contexto. Veo que el padre de David usa el cubo de acero para hacer un tambor. Quizás *cubo* significa un recipiente metálico grande. Cuando termino de leer, veo que tengo razón.**
> Focus Strategy **AUTOCORREGIR**

INTERVENTION PRACTICE BOOK
page 93

Summarize the selection Ask children to think about what happens first, next, and last in the story. Then help them summarize the story in a few sentences.

Answers to *Think About It* Questions

1. David puede crear notas musicales en su tambor. **SUMMARIZE**
2. Se sentía contento y orgulloso. **INTERPRET EVENTS**
3. Las respuestas pueden variar. **TASK**

AFTER

Skill Review
page 225I

USE SKILL CARD 23B

Focus Skill Multiple Meaning Words

RETEACH the skill. Have children look at **side B** of ***Tarjeta de destreza 23: Palabras de significados múltiples*/Skill Card 23: Multiple Meaning Words.** Read the skill reminder with them, and have a volunteer demonstrate drawing the first picture.

After children have completed their multiple-meaning pictures, have them display and explain their work. Encourage each student to show or explain one drawing of their own.

Review Phonics Skill: Hiatos *ae, ea, ee, eo*

RETEACH the skill. Ask children to help you write the words in a chart according to syllables. Show children how to sort words by the number of syllables. Ask them to say which words they wrote in each column. Ask volunteers to come to the board and underline the hiatuses.

2 syllables: caer	creó	creer	leer	traer
3 syllables: torear	correo	ojear	desear	meneo
4 syllables: mareado	geólogo	reelegir	reordenar	
5 syllables: tamborileo	aporreando	geografía		

FLUENCY BUILDER Be sure that children have copies of *Intervention Practice Book* page 91. Explain that today children will practice the sentences on the bottom half of the page by reading them aloud on tape. Assign new partners. Have children take turns reading the sentences aloud to each other and then reading them on tape.

INTERVENTION PRACTICE BOOK
page 91

BEFORE

Drafting a Poem
page 225A

Writing a Poem

Build on prior knowledge Have children tell about poems they have read and discuss how these poems are the same and different; for example, they might have rhyming words, they might have a rhythm, they are on all kinds of subjects, they are short, and so on.

Construct the text "Share the pen" with children. Guide them to think of things that elicit strong feelings, such as summer, that they might write a poem about and around. Possibilities include spring, baseball, Earth, space, and so on. Write a poem together. For example:

La primavera es un tiempo verde.
Siempre cantan los pájaros.
Empiezan a crecer las flores.
La primavera es nuestra estación favorita.

Revisit the text Review the poem that you write as a class, using the following traits of good writing.

- Focus/Ideas: The poem tells about one thing in an interesting way. Ask: **¿Describe el poema una cosa o muchas cosas? ¿Cómo podemos cambiarlo para que sólo describa una cosa?**
- Organization: The poem includes a title and rhyming or sound words, or non-rhyming words. The pattern of words creates a rhythm or the words are organized around a main word. Ask: **¿Hay un ritmo? ¿o rima? ¿o una palabra central?**
- Word Choice: Guide children to add descriptive language.

On Your Own

Have children write a title and a three line poem about their favorite season. Suggest that they try to include descriptive language and varied sentence structure in their poem.

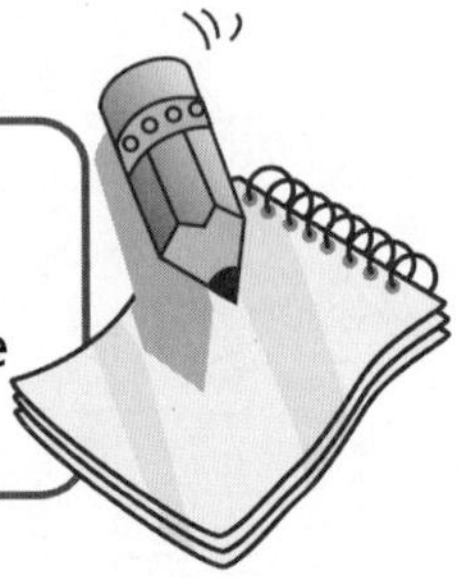

AFTER

Spelling Lesson
page 221H

Connect Spelling and Phonics

RETEACH phonics. Hiatos ae, ea, ee, eo. Write the word *mareado* on the board. Explain that you will say more words which have hiatuses. Have volunteers write each word on the board.

1. *creó**	2. *tamborileó**	3. *golpeó**	4. *tamborilear*
5. *tamborilean**	6. *leer*	7. *creer*	8. *crear*

*** Word appears in *El compositor de música*.**

Dictate the following sentence and have children write it: *Estuvo mareado cuando golpeó el tambor tan fuerte para crear la música nueva.*

Build and Read Longer Words

INTERVENTION ASSESSMENT BOOK

Remind children that they have learned to decode words with hiatuses. Write the words *tamborileo* and *mareado* on the board. Tell children that they can sometime figure out long words by looking for syllables and stem words. Cover *ileo* and have a volunteer read the word *tambor.* Point out that *ileo* has a hiatus, *eo.* Ask students to define *tambor* and then *tamborileo.* Repeat the process with the words *mareado, entreleer y entreabrir.*

FLUENCY BUILDER Have children choose a passage from *El compositor de música* to read aloud to a partner. You may have children choose passages that they found particularly interesting, or have them choose one of the following options:

- Read page 182. (From *Adonde iba David iban también sus palillos*... through ...*Luego los usó para tocar un ritmo en sus cajas.* Total: 65 words)
- Read page 188. (From *El sabado por la noche*... through ...*David deleitó a la multitud cuando hizo música con su tambor de acero* Total: 52 words)

Children should read the selected passage aloud to their partners three times. Have the child rate each reading on a scale from 1 to 4.

BEFORE
Weekly Assessments

Review Vocabulary

To revisit vocabulary prior to the weekly assessment, use these sentences. Have volunteers read them and then together fill-in the missing words as a class. Finally ask other volunteers to read the completed sentences.

1. *El que* (conduce) *abre y cierra las puertas en un tren.*
2. *El loro* (imitaba) *mi voz.*
3. *Él mantiene un* (ritmo) *regular en los tambores.*
4. *Los fuegos artificiales siempre me* (asustan).
5. *El tren retrasado finalmente* (apareció) *en la estación.*
6. *Todo el mundo dijo que la pintura que ella* (creó) *es hermosa.*

You may want to display the vocabulary words and definitions on page 229 and have children copy them to use to study for the vocabulary test.

INTERVENTION PRACTICE BOOK page 94

Focus Skill Review Multiple Meaning Words

To review Multiple Meaning Words before the weekly assessment, distribute Intervention Practice Book p. 94. Have volunteers read aloud the first direction line and the sentences. Guide children by having them read the first sentence together. Discuss which definition of the boldface word makes the most sense.

Review Test Prep

Días maravillosos page 227

Ask children to turn to page 227 of the *Pupil Edition.* Call attention to the Tips for answering the test questions. Tell children that paying attention to these tips can help them answer not only the test questions but also other test questions like these.

Have children follow along as you read each test question and the tip that goes with it. Discuss why the meaning of the word is so important.

INTERVENTION ASSESSMENT BOOK

Self-Selected Reading

Have children select their own books to read independently. They might choose books from the classroom library shelf, or you may wish to offer a group of appropriate books from which children can choose.

- *El deseo de Jenny* See page 2270 of the *Teacher's Edition* for an Independent Reading Plan.
- *El canto del mosquito* por Alma Flor Ada. Santillana USA, 1989.
- *Ramón, el lanzador* por Paul Sharp. Children's Press, 1990.

You may also wish to choose additional books that are the same genre or by the same author, or that have the same kind of text structure as the selection.

After children have chosen their books, give each child a copy of *Mi diario de lectura,* which can be found on page R35 in the back of the *Teacher's Edition.* Have children fill in the information at the top of the form. Then have them use the log to keep track of their reading and to record their responses to the literature.

Conduct student-teacher conferences. Arrange time for each child to conference with you individually about his or her self-selected reading. Have children bring their Reading Logs to share with you at the conference. Children might also like to share a favorite passage to read aloud to you. Ask questions about the book designed to stimulate discussion. For example, **¿Encontraste alguna palabra con significado múltiple? ¿Cómo descubriste el significado correcto? ¿Usaste la estrategia de enfoque, autocorregirse? ¿Cómo sabías que tenías razón?**

FLUENCY PERFORMANCE Have children read aloud to you the passage from *El compositor de música* that they selected and practiced with their partners. Keep track of the number of words the child reads correctly. Ask the child to rate his or her own performance on the 1–4 scale. If children are not happy with their oral reading, give them an opportunity to continue practicing and then to reread the passage to you again.

See *Oral Reading Fluency Assessment* for monitoring progress.

LESSON 24

BEFORE

Building Background and Vocabulary

Use with

"Anthony Reynoso: Charro por tradición"

Introduce Phonics: Dipthongs *ay, ey, oy, uy*

Identify the sound. In order for children to better recognize words with *ay, ey, ay, uy*, show them objects, illustrations or photographs of such items as *rey* and *buey*. Ask them to listen as you say each word. Then have them repeat the words after you as you hold up the objects or pictures.

Associate letters to sound. Write the word *estoy* on the board. Read it aloud and emphasize the syllable containing the sound /oi/. Explain to the children that in some words the sound of two vowels blend to form a new sound. For example, the sound /o/ is blended with the sound /i/ in the word *estoy*. Write the syllables *es* and *toy* separately and demonstrate how to blend them into the word *estoy*. Explain that the /i/ sound is written with *y* in a word ending in *ay, ey, oy, uy*.

Word blending. Indicate the word *soy* and read it aloud. Show children how to blend the sounds and have them read the word at a normal speed. Repeat this procedure for the rest of the one and two-syllable words. Later, point out words at random and ask volunteers to read them.

Apply the skill. Write the word *Paraguay* on the board. Pronounce this word syllable by syllable clapping once as each is read. Ask children to clap along with you and afterwards ask how many syllables they heard. Repeat this procedure with the rest of the words of more than two syllables. Remind children that each syllable includes a vowel sound. Explain that in this case, a triphthong is formed as three vocalic sounds are pronounced in one syllable. Circle the triphthong and say the word again. Repeat the process with the rest of the words. Ask children to copy the words and circle the syllable with the diphthong or triphthong. Afterwards, encourage children to read the words aloud.

Introduce Vocabulary

Write the word.

Say the word.

Track the word and have children repeat it.

Give the meaning or context.

PRETEACH lesson vocabulary. Tell children that they are going to learn five new words that they will see again when they read a story called *Anthony Reynoso: Charro por tradición.* Teach every vocabulary word using the following process.

Use the following suggestions or similar ideas to give the meaning or context.

charrería Use pictures and even a pantomime to show children what charros do.

jaripeo	Again, give children a context for this, show pictures from the text as you repeat the word.
reata	Help students learn this word through synonyms.
rancho	Encourage children to use previous knowledge to try to guess the meaning of this word.
vaquero	Give children a contextual sentence to help them guess the meaning of the word.

For vocabulary activities, see Vocabulary Games on pages 2–7.

Vocabulary Words

charrería actividad de los charros; jinetes expertos

jaripeo diversión de montar toros bravos y otras habilidades

reata cuerda o correa

rancho hacienda para la crianza de caballos, vacas u ovejas

vaquero persona que cuida de las vacas

AFTER

Building Background and Vocabulary

Apply Vocabulary Strategies

Use familiar word parts. Write *vaquero* on the board. Tell children that they can often figure out a word from word parts that they already know.

> MODEL **Cuando veo a la palabra *vaquero*, veo la palabra *vaca*. Sé que una vaca es un animal del rancho. Miro ahora al fin de la palabra y reconozco el sufijo –*ero*. Reconozco este sufijo en palabras como *carpintero* y *cartero*. Entonces *vaquero* debe significar una persona que cuida de las vacas.**

RETEACH **lesson vocabulary.** Have children write each Vocabulary Word on a word card. Have volunteers use each word in a sentence. The rest of the group repeats the Vocabulary Word that was used and holds up the correct word card.

FLUENCY BUILDER Use *Intervention Practice Book* page 95.

Read each word in the first column aloud and have children repeat it. Then have partners read the words in the first column aloud to each other. Tell the children to follow the same procedure with each of the remaining columns. After partners have practiced reading aloud the words in each column, have them practice the entire list.

(Save *Intervention Practice Book* page 95 to use on pages 241 and 243.)

BEFORE

Reading
Anthony Reynoso: Charro por tradición
pages 230–244

USE SKILL CARD 22A

Focus Skill Summarize/Restate

PRETEACH the skill. Tell children that it is not important to remember every single detail of a story. The most important events are the ones they should be sure to recall. Keeping track of these most important events will help them remember the plot of the story.

Have children look at **side A** of ***Tarjeta de destreza 14: Resumir*/Skill Card 24: Summarize/Restate**. Read the definition of Summarize/Restate. Then ask children to look at the picture and determine the main idea. To help them do so, ask:

- **¿Cuál es la idea central? ¿A quién percibes mejor? ¿Es esta persona el enfoque del dibujo?** (*Possible responses: El hombre en el caballo haciendo el jaripeo es el enfoque del dibujo. La idea central es el rodeo.*)
- **¿Qué detalles del dibujo incluirás cuando escribas tu resumen?** (*Possible response: Voy a incluir una descripción sobre el jaripeo, el charro y otras actividades del rodeo.*)

Prepare to Read *Anthony Reynoso: Charro por tradición*

Días maravillosos
pages 230–244

Preview. Tell children that they are going to read *Anthony Reynoso: Charro por tradición*, a nonfiction story about a boy their age. Preview the selection.

- **Page 230:** Veo que esta selección incluye fotos en lugar de dibujos. Es mi primer clave de que esto es no ficción.
- **Page 231:** En estas páginas veo al chico en varias actividades y con mucha gente. Creo que van a explicar su vida, su familia y sus gustos.
- **Pages 232–235:** Ahora veo una explicación de su ropa especial. Anthony es un charro, como dice el título. Veo que voy a aprender qué es un charro y qué hace.

Set purpose. Model setting a purpose for reading *Anthony Reynoso: Charro por tradición.*

MODEL **Desde lo que he visto en las fotos, creo que voy a leer sobre un chico extraordinario. Quiero saber cómo es un chico tan famoso. ¿Qué hace en su tiempo libre? ¿con quién? Entonces, voy a leer para descubrir como es Anthony, sus gustos, su familia y sus actividades especiales.**

AFTER

Reading *Anthony Reynoso: Charro por tradición* pages 230–244

Reread and Summarize

Have children reread and summarize *Anthony Reynoso: Charro por tradición* in sections, as described below.

Pages 231–232

Leemos para descubrir como son las actividades, los gustos y la familia de Anthony.

Summary: Anthony es un chico típico en que le gusta a él su familia, aprende destrezas de ellos y juega a deportes típicos, pero también es un charro famoso.

Pages 233–236

Leemos las páginas 233–236 para descubrir la importancia de su familia grande para Anthony. Leamos para aprender como son.

Summary: La familia de Anthony vive cerca de Anthony. Pasan mucho tiempo juntos. Van siempre a fiestas o al restaurante de sus abuelos.

Pages 237–240

Leemos las páginas 237–240 para aprender más sobre la charrería.

Summary: Anthony y su padre son charros. Esto significa que trabajan con lazos en los rodeos.

FLUENCY BUILDER Use *Intervention Practice Book* page 95, which you used for the previous Fluency Builder activity. Call attention to the sentences on the bottom half of the page. The slashes break the sentences into phrases to allow you to work on natural phrasing. Tell children that their goal is to read each phrase or sentence smoothly. Model appropriate pace, expressions and phrasing as you read each sentence, and have children read it after you. Then have children practice by reading the sentences aloud three times to a partner.

BEFORE

Making Connections
pages 246–247

Directed Reading: *¡El rodeo!* pp. 190–196

Sonidos alegres
pp. 190–196

Have children look at the title and picture on the first page. Challenge them to list all the things they associate with a rodeo. Encourage children who have been to one to share their experiences. Ask: **¿Qué es un rodeo? ¿Qué pasa durante un rodeo? ¿Qué ves en un rodeo?** (*Possible responses: Un rodeo es un espectáculo de charros y vaqueros. Se monta a caballo, al toro y se hace jaripeo. Ves a payasos, charros y vaqueros.*) **MAKE PREDICTIONS**

Have children look at the first sentence on page 190. Model using the Use Decoding/Phonics strategy:

> MODEL **Una palabra en esta frase es nueva para mí. Al principio veo la parte *com* tan como el principio de comer. El resto de la palabra suena como *padre*. Asi que juntos, leo *compadre*.** Focus Strategy **USE DECODING/PHONICS**

Page 191 Inform children that riding in a rodeo is hard work. Ask them to read this page to discover why. Ask: **¿Por qué pueden ser ocho segundos un tiempo muy largo?** (*Possible response: Cuando algo es muy difícil, ocho segundos pueden parecer un tiempo muy largo.*) **DRAW CONCLUSIONS**

Page 192 Call attention to the word *enlazar*. Ask students what word they recognize within it (lazo). Tell students that when they come upon an unfamiliar word, they should look for parts they already know. Say: **Mira a la palabra *enlazar*, ¿cuál palabra reconoces adentro de la palabra? Entonces, ¿qué debe significar *enlazar*?** (*Possible response: Veo la palabra* lazo, *así que* enlazar *debe significar atrapar con un lazo.*) **WORD BITS AND PARTS**

Page 193 By this point children have read enough to practice summarizing and restating information. Model reading the page and summarizing what you have read thus far. Ask: **¿Cuáles son las cosas que hace un vaquero en el rodeo?** (*Possible response: Los vaqueros montan a caballo y a toros. Enlazan a vacas y hacen charrería con los lazos.*)

Page 194 Help children understand the important role that clowns play in the rodeo. Ask: **¿Cómo ayudan los payasos en el rodeo?** (*Possible response: Ayudan porque proporcionan seguridad a los vaqueros cuando los jinetes se caen; los mantienen a los toros alejados de los caballos.*) **IMPORTANT DETAILS**

Page 195

INTERVENTION PRACTICE BOOK
page 97

Encourage children to practice summarizing as they read this page. Ask: **¿Cuándo es el cumpleaños del rodeo? ¿Qué otra cosa tiene el mismo cumpleaños?** (*Possible responses: el 4 de julio y los Estados Unidos*) **SUMMARIZE/RESTATE**

Summarize the selection. Ask children to tell the important things they learned about rodeos. Then help them summarize the selection by restating the main idea and only the most important details. Then have them complete *Intervention Practice Book* page 97.

AFTER

Skill Review
pages 249C–249D

Answers to *Think About It* Questions

1. Manejar el lazo, la reata, montar caballo. **SUMMARIZE**
2. Que los payasos son muy importantes para su seguridad si ellos se caen porque entretienen el toro o caballo y evitan un accidente. **DRAW CONCLUSIONS**
3. Las respuestas pueden variar. **MAIN IDEA**

Focus Skill Review Summarize/Restate

USE SKILL CARD 22B

RETEACH the skill. Have children look at **side B** of ***Tarjeta de destreza: Resumir*/Skill Card 24: Summarize/Restate**. Read the skill reminder with them, and have a volunteer read the paragraph aloud.

After children have completed their webs and summaries, have them display and explain their work.

Review Phonics: Diphthongs *ay, ey, oy, uy*

RETEACH the skill. Have the children write the following words on word cards. Have them mix the cards up. Have them sort the cards into *ay, ey, oy* and *uy* piles. Then have them read each list. Time them, and see if they can do it again more quickly a second time.

hoy	ayer	estoy	muy	
ley	hay	soy	oyendo	
haya	oye	¡Ay!	payaso	leyendo

FLUENCY BUILDER Use *Intervention Practice Book* page 95. Explain that children will practice the sentences on the bottom half of the page by reading them aloud on tape. Assign new partners. Have children take turns reading the sentences aloud to each other and then reading them on tape.

INTERVENTION PRACTICE BOOK
page 95

BEFORE

Drafting a Description of an Event
Page 247A

Writing Process: Description

Build on prior knowledge. Tell children that they are going to talk and write about something interesting that has happened at school. Brainstorm a list of events with children and choose one. Then display information like the following, and have volunteers suggest describing words to add to the lists.

Construct the text. "Share the pen" with children. Guide them to use the words to write a description of the playground.

Escena: El parque
árboles y flores
juguetes
estanque

El parque es mi lugar favorito. Hay muchos árboles y flores hermosas. Me encanta jugar con los juguetes como la pelota redonda y roja y los camiones pequeños y amarillos. Luego, voy al estanque para ver si hay ranas o patos. Un día en el parque es un día feliz.

Revisit the text. Go back and read the sentences together.

- Ask: **¿Cuáles de las palabras hacen imágenes en tu mente?** Underline those words.
- Ask: **¿Cuáles de las palabras no hacen imágenes en tu mente?** Make the appropriate changes.
- Guide children to add more descriptive words to each sentence.
- Have children read the writing aloud and then copy it onto their papers.

On Your Own

Have children draw a picture of something interesting they have done and then write about it. Remind them to include describing words that tell how things looked, sounded, tasted, and so on, and also how they felt about what happened.

AFTER

Spelling Lesson
page 245H

Connect Spelling and Phonics

RETEACH **phonics: Dipthongs *ay, ey, oy, uy*** Write the word *hoy* on the board and tell children that in the words you say, they will hear a dipthong *ay, ey, oy* or *uy.* Have volunteers write each word on the board. Have volunteers write each word on the board.

1. hoy*	**2. ¡Ay!***	**3. ayuda***	**4. muy***
5. payaso*	**6. ayer**	**7. leyes**	**8. estoy**

*** Word appears in *¡El rodeo!***

Tell children that in the following sentence, there are four dipthongs. Dictate the sentence and have children write it: *¡Ay! Me olvidé, hoy me toca a mí ayudar a los payasos.*

INTERVENTION ASSESSMENT BOOK

Build and Read Longer Words

Write the word *rey* on the board. Cover the first letter and ask children: **¿Qué otra palabra de ortografía termina en *ey*?** (*ley*) Repeat the procedure for words ending in a *ay* (*ay, hay, caray*); *oy* (*hoy, voy, soy*); y *uy* (*muy*). Encourage them to say other words they know ending in *ay, ey, oy, uy.*

FLUENCY BUILDER Have children choose a passage from *¡El rodeo!* to read aloud to a partner. You may have children choose passages that they found particularly interesting, or have them choose one of the following options:

- Read pages 193–194. (From *Montar un toro es peligroso...* through *...¡pero alguien tiene que hacerlo!*Total: 68 words.)
- Read pages 190–191. (From *¡Hola, compardre!...* through *...Para ellos, ¡ocho segundos pueden ser mucho tiempo!* Total: 82 words.)

Children should read the selected passage aloud to their partners three times. Have children rate each of their own readings on a scale from 1 to 4.

BEFORE
Weekly Assessments

Review Vocabulary

To review Vocabulary Words prior to the weekly assessment, use these definitions. Encourage children to hold up their word cards for each definition. Then have volunteers write the words and their definitions on the board.

1. fiesta de charros ________ (*charrería*)
2. hacienda con caballos y vacas ________ (*rancho*)
3. habilidad sobre un toro bravo________ (*jaripeo*)
4. una cuerda ________ (*reata*)
5. persona que cuida el ganado ________ (*vaquero*)

You may want to display the Vocabulary Words and definitions on page 239 and have children copy them to use when they study for the vocabulary test.

INTERVENTION PRACTICE BOOK
page 98

Focus Skill Review Summarize/Restate

To review Summarize/Restate before the weekly assessment, distribute Intervention Practice Book page 98. Have volunteers read aloud the first direction line and the paragraph. Guide children by having them discuss what the main idea of the paragraph is.

INTERVENTION ASSESSMENT BOOK

Review Test Prep

Ask children to turn to page 249 of the *Pupil Edition*. Call attention to the Tips for answering the test questions. Tell children that paying attention to these tips can help them answer not only the test questions but also other test questions like these.

Have children follow along as you read the directions, each test item and the tip. Discuss with children why it is important to understand the directions. Discuss how to make sure the response answers the item. (*Possible response: Go back and reread the word by the number and then your answer to see if they have the same sound.*)

Self-Selected Reading

Have children select their own books to read independently. They might choose books from the classroom library, or you may wish to offer appropriate books from which children can choose.

- *En la frontera agreste.* See page 249Q of the *Teacher's Edition* for an Independent Reading Plan.
- *¡Seré mariachi!* por Cecilia Avalos. Modern Curriculum Press, 1991.
- *Fátima-Vanessa: Yo soy de El Salvador.* por Roser Vila Roca Morollón Pardo. La Galera, 1997.

You may also wish to choose additional books that are the same genre or are by the same author.

After children have chosen their books, give each child a copy of *Mi diario de lectura*, which can be found on page R35 in the back of the *Teacher's Edition.* Have children fill in the information at the top of the form. Then have them use the log to keep track of their reading and to record their responses to the literature.

Conduct student-teacher conferences. Arrange time for each child to conference with you about his or her self-selected reading. Have children bring their Reading Logs to share with you at the conference. Children might also like to choose a favorite passage to read aloud to you. Ask questions designed to stimulate discussion about the book. For example, you might ask what the problem and the solution were in a fiction book or how the child figured out a new vocabulary word in a nonfiction book.

FLUENCY PERFORMANCE Have children read aloud to you the passage from *¡El rodeo!* that they practiced. Observe children's pronunciation, intonation, phrasing, and the amount of words, in general, that they read correctly. Ask the child to rate his or her own performance on the 1–4 scale. If children are not happy with their oral reading, give them an opportunity to continue practicing and then to reread the passage to you again.

See *Oral Reading Fluency Assessment* for monitoring progress.

LESSON 25

Use with

"El barrio chino"

BEFORE

Building Background and Vocabulary

Introduce: Consonant blend *dr*

Identify the sound. In order for children to better recognize words with *dr* show them objects, illustrations or photographs of such items as: *dragón, golondrina, padre, madre, cocodrilo, cuadrado, piedra.* Say the words as you hold up the pictures or objects. Ask children to repeat after you.

Associate letters to sound. Explain to children that in some words the sound /d/ blends with the sound /r/ to make the sound /dr/. Tell them this sound is written with the letters *dr* as in *dragón.* Write the words on the board and ask a vounteer to circle the syllables with the consonant blend *dr.*

Word blending. Write the word *madre* on the board and read it aloud. After blending the letters, have children blend the letters to read the word. Repeat this procedure with the rest of the spelling words. Write the following sentences on the board. Read the first sentence as you point to each word. Later, point out the word *hojaldre,* and ask for a volunteer to read it. Continue with the second sentence. Ask children to circle the words with *dr.*

¿Quién ha preparado estos pastelitos de ***hojaldre****?*

Los preparó mi ***padre.***

INTERVENTION PRACTICE BOOK page 100

Apply the skill. Write the word *padrino* on the board. Pronounce this word syllable by syllable clapping once as each is read. Ask children to clap along with you and afterwards ask how many syllables they heard. Repeat this procedure with the words which contain more than two syllables. Circle the letter blend *dr* and say the word again. Repeat the process with the rest of the words. Afterwards, encourage children to read aloud.

padre	**ladrar**	**dragón**	**drama**
adrede	**madre**	**Pedro**	**dromedario**

Introduce Vocabulary

PRETEACH lesson vocabulary. Tell children that they are going to learn six new words that they will see again when they read a story called *El barrio chino.*Teach every vocabulary word using the following process.

Use the following suggestions or similar ideas to give the meaning or context.

celebraciones Encourage children to consider other words with the same stem to guess the meaning of this word. (*celebrar, celebridad*)

desarrollar	Read in syllables. Pronounce this word slowly and have them repeat it. (*de-sa-rro-llar*)
estudiantes	Ask children to give synonyms. (*alumnos, niños*)
furiosos	Challenge children to imitate being *furioso* using the word.
gracia	Ask children to consider all the meanings. (*donaire, beneficio y perdón*)
tienda de abarrotes	Ask them to list what they might find in a *tienda de abarrotes.*

For vocabulary activities, see Vocabulary Games on pages 2–7 (*Intervention Teacher's Guide*).

Write the word.
Say the word.
Track the word and have children repeat it.
Give the meaning or context.

Vocabulary Words

celebraciones reuniones alegres, generalmente para marcar sucesos especiales

desarrollar mejorar algo

estudiantes personas que van a la escuela

furiosos muy enojados

gracia elegancia en el movimiento

tienda de abarrotes una tienda que vende alimentos y productos hogareños

AFTER
Building Background and Vocabulary

Apply Vocabulary Strategies

Use syllabication. Write the word *celebraciones* on the board. Explain that knowing how to pronounce a word can help determine its meaning.

MODEL **Para leer la palabra *celebraciones* en sílabas, miro a cada consonante. Determino dónde está cada pausa en la palabra cuando la leo lentamente y miro a las consonantes. Me doy cuenta de que se lee *celebraciones* por sílabas así:** *ce-le-bra-cio-nes.*

RETEACH **lesson vocabulary.** Have children give examples of each:

1. a *celebración* they enjoy
2. a way they have *desarrollado*
3. something that makes them *furioso*
4. someone or something that has *gracia*
5. a *tienda de abarrotes* their family shops
6. someone who is a *estudiante*

FLUENCY BUILDER Using *Intervention Practice Book* p. 99, read each word aloud in the first column and have children repeat it. Then have children work in pairs to read the words in the first column aloud to each other. Follow the same procedure with each of the remaining columns. After partners have practiced reading aloud the words in each separate column, have them read aloud the entire list.

BEFORE

Reading
El barrio chino
pages 252–270

USE SKILL CARD 25A

Focus Skill Detalles

PRETEACH the skill. Point out to children that the details in a story give extra information about the main idea. Details help to make stories more interesting. Keeping track of the details will help them understand the plot of the story.

Have children look at **side A** of ***Tarjeta de destreza 25: Detalles*/Skill Card 25: Details.** Read the definition of *details.* Have children read through the paragraph. Have them identify the important details. Now call attention to the web. Ask:

- **¿Cómo determinas los detalles sobre cómo y por qué?** (*Possible response: Determino qué hace la gente y de allí puedo determinar cómo y por qué.*)
- **¿Cómo sabes la hora?** (*Possible response: por la posición del sol*)

Prepare to Read *El barrio chino*

Preview. Tell children that they are going to read a selection entitled *El barrio chino* Explain that this is a story about a special section of New York City. Then preview the selection.

Días maravillosos
pages 252–270

- **Pages 252–254:** Veo los colores y decoraciones de una fiesta. Pienso que voy a leer sobre una fiesta.
- **Pages 255–266:** No, me autocorrijo. No es una fiesta. Este cuento trata de un chico, su abuela y su barrio. Veo todas las cosas cotidianas que hacen.
- **Pages 267–270:** Ahora sí, veo una fiesta y un desfile. Toda la gente del barrio festeja algo. Quiero saber lo que festejan.

Set purpose. Model setting a purpose for reading *El barrio chino.*

MODEL **Por lo que he visto en estas páginas, sé que voy a leer sobre un chico, su abuela y su barrio. Veo que voy a leer sobre sus días normales y sus días especiales. Quiero saber más sobre estos dos tipos de días. Voy a leer para descubrir cómo pasan los días cotidianos y los especiales.**

AFTER

Reading
El barrio chino
pages 252–270

Reread and Summarize

Have children reread and summarize *El barrio chino* in sections, as described below.

Pages 252–260
Leemos las páginas 252–260 para ver quién vive en el apartamento y el barrio y qué hacen el niño y la abuela.

Summary: El niño vive en un apartamento con sus padres y su abuela. En el barrio vive mucha gente como el zapatero, y los que hacen tai chi. La abuela y el niño caminan por el barrio todos los días, haciendo compras y comiendo.

Pages 261–265
Leemos las páginas 261–265, que son sobre la comida que comen y compran.

Summary: A veces, el niño y su abuela comen pollo o pato, a veces comen mariscos. Van al mercado al aire libre y compran cangrejos.

Pages 266–270
Leemos las páginas 266–270 para recordar la fiesta del Año Nuevo y los sueños del niño.

Summary: En el Año Nuevo, el niño y su abuela van al desfile de su barrio. Al niño le gustan más los chicos grandes de kung fu. Espera estar en el desfile el año que viene.

FLUENCY BUILDER Be sure children have copies of *Intervention Practice Book* p. 99, which you used for the previous Fluency Builder activity. Call attention to the sentences on the bottom half of the page. The slashes break the sentences into phrases to allow you to work on natural phrasing. Tell children that their goal is to read each phrase or sentence smoothly. Model appropriate pacing, expression, and phrasing as you read each sentence and have children read it after you. Then have children practice by reading the sentences aloud three times to a partner.

BEFORE

Making Connections
pages 274–275

Directed Reading of *Feliz Año Nuevo* pp. 198–204

Sonidos alegres
pp. 198–204

Have children flip through the pages of the story. Ask them to recognize who, what, where and when they'll be reading about. Ask: **¿De qué trata este cuento? ¿Quiénes son los personajes? ¿Cuándo ocurre?** (*Possible responses: Este cuento es de un chico chino y su abuela. Veo que preparan cosas para el Año Nuevo. Veo también abrigos y suéteres. Entonces, sé que están en un lugar donde hace frío en enero.*) Focus Skill **DETAILS**

Pages 198–199

Read to discover what preparations Jimmy and his grandmother make for New Year's Eve. Ask: **¿Qué hacen Jimmy y su abuela para prepararse para la víspera de Año Nuevo? ¿Qué cosas y rituales llevan buena suerte?** (*Possible responses: Preparan la casa; sacan todos los cuchillos para que no corten la suerte. Arreglan naranjas en una mesa también para la suerte.*) **SUMMARIZE**

Pages 200–201

Read about where Jimmy and his grandmother go and what they do in the neighborhood. Ask: **¿Dónde van Jimmy y su abuela? ¿Qué compran y qué hacen allí?** (*Possible responses: Jimmy y su abuela van de compras. Compran fruta y un abrigo nuevo. También van a cortar el pelo de Jimmy.*) **DETAILS**

Now ask a volunteer to read aloud the second paragraph on page 201 while children listen to create a mental image. Model using the Create Mental Images strategy:

> MODEL **Cuando escuché esta sección, oí que "los estudiantes de Kung Fu llevaban una máscara de león de aspecto furioso". Sé que furioso significa "muy enojado", así que me imagino que la máscara es de un león muy enojado.** Focus Strategy **CREATE MENTAL IMAGES**

Discuss whether children agree with your thinking.

Pages 202–204

Ask volunteers to read about how Jimmy feels without his parents with him on New Year's Eve. Ask: **¿Cómo se siente Jimmy sin sus padres? ¿Quién llega a celebrar con la abuela y con Jimmy? ¿Por qué hay unas sillas vacías?** (*Possible response: Jimmy dijo que quería tener a sus padres en casa y veo en la foto que las sillas vacías le hacen sentirse un poco triste. Pero leo también que está feliz comiendo y hablando con sus tíos y primos. Al fin llegan sus padres y sé por las exclamaciones que Jimmy está muy contento ahora.*) **USING DETAILS/INFER**

INTERVENTION PRACTICE BOOK
page 101

Summarize the selection. Ask children to think about why people have different opinions about what a good adventure would be.

Answers to *Think About It* Questions

1. Estaban limpiado el apartamento de la abuela, habían apartado los cuchillos y cualquier otro objeto cortante para no cortar su suerte. Habían servido una fuente con naranjas sobre una mesa bajita, también para la buena suerte. **SUMMARIZE**
2. Porque en esa celebración tiene la oportunidad de estar con su familia y las personas que él quiere. **INTERPRET STORY EVENTS**
3. Las respuestas pueden variar: los pergaminos con letreros de la buena suerte en chino, la máscara de león furioso de la buena suerte, una fuente de naranjas para la buena suerte **TASK**

AFTER
Skill Review
page 275I

USE SKILL CARD 25B

Focus Skill Review Details

RETEACH the skill. Have children look at **side B** of ***Tarjeta de destreza 25: Detalles*/Skill Card 25: Details.** Read the skill reminder with them, and have a volunteer read the paragraph aloud.

Read aloud the set of directions. Explain that children will work with partners to create their own webs. Remind them to write only the important details.

After children have completed their Details webs, have them display and explain their work. Point out that knowing the details in the selection *Feliz Año Nuevo* helps you remember the story.

Review Phonics Skill: Consonant blend *dr*

RETEACH the skill. Write the following words on the board. Ask children to say how these words are similar (all of them have a syllable with the letters *dr*). Ask a volunteer to underline the syllables with *dr*. Remind children that in these words the /d/ sound blends with the /r/ sound to form the sound /dr/.

drama	**draga**	**drenar**	**droga**
dragón	**adrede**	**ladrar**	**ladrón**

FLUENCY BUILDER Be sure that children have copies of *Intervention Practice Book* page 99. Explain that today children will practice the sentences on the bottom half of the page by reading them aloud on tape. Assign new partners. Have children take turns reading the sentences aloud to each other and then reading them on tape.

INTERVENTION PRACTICE BOOK
page 99

BEFORE

Drafting a Summary
page 277C

Daily Writing: Summary

Build on prior knowledge. Tell children that when we write riddles we describe things without telling what they are. Ask children to share riddles they know. Then discuss the different kinds of riddles such as "What am I?" and "I Spy." You can use this as an example:

Subo la escalera sin moverme. ¿Qué soy?
(*la alfombra*)

Construct the text. "Share the pen" with children. Guide them in using sentences to formulate a riddle. Have children brainstorm riddle topics such as animals, toys, things in their rooms/homes/neighborhoods, foods they like, and so on. Write children's responses on chart paper or on the board. Together choose a topic and write a riddle. Challenge children to add to the description.

Revisit the text. Go back and reread the riddle together. Ask: **¿Hay más detalles que podamos incluir? ¿Hay un sonido o color?**

- Guide children in exploring types of riddles, like "What am I?" and "I Spy." Challenge them to make the class riddle one of these types.
- Inform children that often riddles rhyme. Challenge them to help you make the class riddle rhyme. List the suggestions and then together choose the most sensical rhymes.
- Have children read the completed riddle outloud and then copy it onto their own papers.

On Your Own

Have children write their own riddle about a topic that they listed during the class brainstorm. Have them determine a type of riddle and whether their riddle will rhyme. Challenge them to write a holiday riddle or even one about something in one of the two New Year's stories they read.

AFTER

Spelling
page 271H

Connect Spelling and Phonics

RETEACH consonant blend *dr.* Write the word *dragón* on the board. Tell children that in the words you say, the /dr/ sound is spelled *dr.* Dictate the words and have volunteers write them on the board.

1. padre*	**2. madre***	**3. dromedario**	**4. adrede**
5. Andrés	**6. dragón**	**7. padrino**	**8. Padrón**

*** Word appears in *Feliz Año Nuevo.***

Tell children that the /dr/ sound appears 4 times in the following sentence. Dictate the sentence: *Andrés y su madre y padre tomaron viaje en dromedarios.*

INTERVENTION ASSESSMENT BOOK

Build and Read Longer Words

Write the words *madre* and *padre* on the board. Tell children that they can sometimes figure out long words by looking for syllables and suffixes. Cross out the e of *madre* and add *–astra.* Explain that by adding a suffix, we are able to make and read a longer word. Repeat the process for *padre* and *–ino.*

FLUENCY BUILDER Have children choose a passage from *Feliz Año Nuevo* to read aloud to a partner. You may have children choose passages that they found particularly interesting, or have them choose one of the following options:

- Read pages 198–199. (From *Era casi la víspera de Año Nuevo...* through ...*"Que todo sea como tú quieres"*. Total: 98 words.)
- Read pages 203–204. (From *El timbre sonó...* through ...*Año Nuevo es también mi celebración favorita.* Total: 103 words.)

Children should read the selected passage aloud to their partners three times. Have the child rate each reading on a scale from 1 to 4.

BEFORE

Weekly Assessments

Review Vocabulary

To revisit vocabulary prior to the weekly assessment, use these sentences. Ask children to determine whether they are true or false. Write the sentences and the children's responses on the board.

1. Puedes comprar un avión en una tienda de abarrotes. (*falso*)
2. Desarrollar es igual a mejorar. (*verdadero*)
3. Una persona furiosa es feliz. (*falso*)
4. Las celebraciones son sucesos tristes. (*falso*)
5. Los bailarines con gracia son bailarines elegantes. (*verdadero*)
6. Los estudiantes son gente de todas las edades que va a la escuela. (*verdadero*)

You may want to display the vocabulary words and definitions on page 249 and have children copy them to use when they study for the vocabulary test.

INTERVENTION PRACTICE BOOK
page 102

Focus Skill Review Details

To review details before the weekly assessment, distribute *Intervention Practice Book* page 102. Guide children by having them draw a sample web on the board and find the first detail.

Review Test Prep

Ask children to turn to page 277 of the *Pupil Edition*. Call attention to the Tips for answering the test questions. Tell children that paying attention to these tips can help them answer not only the test questions but also other test questions like these.

Dias maravillosos

Have children follow along as you read each test question and the tip that goes with it. Discuss why it is important to pay attention to the important details of the story. (*Possible response: Los puedes recordar.*) Discuss why it is important to reread the story. (*Possible response: Puedes regresar y verificar si tu respuesta es correcta.*)

INTERVENTION ASSESSMENT BOOK

Self-Selected Reading

Have children select their own books to read independently. They might choose books from the classroom library shelf, or you may wish to offer a group of appropriate books from which children can choose.

- *¡Feliz Año Nuevo Chino!* See page 277 O of the *Teacher's Edition* for an Independent Reading Plan.
- *Perez y Martina: un cuento folklórico puertorriqueño* por Pura Belpré. Viking Penguin, 1991.
- *La alegría de ser tú y yo* por W. Nikola-Lisa. Lee & Low, 1996.

You may also wish to choose additional books that are the same genre or by the same author, or that have the same kind of text structure as the selection.

After children have chosen their books, give each child a copy of *Mi diario de lectura*, which can be found on page R35 in the back of the *Teacher's Edition.* Have children fill in the information at the top of the form. Then have them use the log to keep track of their reading and to record their responses to the literature.

Conduct student-teacher conferences. Arrange time for each child to conference with you individually about his or her self-selected reading. Have children bring their Reading Logs to share with you at the conference. Children might also like to share a favorite passage to read aloud to you. Ask questions about the book designed to stimulate discussion. For example, you might want to ask what the problem and the solution were in a fiction text or how they figured out a new vocabulary word in a nonfiction text.

FLUENCY PERFORMANCE Have children read aloud to you the passage from *Feliz Año Nuevo* that they selected and practiced with their partners. Keep track of the number of words the child reads correctly. Ask the child to rate his or her own performance on the 1–4 scale. If children are not happy with their oral reading, give them an opportunity to continue practicing and to read the passage to you again.

See *Oral Reading Fluency Assessment* for monitoring progress.

LESSON 26

BEFORE

Building Background and Vocabulary

Use with

"Abuela"

Review Phonics: Combinación de consonantes: *cl, cr*

Identify the sound. Have children repeat the following sentence three times: *No puedo ir en bicicleta porque tengo que llevar mi clarinete de cristal y se rompería.* Ask them which words in the sentence have the *cl* sound that children hear in *clase.* (*bicicleta*, *clarinete*) Then ask which words have the *cr* sound that they hear in *cráneo.* (*cristal*)

Associate letters to sounds. On the board, write: *No puedo ir en bicicleta porque tengo que llevar mi clarinete de cristal y se rompería.* Circle the words *bicicleta* and *clarinete.* Ask children to tell how the words are alike. (*both have the cl sound*) Underline the letters *cl* in *bicicleta* and *clarinete.* Tell children that the letters *cl* stand for the *cl* sound they hear in *bicicleta* and *clarinete.* Then follow a similar procedure to introduce the *cr* sound in the words *cristal.*

Word blending. Model how to blend and read the word *cruz.* Slide your hand under the letters as you slowly elongate the sounds */crruuzz/.* Then read *cruz* naturally. Follow a similar procedure for *cráneo, cráter, clavo*, and *clavel.*

INTERVENTION PRACTICE BOOK page 104

Apply the skill. Write the following words on the board, and have children read them aloud. Make the changes necessary to form the words in parentheses. Have children read each new word.

clave (clavel)	**bicicleta** (tricicleta)	**clase** (clásico)	**crema** (cremoso)
crear (creación)	**credo** (crédito)	**creer** (creíble)	**cristal** (cristalización)

Introduce Vocabulary

PRETEACH lesson vocabulary. Tell children that they are going to learn five new words that they will see again when they read a story called *Abuela.*

Use the following suggestions or similar ideas to give the meaning or context:

> Write the word.
> Say the word.
> Track the word and have children repeat it.
> Give the meaning or context.

bandada Relate with simple drawings of a flock of birds and only one bird. Have children contrast the two drawings.

crestas Invite children to draw pictures of waves and label them with *crestas.*

puerto Relate by showing a picture or photograph. Discuss where ships go when they are not sailing.

elevarnos Relate by using a toy or paper airplane and demonstrating the act of soaring.

ondeando Point out the *-ando* ending. Relate by using a toy or paper airplane and demonstrating the act of swooping.

For vocabulary activities, see Vocabulary Games on pages 2–7.

Vocabulary Words

bandada grupo de pájaros

puerto lugar donde amarran los barcos

crestas bordes espumosos de las olas

elevarnos subirnos

ondeando formando ondas

AFTER

Building Background and Vocabulary

Apply Vocabulary Strategies

Use familiar patterns. Write the word *crestas* on chart paper and underline the letters *cr.* Tell children that they can sometimes figure out the meaning of the word by looking for letter patterns that they know.

> MODEL **La combinación de consonantes *cr es* familiar para mí porque la he visto en palabras como *creer.* He visto la combinación de letras e-s-t-a que forman la palabra *esta.* Cuando combino *cr* con *esta,* leo *cresta.***

Guide children in using a similar procedure to decode the words *elevarnos* and *ondeando.*

RETEACH lesson vocabulary. Have children listen to each of the following questions. Tell them to hold up the word card that answers each question. Reread the questions aloud with the correct answers. Then discuss how children made their choices.

1. ¿Qué palabra nombra el lugar donde podrías hallar barcos amarrados? (*puerto*)
2. ¿Qué palabra describe un grupo de pájaros? (*bandada*)
3. ¿Qué palabra habla del *borde espumoso de las olas?* (*crestas*)
4. ¿Qué palabra describe el movimiento de algo formando ondas? (*ondeando*)
5. ¿Qué palabra significa *irnos hacia arriba?* (*elevarnos*)

FLUENCY BUILDER Using *Intervention Practice Book* page 103, read aloud each word in the first column and have children repeat it. Then have children work in pairs to read the words in the first column aloud to each other. Follow the same procedure with each of the remaining columns. After partners have practiced reading aloud the words in each separate column, have them practice the entire list. Save Intervention Practice Book page 103 for use on pages 261 and 263.

BEFORE

Reading *Abuela*
pages 282–299

Focus Skill Make Inferences

PRETEACH the skill. Point out to children that readers use story clues and what they already know to decide if something is real or make-believe in a story. Discuss how readers make these decisions, or make inferences, to figure out what is happening in a story. Guide children to see that an author does not always tell readers everything that is happening, but readers can use their own personal experience to help them understand the story.

USE SKILL CARD 26A

Have children look at **side A** of ***Tarjeta de destrezas 26: Hacer inferencias/* Skill Card 26: Make Inferences.** Read the definition of Make Inferences. Next read the story and have children read it with you.

Now call attention to the chart and have volunteers take turns reading the information aloud. Ask:

- **¿Qué dice el cuento sobre lo que hace el nieto?** (*Possible response: Llama a su abuela todas las noches.*)
- **¿Por qué llamarías a alguien todas las noches?** (*Possible response: Porque lo amo mucho y quiero hablar con él o ella.*)

Prepare to Read *Abuela*

Días maravillosos
pages 282–301

Preview. Tell children that they are going to read a selection titled *Abuela.* Explain that this is a fantasy story. Tell children that *Abuela* tells about a make-believe trip a girl takes with her grandmother. Then preview the selection.

- **Pages 282–283:** Veo el título, *Abuela*, y el nombre del autor en las páginas 282–283. Veo un dibujo de una mujer vieja y una chica joven volando en los cielos. Pienso que este cuento va a tratar de estas dos personas y cuenta por qué vuelan.
- **Pages 284–285:** En estas páginas, leo sobre la chica y su abuela. Leo palabras inglesas y españolas. Pienso que unas partes del cuento van a estar en inglés y el resto en español.
- **Pages 286–287:** En estas páginas, leo que la chica quiere saber qué pasaría si ella y su abuela pudieran volar. Veo el dibujo de la chica y la abuela volando juntas. Pienso que voy a leer y ver más sobre su vuelo.

Set purpose. Model setting a purpose for reading *Abuela.*

MODEL **Por lo que he visto en estas páginas, pienso que voy a leer más sobre dónde va la chica y su abuela en su fantasía. Voy a leer para ver qué ven cuando vuelan y si les gusta volar.**

AFTER

Reading *Abuela*
pages 282–299

Reread and Summarize

Have children reread and summarize *Abuela* in sections, as described below.

Pages 284–285
Leamos las páginas 284–285 para recordar quiénes son los personajes en el cuento y qué hacen juntos en sus vidas reales.

Summary: El cuento es sobre una chica y su abuela quiénes van al parque juntas y dan de comer a los pájaros.

Pages 286–293
Leamos las páginas 286–293 para recordar qué pasa en la fantasía de la chica.

Summary: La chica imagina que ella y Abuela vuelan por toda la ciudad.

Pages 294–296
Leamos las páginas 294–296 para recordar algunas de las cosas que ven en los cielos. Tratemos de recordar las palabras en inglés.

Summary: La chica y Abuela ven las nubes; una de las nubes se parece a un gato; una de las nubes se parece a un oso; otra de las nubes se parece a una silla.

Pages 297–298
Leamos las páginas 297–298 para recordar qué le pasa a la chica y a su abuela al final del cuento.

Summary: Vuelven al parque. Caminan cerca del lago y Abuela quiere remar en un bote y tener otra aventura.

FLUENCY BUILDER Use *Intervention Practice Book* page 103. Call attention to the sentences on the bottom half of the page. The slashes break the sentences into phrases to allow you to work on natural phrasing. Tell children that their goal is to read each phrase or sentence smoothly. Model appropriate pace, expression and phrasing as you read each sentence and have children read it after you. Then have children practice by reading the sentences aloud three times to a partner.

BEFORE

Making Connections
pages 302–303

Directed Reading of *Si yo pudiera volar*

Sonidos alegres
pp. 206–212

Ask a volunteer to read aloud the title on page 206. Ask children why they think people might want to fly. Then have children read page 206 to find out about Lucas. Ask: **¿Qué dice el cuento sobre dónde quisiera volar Lucas si pudiera hacerlo? ¿Qué sabes de gente que quieren visitar grandes ciudades? ¿Qué tipo de persona es Lucas?** (*Possible response: El cuento me dice que Lucas quisiera volar sobre una ciudad grande porque nunca ha visto una. La gente que quiere ir a ciudades grandes prefiere a mucha gente, el ruido y las aventuras. Es posible que Lucas esté curioso por conocer lugares nuevos.*) Focus Skill **MAKE INFERENCES**

Page 207

Have children read page 207. Ask: **¿Qué quiere decir Lucas cuándo dice que *navegaría por encima de los edificios?*** (*Possible response: Volaría en lo alto del cielo, encima de la ciudad.*) **UNDERSTAND FIGURATIVE LANGUAGE**

Reread page 207 aloud. Model using the Look at Word Bits and Parts strategy in order for children to understand how to read and figure out the meanings of long or unfamiliar words.

> MODEL **Cuando leo, no conozco todas las palabras. Si tengo que leer una palabra larga, miro las sílabas conocidas. Por ejemplo *re* y *pasar* forman *repasar*.** Focus Strategy **LOOK AT WORD BITS AND PARTS**

Page 208

Have children look at the illustration to predict where Fátima would fly. Then have them read page 208 to confirm their predictions. Ask: **¿Dónde iría Fátima si pudiera volar?** (*Possible response: Volaría a un país donde a la gente le gustara jugar.*) **MAKE PREDICTIONS**

Page 209

Have children read page 209 to find out what Fátima would do in that country. Ask: **¿Enseñaría a la gente a volar?** (*Possible response: Sí.*) **INTERPRET STORY EVENTS** Ask: **¿Qué haría la gente y Fátima?** (*Possible response: Tendrían una gran fiesta en el cielo; comerían pastel por encima de los árboles; bailarían en las nubes.*) **NOTE DETAILS**

Page 210

Have children read page 210 to find out where Sally would go if she could fly. Ask: **¿Dónde iría Sally si pudiera volar y por qué?** (*Possible response: Iría a ver a su abuela porque se ha mudado lejos y la extraña mucho.*) **UNDERSTAND CHARACTERS' MOTIVES**

Page 211

Have children read page 211 to find out what Sally would do with her grandma after they ate. Ask: **¿Qué haría Verónica con su abuela?** (*Possible response: Ellas irían a pasear, a pescar, a buscar ballenas, a ver la puesta del sol y a leer libros juntas.*) **SUMMARIZE** Ask: **¿Cuáles son las similitudes y diferencias entre la aventura de Verónica y las de Lucas y Fátima?** (*Possible response: Las aventuras son similares porque a todos les gusta volar. La aventura de Verónica es diferente porque fue más realista.*) **COMPARE AND CONTRAST** Ask: **¿Por qué es la aventura de Verónica la mejor para ella?** (*Possible response: Las respuestas variarían.*)

Summarize the selection. Ask children to think about why people have different opinions about what a good adventure would be.

Answers to *Piénsalo* Questions

1. Lucas volaría a la ciudad, buscaría los mejores juguetes en las vidrieras de todas las tiendas. Fátima se uniría a una **bandada** de pájaros en el **puerto.** Cruzaría el peligroso mar, comería pastel por encima de los árboles, bailaría en las nubes, hasta que llegara a un país donde a la gente le encantara jugar. Verónica visitaría a su abuelita porque se mudó lejos y ella la extraña mucho. **SUMMARY**
2. Verónica quiere mucho a su abuelita. Lo sé porque quiere ir a visitarla. **INTERPRETATION**
3. Las respuestas pueden variar. **TASK**

AFTER

Skill Review
page 305C–305D

USE SKILL CARD 26B

Focus Skill Make Inferences

RETEACH the skill. Have children look at **side B** of ***Tarjeta de destrezas 26: Hacer inferencias*/Skill Card 26: Make Inferences.** Read the skill reminder with them, and have a volunteer read the story aloud.

Read aloud the set of directions. Explain that children will work with partners to create their own charts. Remind them to think about the clues in the story as well as what they know as they read the story.

After children have completed their Make Inferences charts, have them display and explain their work. Point out that many inferences could be made about the selection *Si yo pudiera volar.* Ask volunteers to make some inferences about the characters in *Si yo pudiera volar.*

Focus Skill Review Phonics Skill from *Abuela*

RETEACH Combinación de consonantes *cl, cr.* Read aloud the following sentence: *En mi clase de cocina, aprendí el secreto de hacer una crema clara.* Have children listen for the *cl* and *cr* blend. Then read this list aloud and have children raise their hands when they hear the *cl* or *cr* blend: *clavel, crema, estrellas, clavo, clase, cocodrilos, clarinete, bicicleta, cráter, claro, círculo, cráneo.*

FLUENCY BUILDER Use *Intervention Practice Book* page 103. Explain that today children will practice the sentences on the bottom half of the page by reading them aloud on tape. Assign new partners. Have children take turns reading the sentences aloud to each other and then reading them on tape.

INTERVENTION PRACTICE BOOK
page 103

BEFORE

Drafting a Personal Narrative Paragraph
page 305E

Writer's Craft: Personal Narrative Paragraph

Build on prior knowledge. Tell children that they are going to talk about and write personal narrative paragraphs. Explain that personal narrative paragraphs tell about things the writer did or things that happened to the writer. Tell children that the events in the personal narrative paragraph happen in an order that makes sense. Have children share ideas for a personal narrative paragraph. Guide them to use time-order words in their narratives when they describe the events that occurred.

Mi familia se comió la torta.

Miré en un libro de cocina.

Elegí una receta.

Hice una torta.

Puse todos los ingredientes en la mesa.

Construct the text. "Share the pen" with children. Tell them that the list names events that took place in a personal narrative. Help children organize the items on the list into a personal narrative paragraph. Guide them to focus on the logic behind the order of the events. For example:

> Miré en un libro de cocina. Elegí una receta. Puse todos los ingredientes en la mesa. Hice una torta. Mi familia se comió la torta.

Revisit the text. Go back and read the personal narrative paragraph together. Ask: **¿Qué pasó primero?** (Miré en un libro de cocina.) **Luego, ¿qué pasó?** (Elegí una receta.)

- Guide children to use time-order words to show the order of events. Ask: **¿Cómo podemos usar palabras de tiempo para mostrar el orden de los sucesos?** (*Primero, miré en un libro de cocina. Luego, elegí una receta. Entonces, puse todos los ingredientes en la mesa. Después, hice una torta. Al final, mi familia se comió la torta.*) Make appropriate changes.
- Ask: **¿Qué pasaría si los sucesos estuvieran en un orden distinto?** (*El cuento no tendría sentido.*)
- Have children read the completed personal narrative paragraph aloud and then copy it on their papers.

On Your Own

Have children write a list of events that could take place in a personal narrative paragraph. Tell them to put their list in the order in which they happen.

AFTER

Spelling Lesson
page 301H

Connect Spelling and Phonics

RETEACH phonics. Tell children to number their papers 1–8. Dictate the following words, and have children write them. After each word is written, write it on the board so children can proofread their work. They should draw a line through a misspelled word and write the correct spelling below it.

1. creería*	**2. cruzaríamos***	**3. crestas***	**4. clase**
5. claro	**6. cristal**	**7. clavo**	**8. increíble**

*** Word appears in *Si yo pudiera volar.***

Dictate this sentence and have children write them: *Claro, es increíble, pero creería que las crestas en las olas fueron de cristal.*

Build and Read Longer Words

Remind children that they have learned how to decode words with the *cl* or *cr* blend. Explain that now they will use what they have learned to help them read some longer words.

INTERVENTION ASSESSMENT BOOK

Write the word *creación* on the board. Remind children that they can often figure out longer words by looking for smaller words in them. Cover the word part */ción/,* and have children read the small word that is left. Model how to blend the two word parts to read aloud the longer word *creación.* Do the same to have children blend word parts to read these longer words: *creíble, cremoso, cristalización.*

FLUENCY BUILDER Have children choose a passage from *Si pudiera volar* to read aloud to a partner. You may have children choose passages that they found particularly interesting, or have them choose one of the following options:

- Read pages 206–207. (From *¿Adónde irían…* through *…ondeando al viento!* Total: 96 words.)
- Read pages 209–211. (From *A mí me parece que no…* through *…si hay ballenas!* Total: 90 words.)

Children should read the selected passage aloud to their partners three times. Have the child rate each reading on a scale from 1 to 4.

BEFORE

Weekly Assessments

Review Vocabulary

To revisit vocabulary words prior to the weekly assessment, use these clues. Have volunteers take turns reading aloud the clues. Children say and then write the word or words that best answer the clue.

1. Esta palabra habla de los bordes de la olas. (*crestas*)
2. Esta palabra rima con *cantando.* (*ondeando*)
3. Esta palabra significa lo mismo que la palabra *subirnos.* (*elevarnos*)
4. Esta palabra tiene el mismo comienzo que la palabra *banda.* (*bandada*)
5. Esta palabra termina igual que la palabra *huerto.* (*puerto*)

You may want to display the Vocabulary Words and definitions on page 259 and have children copy them to use when they study for the vocabulary test.

INTERVENTION PRACTICE BOOK
page 106

Focus Skill Review Make Inferences

To review make inferences before the weekly assessment, distribute *Intervention Practice Book* page 106. Have volunteers read aloud the direction line and the story. Guide children to think about their own personal experience as they make their inferences.

INTERVENTION ASSESSMENT BOOK

Review Test Prep

Días maravillosos
pages 282–299

Ask children to turn to page 305 of the *Pupil Edition*. Call attention to the Tips for answering the test questions. Tell children that paying attention to these tips can help them answer not only the test questions but also other test questions like these.

Have children follow along as you read each test question and the tip that goes with it. Tell children to take their time as they think about each choice.

Self-Selected Reading

Have children select their own books to read independently. They might choose books from the classroom library shelf, or you may wish to offer a group of appropriate books from which children can choose.

- *Vuela, Catarina, vuela* See page 305A of the *Teacher's Edition* for plan.
- *El tapiz de abuela* por Omar S. Castañeda. Lee & Low, 1993.
- *Las abuelas de Liliana* por Leyla Torres. Farrar, Straus & Giroux.

After children have chosen their books, give each child a copy of *Mi diario de lectura,* which can be found on page R35 in the back of the *Teacher's Edition.* Have children fill in the information at the top of the form. Then have them use the log to keep track of their reading and to record their responses to the literature.

Conduct student-teacher conferences. Arrange time for each child to conference with you individually about his or her self-selected reading. Have children bring their Reading Logs to share with you at the conference. Children might also like to choose a favorite passage to read aloud to you. Ask questions about the book designed to stimulate discussion. For example, you might ask if children would like to fly and where they would like to go.

FLUENCY PERFORMANCE Have children read aloud to you the passage from *Si yo pudiera volar* that they selected and practiced with their partners. Keep track of the number of words the child reads correctly. Ask the child to rate his or her own performance on the 1–4 scale. If children are not happy with their oral reading, give them an opportunity to continue practicing and then to reread the passage to you again.

See *Oral Reading Fluency Assessment* for monitoring progress.

LESSON

27

BEFORE

Building Background and Vocabulary

Use with

"Atlas mundial para principiantes"

Review Phonics: Prefijos: re, des, in/Sufijo: mente

Identify the sound. Have children repeat the following sentence three times: *Recalentamos la sopa rápidamente para la niña desnutrida.* Ask them which words in the sentence have the prefixes *re, des* and the suffix *mente.* (*recalentamos, desnutrida, rápidamente*)

Associate letters to sound. On the board, write: *Recalentamos la sopa rápidamente para la niña desnutrida.* Have a volunteer underline the words that contain the prefixes *re, des* and the suffix *mente.* Review the sounds of each prefix and suffix with the children.

Word blending. Model how to blend and read the word *recalentamos.* Slide your hand under the letters as you slowly elongate the sounds /reecaaleentaamoss/. Then read *recalentamos* naturally. Follow a similar procedure for *desnutrida* and *rápidamente.*

INTERVENTION PRACTICE BOOK

page 108

Apply the skill. *Consonant and Vowel Substitution. Write the following words on the board, and have children read them aloud. Make the changes necessary to form the words in parentheses. Have children read each new word.*

nutrida (desnutrida)	**ahogar** (desahogar)	**rápido** (rápidamente)
olvidar (inolvidable)	**animar** (desanimar)	**hecho** (deshecho)
directo (directamente)	**duro** (duramente)	

Introduce Vocabulary

PRETEACH lesson vocabulary. Tell children that they are going to learn five new words that they will see again when they read a story called *Atlas mundial para principiantes*. Teach every vocabulary word using the following process.

Write the word.

Say the word.

Track the word and have children repeat it.

Give the meaning or context.

Use the following suggestions or similar ideas to give the meaning or context:

conecta Relate movement by having a volunteer connect two children's hands. Say: *Él o ella conecta a los dos niños*. Repeat the process by having volunteers connect other classroom objects.

distancia Relate to measurement by using a yardstick to measure the distance between two classroom desks.

características Relate to physical feature by having children touch the fea-

características	Relate to physical feature by having children touch the features on their face; then point to the features on a map.
cartógrafo	Have children role-play being mapmakers as they draw maps of the classroom or their neighborhood.
pelar	Relate to peeling an orange.

For vocabulary activities, see Vocabulary Games on pages 2–7.

Vocabulary Words

conecta une, reúne

distancia cuán lejos está un lugar de otro

características detalles, particularidades

cartógrafo una persona que hace mapas

pelar sacar, sacar la piel

AFTER

Building Background and Vocabulary

Apply Vocabulary Strategies

Use synonyms. Write the word *conecta* on chart paper and help children define it. Tell children that they can sometimes figure out the meaning of the word if they know its synonyms. A synonym is a word that means nearly the same as another word.

> MODEL **Si quiero saber qué significa la palabra *conecta*, puedo buscar sinónimos u otras palabras que tienen el mismo significado. *Conecta* y *une* son sinónimos. Reconozco la palabra *une*. Ahora sé que la palabra *conecta* significa lo mismo que *une*.**

Guide children in using a similar procedure to decode the words *características* and *pelar*. (*rasgos,descascarar*)

RETEACH **lesson vocabulary.** Have children listen to each of the following questions. Tell them to hold up the word card that answers each question. Reread the questions aloud with the correct answers. Then discuss how children made their choices.

1. ¿Qué palabra dice algo que podrías hacer con una fruta? (*pelar*).
2. ¿Qué palabra describe una persona que trabaja con mapas? (*cartógrafo*).
3. ¿Qué palabra se refiere a los rasgos físicos de una cara o de un mapa? (*características*).
4. ¿Qué palabra es otra manera de decir *que une*? (*conecta*).
5. ¿Qué palabra describe la medida de un lugar a otro? (*distancia*).

FLUENCY BUILDER Use *Intervention Practice Book* page 107. Read each word aloud in the first column and have children repeat it. Then have children work in pairs to read the words in the first column aloud to each other. Follow the same procedure with each of the remaining columns. After partners have practiced reading aloud the words in each column separately, have them practice the entire list.

(Save *Intervention Practice Book* page 107 for use on pages 271 and 273.)

BEFORE

Reading *Atlas mundial para principiantes* pages 308–331

USE SKILL CARD 27A

Focus Skill Locate Information

PRETEACH the skill. Point out to children that readers can use the table of contents to locate information in books such as atlases. Discuss how a table of contents is organized. Guide children to see that using a table of contents saves readers time.

Have children look at **side A** of **Skill Card 27: Locate Information.** Read the definition of Locate Information. Next read the table of contents and have children read it with you.

Now call attention to the chart and have volunteers take turns reading the information aloud. Ask:

- **¿Qué ves en un mapa?** (*Possible response: continentes, océanos y características físicas de los lugares*)
- **¿Cómo se llaman los ríos, los lagos y las montañas en un mapa?** (*Possible response: características físicas*)

Prepare to Read *Atlas mundial para principiantes*

Preview. Tell children that they are going to read a selection entitled *Atlas mundial para principiantes*. Explain that this is an informational story. Tell children that *Atlas mundial para principiantes* tells facts about the places in the world. Then preview the selection.

Días maravillosos pages 308–331

- **Pages 308–309:** Veo el título, *Atlas mundial para principiantes*, en las páginas 308–309. Veo una foto de niños, animales y el planeta Tierra. Pienso que la selección va a contar hechos sobre el planeta Tierra.
- **Pages 310–311:** En estas páginas, aprendo acerca de los mapas. Veo fotos que muestran vistas diferentes de un lugar, y leo acerca de la vista que muestra un mapa. Pienso que voy a aprender más acerca de los mapas al leer esta selección.
- **Pages 312–313:** En estas páginas, leo sobre cómo encontrar lugares en un mapa. Veo fotos que me ayudan a entender las características de un mapa. Creo que voy a usar mapas para encontrar información a medida que lea la selección.

Set Purpose. Model setting a purpose for reading *Atlas mundial para principiantes.*

MODEL **Según lo que he visto en estas páginas, creo que voy a leer más sobre los mapas y cómo usarlos para encontrar información sobre la Tierra, la gente y los animales que viven allí. Voy a leer para descubrir qué otro tipo de información se puede encontrar en un atlas.**

AFTER

Reading ***Atlas mundial para principiantes pages 308–331***

Reread and Summarize

Have children reread and summarize *Atlas mundial para principiantes* in sections, as described below.

Pages 310–313 **Leamos las páginas 310–313 para recordar hechos sobre los mapas.**

Summary: Un mapa es un dibujo de un lugar visto desde arriba. Un mapa te puede ayudar a encontrar lugares. Los mapas tienen una brújula, una escala y una clave del mapa que dan información sobre dirección, distancia y otras cosas que se encuentran en un mapa.

Pages 314–319 **Leamos las páginas 314–319 para recordar la diferencia entre un mapa y un globo y para recordar las características físicas del mundo.**

Summary: Un globo es un mapa redondo. Algunas características físicas del mundo son los continentes, las islas, los océanos, los lagos y ríos.

Pages 320–321 **Leamos las páginas 320–321 para recordar los símbolos en el mapa.**

Summary: Las montañas, los desiertos, los bosques de coníferas, los bosques de árboles de hojas que cambian todos los años, los bosques tropicales, los casquetes polares, las tundras, las tierras pantanosas y los pastizales tienen símbolos especiales en un mapa.

Pages 322–328 **Leamos las páginas 322–328 para recordar algunos hechos de América del Norte.**

Summary: América del norte tiene la forma de un triángulo. Tiene montañas y tierras pantanosas. Los Grandes Lagos son el grupo de lagos de agua dulce más grande del mundo. Hace mucho frío en el norte, y las temperaturas se vuelven cada vez más templadas hacia el sur. Hay una gran variedad de animales. La Ciudad de México es la más grande de América del Norte. Los antepasados de la mayoría de los habitantes de América del Norte son de Europa. Los principales idiomas son inglés y español.

FLUENCY BUILDER Use *Intervention Practice Book* page 107. Call attention to the sentences on the bottom half of the page. The slashes break the sentences into phrases to allow you to work on natural phrasing. Tell children that their goal is to read each phrase or sentence smoothly. Model appropriate pace, expression and phrasing as you read each sentence and have children read it after you.

BEFORE

Making Connections
pages 332–333

Directed Reading of *Juegos con mapas*

Sonidos alegres
pages 214–221

Pages 214–215

Ask a volunteer to read aloud the title on page 214. Ask children what a globe is like. Then have children read pages 214–215 to find out. Ask: **¿Quién hace los globos? ¿En qué se parecen los mapas y los globos?** (*Possible response: un cartógrafo; un globo es como un mapa redondo*) Focus Skill **NOTE DETAILS**

Pages 216–217

Have children read pages 216–217. Ask: **¿Qué libro contiene estos hechos? ¿Cómo buscas información en este libro?** (*Possible response: un atlas; Voy a usar la tabla de contenido.*)

Focus Skill **Locate Information.** Ask: **¿Qué haces primero en el juego de globos? ¿Luego qué haces?** (*Possible response: Primero dale vueltas al globo, luego, detén el globo.*) **SEQUENCE OF EVENTS**

Page 218

Have children read page 218. Model using the Decoding/Phonics strategy in order for children to understand how to figure out long or unfamiliar words.

> MODEL **Cuándo veo a la palabra *continentes,* no estoy segura cómo leerla. Empiezo por pronunciar los sonidos y romperla en sílabas. Reconozco las letras *ente* porque las he visto en palabras como *mente* y *fuente.* He visto la *s* al final de palabras plurales como *gatos* y *perros.* He visto las letras *con* en palabras como *conectar* y *contrastar.* Ahora sé que la palabra es *continentes.*** Focus Strategy **DECODING PHONICS**

Page 219

Have children read page 219 to find out how to play What Is It Like There? Ask: **¿Cómo se juega el nuevo juego?** (*Possible response: Haz preguntas acerca de los lugares del mapa. Cada jugador escribe su respuesta. Luego buscan en libros sobre el lugar para averiguar quién tiene razón.*) **NOTE DETAILS**

Page 220

INTERVENTION PRACTICE BOOK page 109

Have children read page 220 to find out why people might want to play and make up new map games. Ask: **Además de ser divertidos, ¿por qué son importantes estos juegos?** (*Possible response: Se puede aprender cosas sobre el mundo cuando se juega.*) SPECULATE

Summarize the selection. Ask children to think about why people like to use maps and globes and atlases.

AFTER

Skill Review *page 333I*

USE SKILL CARD 27B

Focus Skill Locate Information

RETEACH the skill. Have children look at **side B** of **Skill Card 27: Locate Information.** Read the skill reminder with them, and have a volunteer read the table of contents aloud.

Read aloud the set of directions. Explain that children will work with partners to create their own charts. Remind them to look for clue words in the questions that match the information found on each page.

After children have completed their Locate Information charts, have them display and explain their work. Point out that a table of contents could be made for the selection *Juegos con mapas.* Ask volunteers to suggest headings for a table of contents for *Juegos con mapas.*

Review the Phonics Skill from *Atlas mundial para principiantes:*

RETEACH Prefijos: ***re, des, in*****/Sufijo:** ***mente.*** Read aloud the following sentence: *Podemos rehacer la tarea fácilmente si no te desanimas ni estás inquieto.* Have children identify the words with prefixes and suffixes.

FLUENCY BUILDER Be sure that children have copies of *Intervention Practice Book* page 107. Explain that today children will practice the sentences on the bottom half of the page by reading them aloud on tape. Assign new partners. Have children take turns reading the sentences aloud to each other and then reading them on tape.

INTERVENTION PRACTICE BOOK page 107

BEFORE

Drafting a Paragraph of Information
Page 335C

Writer's Craft: Paragraph of Information

Build on prior knowledge. Tell children that they are going to talk about and write a paragraph of information, or an informational paragraph. Explain that informational paragraphs should be interesting and tell about one topic. Tell children that the ideas in an informational paragraph must be grouped in a way that makes sense. Explain that when writing an informational paragraph, it is often helpful to organize ideas by using time-order words. Have children discuss time-order words and how they think these words would be helpful in an informational paragraph.

otoño
primavera
verano
invierno

Construct the text. "Share the pen" with children. Tell them that the list names seasons of the year and that different places in the world experience the seasons at different times. Help children to organize the seasons on the list into an informational paragraph about the sequence of seasons around the world. Guide them to focus on the order of the seasons that happen where they live. For example:

Cuando es invierno donde yo vivo, es verano en Australia. Cuando es primavera donde yo vivo, es otoño el Australia. Cuando es verano donde yo vivo, es invierno en Australia. Cuando es otoño donde yo vivo, es primavera en Australia.

Revisit the text. Go back and read the informational paragraph together. Ask: **¿Por qué el párrafo empieza con el invierno?** (*El invierno es la primera estación del año donde vivo yo.*) **¿Por qué la primavera es el tema siguiente?** (*La primavera viene después del invierno.*)

- Guide children to use time-order words to show the order of events. Ask: **Cómo puedo usar palabras de tiempo para mejorar este párrafo?** (*Cuando es invierno donde yo vivo, es verano en Australia. Luego, cuando es primavera donde yo vivo, es otoño el Australia. Entonces, cuando es verano donde yo vivo, es invierno en Australia. Finalmente, cuando es otoño donde yo vivo, es primavera en Australia.*) Make appropriate changes.
- Ask: **¿Qué pasaría si usara un orden diferente?** (*El párrafo no tendría sentido.*)
- Have children read the completed informational paragraph aloud and then copy it on their papers.

AFTER

Spelling Lesson
page 331H

Connect Spelling and Phonics

RETEACH phonics: Prefijos: *re, des, in*/Sufijo: *mente* Tell children to number their papers 1–8. Dictate the following words, and have children write them. After each word is written, write it on the board so children can proofread their work. They should draw a line through a misspelled word and write the correct spelling below it.

1. regresar*	**2. fácilmente**	**3. rápidamente**	**4. contentamente**
5. inútil	**6. deshecho**	**7. recalentar**	**8. desemboca**

*** Word appears in *Juegos con mapas.***

Dictate these sentences and have children write them: *Podemos hacer la tarea fácilmente. Los pantalones son descosidos.*

Build and Read Longer Words

Remind children that they have learned how to decode words with the prefixes: *re, des, in,* and *sufixe mente.* Explain that now they will use what they have learned to help them read some longer words.

Write the word *fácilmente* on the board. Cover the first part of the word *fácil* then read *mente.* Cover the second part of the word and read fácil. Explain that when we add mente to a word, we use the feminine form of that word (rápido, rápidamente) Follow the same procedure to have children build and read these longer words: *lentamente* and *tristemente.*

FLUENCY BUILDER Have children choose a passage from *Juegos con mapas* to read aloud to a partner. You may have children choose passages that they found particularly interesting, or have them choose one of the following options:

- Read page 214. (From *Tú puedes usar*... through ...uno o más amigos de tu edad. Total: 81 words.)
- Read pages 217–218. (From *Mira el globo*... through ...*otras partes del mundo.* Total: 72 words.)

Children should read the selected passage aloud to their partners three times. Have the child rate each reading on a scale from 1 to 4.

BEFORE
Weekly Assessments

Review Vocabulary

To revisit Vocabulary Words prior to the weekly assessment, use these sentence frames. Have volunteers take turns reading aloud the sentence stems and choices. Students identify the correct choice and explain why that choice makes sense in the sentence.

1. Cuando vas a **pelar** una naranja, vas a
   a. dejar la cáscara   b. quitar la cáscara
2. Si sabes la **distancia** entre dos lugares, sabes
   a. la altura de los lugares   b. cuán lejos están el uno del otro
3. Un **cartógrafo** es una persona que
   a. hace mapas   b. viaja en avión
4. Unas **características** físicas de un continente son
   a. montañas y desiertos   b. palabras y párrafos
5. Cuando una persona **conecta** dos cosas, lo que hace es
   a. separarlas   b. unirlas

Correct responses: 1.b, 2.b, 3.a, 4.a, 5.b.

You may want to display the vocabulary words and definitions on page 269 and have children copy them to use when they study for the vocabulary test.

INTERVENTION PRACTICE BOOK
page 110

Focus Skill Review Locate Information

To review Locate Information before the weekly assessment, distribute *Intervention Practice Book* page 110. Have volunteers read aloud the direction line and the table of contents. Guide children to look for clue words in the questions that match the headings in the table of contents.

INTERVENTION PRACTICE BOOK

Review Test Prep

Días maravillosos
page 335

Ask children to turn to page 335 of the *Pupil Edition.* Call attention to the Tips for answering the test questions. Tell children that paying attention to these tips can help them answer not only the test questions but also other test questions like these.

Have children follow along as you read each test question and the tip that goes with it. Tell children to check over their answers after they have completed the test.

Self-Selected Reading

Have children select their own books to read independently. They might choose books from the classroom library shelf, or you may wish to offer a group of appropriate books from which children can choose.

- *El camino de las mariposas monarca.* See page 335O of the *Teacher's Edition* for an Independent Reading Plan.
- *Mapa rompecabezas de los Estados Unidos* por Nany L. Clouse. Henry Holt, 1990.
- *Mapas y globos terráqueos* por Jack Knowlton. HarperCollins, 1996.

After children have chosen their books, give each child a copy of *Mi diario de lectura,* which can be found on page R35 in the back of the *Teacher's Edition.* Have children fill in the information at the top of the form. Then have them use the log to keep track of their reading and to record their responses to the literature.

Conduct student-teacher conferences. Arrange time for each child to conference with you individually about his or her self-selected reading. Have children bring their *Diarios de lectura* to share with you at the conference. Children might also like to choose a favorite passage to read aloud to you. Ask questions designed to stimulate discussion about the book. For example, you might ask children to share which places in the world they would like to visit, and what they know about those places.

FLUENCY PERFORMANCE Have children read aloud to you the passage from *Juegos con mapas* that they selected and practiced with their partners. Keep track of the number of words the child reads correctly. Ask the child to rate his or her own performance on the 1–4 scale. If children are not happy with their oral reading, give them an opportunity to continue practicing and to read the passage to you again.

See *Oral Reading Fluency Assessment* for monitoring progress.

LESSON 28

BEFORE

Building Background and Vocabulary

INTERVENTION PRACTICE BOOK page 112

Use with

"El viaje de los dinosaurios"

Review Phonics: Consonants *x, z*

Identify the sound. Have children repeat the following sentence three times: *Dejé mis zapatos y mi saxofón en el taxi.* Ask children to identify the words that have an *x* or *z*. (*zapatos, saxofón, taxi*)

Associate letters to sound. On the board, write: *Dejé mis zapatos y mi saxfón en el taxi.* Circle the words *taxi* and *saxofón.* Ask children to tell how the words are alike. (*los dos tienen una x*) Underline the letter *x* in *taxi* and *saxofón.* Then follow a similar procedure for the *z* sound in the word *zapatos.*

Word blending. Model how to blend and read the word *zapatos.* Slide your hand under the letters as you slowly elongate the sounds /saapaato/. Then read *zapato* naturally. Follow a similar procedure for *saxófono* and *taxi.*

Apply the skill. *Vowel and Consonant Substitution* Write the following words on the board, and have children read them aloud. Make the changes necessary to form the words in parentheses. Have children read each new word.

ves (vez)	**sana** (manzana)	**quiso** (quizá)	**taco** (taxi)
conoce (conozca)	**parecen** (parezcan)	**bolea** (boxeo)	**entra** (extra)

Introduce Vocabulary

PRETEACH lesson vocabulary. Tell children that they are going to learn five new words that they will see again when they read a story called *El viaje de los dinosaurios.* Teach each vocabulary word using the following process.

Write the word.
Say the word.
Track the word and have children repeat it.
Give the meaning or context.

Use the following suggestions or similar ideas to give the meaning or context:

grabadora Relate by demonstrating how to use an actual cassette recorder.

amigos Relate by having children role-play being companions or friends.

equipaje Relate by showing a picture or having children role-play packing using actual suitcases or boxes.

familiares	Relate by having children name their family members and draw family trees.
ligero	Relate by contrasting light and heavy classroom objects.

For vocabulary activities, see Vocabulary Games on pages 2–7.

Vocabulary Words

grabadora máquina con una cinta dentro que se usa para grabar

amigos compañeros, personas con quienes se tiene amistad

equipaje maletas o cajas que usan los que viajan

familiares gente que pertenece a la misma familia

ligero liviano, de poco peso

AFTER

Building Background and Vocabulary

Apply Vocabulary Strategies

Use antonyms. Write the word *ligero* on chart paper and help children define it. Tell children that they can sometimes figure out the meaning of the word if they know its antonym. An antonym is a word that means the opposite of another word.

> MODEL **La palabra *ligero* significa liviana, y esto significa "no pesado". El papel es ligero. Un lápiz es ligero. Ahora sé que el antónimo de *ligero* es *pesado.* Como *liviana, ligero* también significa "no pesado".**

Guide children to use a similar process to remember the meaning of *amigos.* For example, say: *amigos* no son enemigos.

RETEACH **lesson vocabulary.** Have children listen to each of the following groups of words. Tell them to hold up the word card that goes with each group. Reread the groups aloud with the correct answer. Then discuss how children made their choices.

1. maletas	**cajas**	**viajar** (*equipaje*)
2. música	**casete**	**voz** (*grabadora*)
3. compañeros	**te ayudan**	**viene contigo** (*amigos*)
4. liviana	**pequeño**	**no pesado** (*ligero*)
5. familia	**padres**	**hermanos** (*familiares*)

FLUENCY BUILDER Use *Intervention Practice Book* page 111. Read each word in the first column aloud and have children repeat it. Then have children work in pairs to read the words in the first column aloud to each other. Follow the same procedure with each of the remaining columns. After partners have practiced reading aloud the words in each column separately, have them practice the entire list. Save *Intervention Practice Book* page 111 for use on pages 281 and 283.

INTERVENTION PRACTICE BOOK page 111

BEFORE

Reading *El viaje de los dinosaurios* pages 338–357

USE SKILL CARD 28A

Focus Skill Author's Purpose

PRETEACH the skill. Point out to children that the author's purpose is the reason why the author wrote the story. Explain that authors may have more than one reason or purpose for writing. Give examples of author's purposes, such as *to give information*, or *to entertain.* Discuss why it helps authors to have a purpose before they begin to write.

Have children look at **side A** of **Skill Card 28: Author's Purpose.** Read the definition of author's purpose. Next read the story and then have children reread it with you. Then have volunteers take turns reading the information aloud. Ask:

- **¿Cuál sería el propósito del autor si el cuento fuera de un marciano que lava un perro verde?** (*Possible response: para entretener.*)
- **¿Cómo las pistas te ayudan a entender el propósito del autor?** (*Possible response: Apoyan el propósito del autor.*)

Prepare to Read: *El viaje de los dinosaurios*

Preview. Tell children that they are going to read a selection entitled *El viaje de los dinosaurios.* Explain that this is an informational story. Tell children that *El viaje de los dinosaurios* gives information about how to travel. Then preview the selection.

Días maravillosos
pages 338–357

- **Pages 338–339:** Veo el título, *El viaje de los dinosaurios,* y el nombre de los autores en las páginas 338–339. Leo el subtítulo, *Guía para familias viajeras* y esto me dice que voy a aprender cómo las familias pueden viajar. Creo que voy a ver más dibujos de dinosaurios que están viajando.
- **Pages 340–341:** En estas páginas, leo sobre los lugares donde se puede viajar. Veo dibujos de dinosaurios que están viajando. Aunque sé que los dinosaurios no pueden viajar, es gracioso verlos, y sé que están haciendo algo que a la gente le gusta hacer.
- **Pages 342–343:** En estas páginas, leo acerca de cómo prepararse para un viaje. Creo que voy a aprender más sobre cómo planear un viaje.

Set Purpose. Model setting a purpose for reading *El viaje de los dinosaurios.*

MODEL **Por lo que he visto en estas páginas, creo que voy a leer más sobre cómo viajar y qué podría pasar durante un viaje. También leeré para entretenerme con los dinosaurios graciosos que me ayudan a aprender cómo hacer un viaje.**

AFTER

Reading ***El viaje de los dinosaurios pages 338–357***

Reread and Summarize

Have the children reread and summarize *El viaje de los dinosaurios* in sections, as described below.

Pages 340–343 **Leamos las páginas 340–343 para recordar por qué la gente viaja y cómo prepararse para un viaje.**

Summary: La gente viaja porque quiere tener aventuras. Los libros y los mapas te pueden ayudar a prepararte para un viaje. Debes buscar a alguien que pueda cuidar a tus mascotas mientras no estés. Debes traer las direcciones de tus amigos y familiares para que puedas escribirles durante el viaje. Debes empacar cosas pequeñas, livianas y duraderas.

Pages 344–347 **Leamos las páginas 344–347 para recordar cómo viajar de un lugar a otro y por qué es bueno viajar de esta manera.**

Summary: Se puede caminar o montar en bicicleta. Caminando se puede parar y ver mucho y tu cuerpo es el único equipo. Las bicicletas van más rápidas y se puede llegar a casi a donde quieras en éstas.

Pages 348–353 **Leemos las páginas 350–353 para recordar otras maneras de viajar y por qué son buenas.**

Summary: En la ciudad, se puede viajar en metro o en autobús. Los transportes subterráneos son rápidos, y algunos autobuses tienen que señalen los sitios de interés. Viajar en tren es una manera nueva de ver nuevos lugares. Se puede sentarse hacia el frente o hacia atrás en un tren. En avión, se puede volar encima de las nubes.

Páginas 354–355 **Leamos las páginas 354–355 para recordar qué pasa a la hora de volver.**

Summary: Hay que recordar empacar todas tus cosas. Quizás quieras traer un regalo para tus amigos. Puedes sacar fotos para recordar tu viaje.

FLUENCY BUILDER Use *Intervention Practice Book* page 111. Call attention to the sentences on the bottom half of the page. The slashes break the sentences into phrases to allow you to work on natural phrasing. Tell children that their goal is to read each phrase or sentence smoothly. Model appropriate pace, expression and phrasing as you read each sentence and have children read it after you. Then have children practice by reading the sentences aloud three times to a partner.

BEFORE
Making Connections
pages 360–361

Directed Reading of *Cuando visitas a tus familiares*

Sonidos alegres
pages 222–229

Page 222

Read aloud the title of the story. Ask children to name some *relatives* that they might like to visit. Then have children read page 222 to find out what to do before visiting relatives. Ask: **¿Qué se debe hacer antes de visitar a los familiares?** (*Possible response: llamarlos por teléfono.*) **SEQUENCE**

Ask: **¿Por qué hay que llamar primero?** (*Possible response: para darles tiempo a los familiares a prepararse para tu visita*) **CAUSE AND EFFECT**

Page 223

Have children read the heading on page 223. Ask: ¿Cómo los títulos te ayudan a entender el propósito del autor? (*Possible response: Los títulos me muestran que el autor quiere organizar la información para enseñar cómo hacer algo.*) Focus Skill **AUTHOR'S PURPOSE**

Have children read page 223. Model how to use the Use Context to Confirm Meaning strategy in order to understand the word *compañero.*

> MODEL **Si no entiendo qué significa una palabra, puedo usar las otras palabras en la oración o el párrafo para ayudarme a entender el significado de la palabra. Después de leer la palabra *compañero* en el título, leo la próxima frase. Esta frase dice que se puede invitar a un amigo en vez de viajar solo. Esto me ayuda a confirmar que en el título, *compañeros* probablemente significa *amigos.*** Focus Strategy **Use Context to Confirm Meaning**

Page 224

Have children read page 224. Ask: **¿Qué debes hacer si montas en bicicleta?** (*Possible response: Montar cuando hace buen tiempo; no viajar muy lejos; no montar cerca de autos; montar en caminos seguros; llevar una merienda.*) **SUMMARIZE**

Page 225

Have children read the heading on page 225. Ask children what luggage is. Then have them read page 225 to find out what to pack for a trip. Ask: **¿Qué se debe empacar para un viaje?** (*Possible response: la ropa, unos juguetes, un impermeable*) **NOTE DETAILS**

Page 226

Have children read the heading on page 226. Then have them read page 226 to find out what rules to follow. Ask: **¿Qué regla te parece la más importante?** (*Possible response: La respuestas pueden variar.*) **MAKE JUDGEMENTS**

Page 227

Have children read the heading on page 227. Then have them read page 227 to learn how to help out. Ask: **¿Cuáles son algunas maneras de ayudar a los familiares?** (*Possible response: Puedes hacer tu cama; recoger los juguetes; preparar el almuerzo; lavar los platos.*) **NOTE DETAILS** Ask: **¿Qué otras cosas se pueden hacer para ayudar?** (*Possible response: La respuestas pueden variar.*) **EXTEND THE STORY**

Page 228

Have children read the heading on page 228. Then have them read the page to find out how to thank their relatives. Ask: **¿Cuáles son algunas**

formas de decir *gracias*? (*Possible response: Puedes decir a los familiares que te divertiste mucho; agradecerles por invitarte; invitarles a visitarte; mandarles una nota de agradecimiento.*) **NOTE DETAILS**

Summarize the Selection Ask children to think about why people want to travel to see their relatives and what they like to do once they get there.

INTERVENTION PRACTICE BOOK
page 113

Answers to *Piénsalo* Questions

1. Llamar antes, diles de tus planes y cómprales un regalo. Las dos cosas que debes hacer cuando estés con ellos es respetar las reglas y ayudarlos. **SUMMARY**
2. Porque puede llover y puedes necesitarlo. **INTERPRETATION**
3. Las respuestas pueden variar. **TASK**

AFTER

Skill Review
pages 363C

USE SKILL CARD 28B

Focus Skill AUTHOR'S PURPOSE

RETEACH the skill. Have children look at **side B** of **Skill Card 28: Author's Purpose.** Read the skill reminder with them, and have a volunteer read the story aloud.

Read aloud the directions. Read aloud the set of directions. Explain that children will work with partners to create their own charts. Remind them to remember the difference between the author's purpose and the clues to the purpose.

After children have completed their author's purpose charts, have them display and explain their work. Point out that the selection *El viaje de los dinosaurios* has an author's purpose and clues to that purpose. Ask volunteers to name the author's purpose and some clues to that purpose found in the selection.

Focus Skill Review the Phonics Skill from *El viaje de los dinosaurios*

RETEACH ***Consonantes x, z*** Read aloud the following sentence: *Tomé el zumo en el taxi*. Have children listen for the *x* and *z* sounds. Then read this list aloud and have children raise their hands when they hear the *x* sound: *saxofón, buscar, próximo, máximo, aceite, éxito, mal, niño.* Then have them raise their hands when they hear the *z* sound: *dureza, amor, zoológico, preguntar, zapato, empieza, piezas, naranjas, manzanas.*

FLUENCY BUILDER Be sure that children have copies of *Intervention Practice Book* page 111. Explain that today children will practice the sentences on the bottom half of the page by reading them aloud on tape. Assign new partners. Have children take turns reading the sentences aloud to each other and then reading them on tape.

INTERVENTION PRACTICE BOOK
page 111

BEFORE

Drafting a Research Report
pages 363G

Writing Process: How-to Paragraph

Build on Prior Knowledge. Tell children that they are going to talk about and write how-to paragraphs. Explain that how-to paragraphs tell directions or instructions that must be followed to make or do something. Tell children that the directions or instructions in the how-to paragraph are listed in an order that makes sense. Have children share ideas for a how-to paragraph.

Tarea: planear una comida campestre

Materiales:

1. canasta	**4. bebidas**
2. manta	**5. loción del sol**
3. comida	**6. bolsas**

Construct the text. "Share the pen" with children. Guide them in using the list to formulate steps for planning a picnic. For example:

1. **Preparar la comida.**
2. **Poner la comida en bolsas.**
3. **Poner las bolsas de bocaditos en la canasta.**
4. **Poner las bebidas en la canasta.**
5. **Poner loción del sol en la canasta.**
6. **Llevar la canasta y la manta al parque y disfrutar de la comida campestre.**

Revisit the text. Go back and read the list of steps together. Ask: **¿Qué pasa primero?** (*Hacer comida.*) **¿Qué pasa luego?** (*Poner la comida en sacos.*)

- Guide children to use time-order words to show the sequence of the steps. Ask: **¿Cómo puedo usar palabras de tiempo para planear un picnic?** (*Usa palabras como* primero, luego, después, entonces, *y* finalmente.) Make appropriate changes.
- Ask: **¿Qué pasaría si escribiera los pasos en otro orden?** (*Las instrucciones no tendrían sentido.*)
- Have children read the how-to paragraph aloud and then copy it on their papers.

On Your Own

Have children write three or four steps for something they know how to do or make. Guide them to write their steps in an order that makes sense.

AFTER

Spelling Lesson
pages 357H

Connect Spelling and Phonics

RETEACH phonics. Tell children to number their papers 1–8. Write *éxito* and *zapato* on the board, and tell children that in the words you will say, they will hear an *x* or a *z*. Dictate the following words, and have children write them. After each word is written, write it on the board so children can proofread their work. They should draw a line through a misspelled word and write the correct spelling below it.

1. hazles*	**2. vez***	**3. haz ***	**4. danzas**
5. cabezas	**6. zumo**	**7. exclamó**	**8. exclamación**

* Word appears in *Cuando visitas a tus familiares.*

Dictate these sentences and have children write them: *No tuve mucho éxito. El saxófono me costaba mucho aprender. Voy a practicar danza.*

Build and Read Longer Words

Remind children that they have learned how to decode words with the consonants *x* and *z*. Explain that now they will use what they have learned to help them read some longer words.

INTERVENTION ASSESSMENT BOOK

Write the word *exclamación* on the board. Remind children that they can often figure out longer words by looking for small words or word parts in them. Cover the word part *ción*, and have children read the small word that is left. Follow a similar procedure to have them read the word part *exclama.* Model how to blend the two smaller words to read aloud the longer word *exclamación*. Follow a similar procedure to have children read these longer words: *exageración* and *zapatería*.

FLUENCY BUILDER Have children choose a passage from *Cuando visitas a tus familiares* to read aloud to a partner. You may have children choose passages that they found particularly interesting, or have them choose one of the following options:

- Read pages 222–223. (From *Llama antes*… through …*¡Me encantaría, Ernesto!* Total: 80 words.)
- Read pages 224–225. (From *Sacas esas ruedas*… through …*son viajeros contentos.* Total: 88 words.)

Children should read the selected passage aloud to their partners three times. Have the child rate each reading on a scale from 1 to 4.

BEFORE
Weekly Assessments

Review Vocabulary

To revisit Vocabulary Words prior to the weekly assessment, use these questions. Have volunteers take turns reading aloud the questions and choices. Tell children to identify the correct choice and explain how they made their decision.

1. ¿Qué palabra es el opuesto de *pesado?*
   a. familiares **b.** ligero
2. ¿Qué palabra describe a tu madre, padre, hermanos y hermanas?
   a. ligero **b.** familiares
3. ¿Qué palabra describe un equipo que produce música?
   a. grabadora **b.** nevera
4. ¿Qué palabra describe a los niños con quienes juegas y te diviertes?
   a. equipaje **b.** amigos
5. ¿Qué palabra describe el lugar donde guardas tus ropas de viaje?
   a. grabadora **b.** equipaje

Correct responses: 1.b, 2.b, 3.a, 4.b, 5.b.

You may want to display the vocabulary words and definitions on page 279 and have children copy them to use when they study for the vocabulary test.

INTERVENTION PRACTICE BOOK
page 114

Focus Skill Review Author's Purpose

To review Author's Purpose before the weekly assessment, distribute *Intervention Practice Book* page 114. Have volunteers read aloud the direction line and the story. Guide children to think about all the reasons authors write stories.

Review Test Prep

INTERVENTION ASSESSMENT BOOK

Ask children to turn to page 363 of the *Pupil Edition.* Call attention to the Tips for answering the test questions. Tell children that paying attention to these tips can help them answer not only the test questions but also other test questions like these.

Have children follow along as you read each test question and the tip that goes with it. Tell children to get a good night's rest and eat a good breakfast before taking a test.

Días maravillosos
page 363

Self-Selected Reading

Have children select their own books to read independently. They might choose books from the classroom library shelf, or you may wish to offer a group of appropriate books from which children can choose.

- *Un viaje en Aerolíneas Dinosaurio.* See page 363S of the *Teacher's Edition* for an *Independent Reading Plan.*
- *Destello el dinosaurio* por Marcus Pfister. North-South, 1995.
- *Viajo en avión* por Montserrat Viza. Parramón Ediciones, 1987.

After children have chosen their books, give each child a copy of *Mi diario de lectura*, which can be found on page R35 in the back of the *Teacher's Edition.* Have children fill in the information at the top of the form. Then have them use the log to keep track of their reading and to record their responses to the literature.

Conduct Student-Teacher Conferences Arrange time for each child to conference with you individually about his or her self-selected reading. Have children bring their Reading Logs to share with you at the conference. Children might also like to choose a favorite passage to read aloud to you. Ask questions designed to stimulate discussion about the book. For example, you might ask which method of travel children would like to experience and why.

FLUENCY PERFORMANCE Have children read aloud to you the passage from *Cuando visitas a tus familiares* that they selected and practiced with their partners. Keep track of the number of words the child reads correctly. Ask the child to rate his or her own performance on the 1–4 scale. If children are not happy with their oral reading, give them an opportunity to continue practicing and then to reread the passage to you again.

See *Oral Reading Fluency Assessment* for monitoring progress.

LESSON 29

BEFORE

Building Background and Vocabulary

Use with

"Monterino en alta mar"

Review Phonics: Diminutivos

Identify the sound. Have children repeat the following sentence three times: *El conejito y el caballito son amiguitos.* Ask children to identify the words that have dimuntives. (*conejito, caballito* y *amiguitos*)

Associate letters to sound. On the board, write: *El conejito y el caballito son amiguitos.* Circle the words *conejito, caballito* and *amiguitos*. Ask children to tell how the words are alike. (*los dos son diminutivos*) Underline the letters *ito* in the words. Tell children that the letters *ito* stand for something small or dear.

Word blending. Model how to blend and read the word *bebito*. Slide your hand under the letters as you slowly elongate the sounds. Then read *bebito* naturally. Follow a similar procedure for *calentito, perrito* and *amiguito*.

INTERVENTION PRACTICE BOOK

page 116

Apply the skill. *Vowel and Consonant Substitution* Write the following words on the board, and have children read them aloud. Make the changes necessary to form the words in parentheses. Have children read each new word.

gato (gatito)	**pato** (patito)	**caliente** (calentito)
abuelo (abuelito)	**ratón** (ratoncito)	**perro** (perrito)

Introduce Vocabulary

PRETEACH lesson vocabulary. Tell children that they are going to learn six new words that they will see again when they read a story called *Monterino en alta mar.* Teach every vocabulary word using the following process.

Write the word.
Say the word.
Track the word and have children repeat it.
Give the meaning or context.

Use the following suggestions or similar ideas to give the meaning or context:

acogedora Relate by role-playing how a person feels in a cozy place.

deriva Relate by demonstrating with a toy or paper boat in the classroom sink or a bucket.

flota Relate by drawing a simple picture of many boats. Have children contrast it with a simple picture of one boat.

navegaban Act out sailing a boat. Have children join you.

escabulló Relate with synonyms (*huir, escapar*).

inundada Speak about the effects of small and large floods on people's lives and homes.

For vocabulary activities, see Vocabulary Games on pages 2–7.

Vocabulary Words

acogedora tibia y cómoda

deriva arrastrado por el agua en movimiento

escabulló salir o meterse dentro silenciosamente

flota grupo de naves

inundada llena de agua

navegaban viajaban en el agua

AFTER

Building Background and Vocabulary

Apply Vocabulary Strategies

RETEACH lesson vocabulary. Write the word *escabulló* on chart paper and help children define it. Tell children that they can sometimes figure out the meaning of the word if they know its synonyms. A synonym is a word that means nearly the same as another word.

> MODEL **Si quiero entender el significado de la palabra *escabulló* busco sinónimos u otras palabras conocidas que tienen el mismo significado. *Escabulló y escapó* son sinónimos. Reconozco la palabra *escapó*. Así que sé que *escabulló* significa lo mismo que *escapó*.**

Guide children in using a similar procedure to understand other words when you read.

Vocabulary activity. Have children listen to each of the following questions. Tell them to hold up the word card that answers each question. Reread the questions aloud with the correct answer. Then discuss how children made their choices.

1. ¿Qué palabra describe una cama calentita y cómoda? (*acogedora*)
2. ¿Qué palabra dice lo que hacían los barcos en el agua? (*navegaban*)
3. ¿Qué palabra describe un grupo de muchos barcos? (*flota*)
4. ¿Qué palabra significa empujado por el agua en movimiento? (*deriva*)
5. ¿Qué palabra significa ***llena de agua***? (*inundada*)
6. ¿Qué palabra quiere decir salir o meterse dentro silenciosamente? (*escabulló*)

FLUENCY BUILDER Using *Intervention Practice Book* page 115, read each word in the first column aloud and have children repeat it. Then have children work in pairs to read the words in the first column aloud to each other. Follow the same procedure with each of the remaining columns. After partners have practiced reading aloud the words in each column separately, have them practice the entire list. Save Intervention Practice Book page 115 for use on pages 291 and 293.

BEFORE

Reading *Monterino en alta mar* pages 366–379

USE SKILL CARD 29A

Focus Skill Homophones

PRETEACH the skill. Point out to children that homophones are words that sound alike but have different meanings. Explain that readers can recognize homophones by reading words aloud. Give examples of homophones, such as *¡ay!* and *hay*. Discuss why it is important for readers to know the exact meanings of words.

Have children look at **side A** of **Skill Card 29: Homophones**. Read the definition of homophones. Next, read the story and then have children reread it with you.

Now call attention to the chart and have volunteers take turns reading the information in the boxes aloud. Ask:

1. **¿Por qué son homófonos las palabras *a* y *ha*?** (*Possible response: Suenan iguales pero tienen significados diferentes.*)
2. **¿Cómo te ayuda el cuento a confirmar los significados de los homófonos?** (*Possible response: Hay claves en cada frase y en español muchas veces hay un acento en una de las palabras para distinguirlas.*)

Prepare to Read: *Monterino en alta mar*

Días maravillosos pages 366–379

Preview. Tell children that they are going to read a selection entitled *Monterino en alta mar*. Explain that this is a story with characters, a setting, and a plot. Tell children that *Monterino en alta mar* is set on the high seas. Then preview the selection.

- **Pages 366–367:** Veo el título *Monterino en alta mar*, y el nombre del autor en las páginas 366–367. Veo un dibujo de un topo flotando en el mar en una botella. Pienso que el topo puede ser Monterino.
- **Pages 368–369:** En estas páginas, veo un dibujo del topo dormido en su acogedora madriguera. Leo que él tiene que encontrar un nuevo hogar. Sé que algo importante va a ocurrir.
- **Pages 370–371:** En estas páginas, leo que Monterino ha estado arrastrado por el mar. Leo que una ballena lo lanza por los aires. Pienso que Monterino va a tener otras aventuras en el mar.

Set purpose. Model setting a purpose for reading *Monterino en alta mar.*

MODEL **Por lo que he visto en estas páginas, creo que voy a leer más sobre lo que hace Monterino en alta mar. Voy a leer para entretenerme con las aventuras del topo. También voy a leer para conocer a los otros personajes del cuento y para saber qué pasa cuándo ellos se encuentran con el topo.**

AFTER

Reading ***Monterino en alta mar*** ***pages 366–379***

Reread and Summarize

Have children reread and summarize *Monterino en alta mar* in sections, as described below.

Pages 366–371
Leemos las páginas 366–371 para recordar quién es Monterino, por qué tenía que salir de su acogedora madriguera y dónde fue.

Summary: Monterino es un topo que tuvo que irse de su acogedora madriguera a causa de una inundación de lluvia. Entró en una casa curiosa y durmió allí, pero mientras dormía, estuvo arrastrado por el mar. Una ballena lanzó el topo por los aires.

Pages 372–374
Leemos las páginas 372–374 para recordar cómo llegó Monterino a estar en un barco.

Summary: Él estaba en una botella que fue tragada por un pez. El pez fue atrapado en una red de un barco. Monterino se cayó de la boca del pez.

Pages 375–376
Leemos las páginas 375–376 para recordar por qué los ratones querían irse del barco.

Summary: Los ratones querían irse porque Percebes, el gato, quisiera eliminarlos. Hicieron una flota de barcos para escapar.

Pages 377–378
Leemos las páginas 377–378 para recordar qué pasó a Monterino al final del cuento.

Summary: Él escapó con los ratones y llegó a ser su capitán. Les guió hasta que llegaron a la tierra. Los ratones cargaron a Monterino en hombros y le pidieron que viviera con ellos. Hicieron casas y a Monterino le encantaba su casa nueva. Conservó su botella y su vela por si algún día sinitera el llamado de alta mar.

FLUENCY BUILDER Be sure children have copies of *Intervention Practice Book* page 115, which you used for yesterday's Fluency Builder activity. Call attention to the sentences on the bottom half of the page. The slashes break the sentences into phrases to allow you to work on natural phrasing. Tell children that their goal is to read each phrase or sentence smoothly. Model appropriate pace, expression, and phrasing as you read each sentence and have children read it after you. Then have children practice by reading the sentences aloud three times to a partner.

INTERVENTION PRACTICE BOOK
page 115

BEFORE

Making Connections
pages 380–381

Directed Reading: *Zelda se muda al desierto,* pp. 230–236

Sonidos alegres
pages 230–236

Help children read the title of the story aloud. Then have them decide what they see in the illustration. Point to the bat and tell children that this is Zelda, the main character. Ask children what kind of weather they see outside the cave. (*lluvia*) Then have children read page 230 to learn more about Zelda. Ask: **¿Qué hace Zelda por la noche?** (*Possible response: Sale volando en búsqueda de insectos.*) **NOTE DETAILS** Ask: **¿Cuál es la diferencia entre *casa* y *caza*?** (*Possible response: Una* casa *es un lugar dónde vivir.* Caza *es una forma del verbo* cazar *que significa capturar.*) Focus Skill **HOMOPHONES**

Page 231

Have children read page 231. Model how to use the Create Mental Images strategy in order to understand that Zelda's cave will soon be flooded.

> **MODEL** **Si no entiendo qué pasa en el cuento, trato de crear una imagen en mi mente. Sé que la lluvia cae fuerte y el agua sube y sube. Pronto el agua va a llegar a la cueva de Zelda. Si imagino esto en mi mente, puedo entender que pronto la casa de Zelda va a estar inundada.** Focus Strategy **CREATE MENTAL IMAGES**

Pages 232–233

Have children read pages 232–233 to find out what Zelda does next. Ask: **¿Qué dicen los ratones a Zelda?** (*Possible response: que ella tiene que buscar una casa nueva.*) **NOTE DETAILS** Ask: **¿Qué va a hacer Zelda?** (*Possible response: Va a irse del bosque para buscar una casa nueva.*) **MAKE PREDICTIONS**

Page 234

Have children read page 234 to find out what Zelda has learned. Ask: **¿Cómo la inundación enseña a Zelda que el mar no es una buena casa para ella?** (*Possible response: Las casas mojadas no son buenas para ella y el mar es demasiado mojado.*) **CAUSE AND EFFECT**

Page 235

Have children read page 235 to find out where Zelda makes her new home. Ask: **¿Por qué el desierto es una buena casa para Zelda?** (*Possible response: Está seco y tiene una cueva cómoda y pequeña.*) **INTERPRET STORY EVENTS**

INTERVENTION PRACTICE BOOK
page 117

Summarize the selection. Ask children to think about Zelda's problem and how she has solved it. Invite them to share their impressions about Zelda and the kind of character she is.

Answers to *Piénsalo* Questions

1. Porque su cueva ya no era segura y se estaba inundando. **SUMMARY**
2. No. A Zelda le gustan los lugares secos. **INTERPRETATION**
3. Las respuestas pueden variar: Se sentirá contenta, o a lo mejor tendrá mucho calor. Puede que extrañe su casa anterior. **TASK**

AFTER

Skill Review
pages 38II

USE SKILL CARD 29B

Focus Skill Review HOMOPHONES

RETEACH the skill. Have children look at **side B** of **Skill Card 29: Homophones**. Read the skill reminder with them, and have a volunteer read the story aloud.

Read aloud the set of directions. Explain that children will work with partners to create their own charts. Encourage them to say the story aloud quietly to themselves in order to hear which words sound alike.

After children have completed their Homophones charts, have them display and explain their work. Point out that the selection *Monterino en alta mar* has some homophones in it. Ask volunteers to name the homophones, give their meanings, and tell how the story helps them figure out these meanings.

Focus Skill Review Phonics Skill from *Monterino en alta mar*

RETEACH diminutivos. Read aloud the following sentence: *La cuevita está cequita y comodita.* Have children listen for the diminutives. Then read this list aloud and have children raise their hands when they hear a diminutive: *casa, tortuguita, cueva, perrito, amiguito, amorcito, lugar.*

FLUENCY BUILDER Be sure children have copies of *Intervention Practice Book* page 115. Explain that they will practice the sentences at the bottom of the page by recording them on tape. Have children choose new partners. Tell the partners to take turns reading the sentences aloud to each other and then recording them. Have children listen to the tape and tell how they think their reading has improved. Then have them record the sentences one more time.

BEFORE

Drafting Directions
page 381A

Writing Process: Directions

Build on prior knowledge. Tell children that they are going to talk and write about directions. Explain that directions are a set of steps or information that people follow in order to make or do something or go somewhere. Tell children that directions need to use exact words so that readers do not get confused. Guide children to see the difference between exact and general words, such as *Calle Colón 111* versus *la calle.*

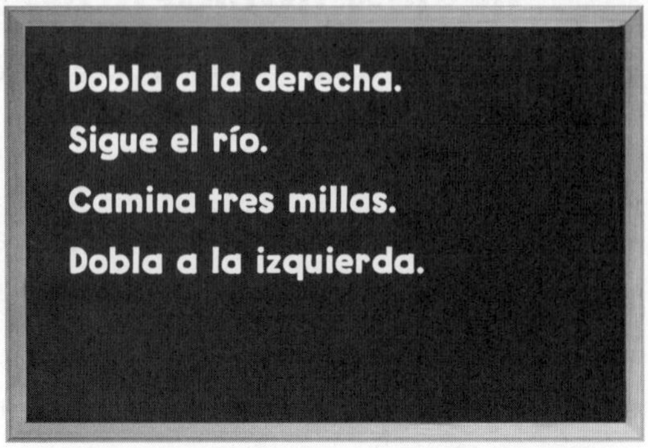

Construct the text. "Share the pen" with children. Tell them that the list shows directions for how to get to the desert. Guide them in using the list to formulate four steps in a set of directions. For example:

1. Dobla a la derecha.
2. Sigue el río.
3. Camina tres millas.
4. Dobla a la izquierda

Revisit the text. Go back and read the list of steps together. Ask: **¿Cómo te ayudan los números?** (*Dicen en qué orden debes dar los pasos.*)

- Guide children to use exact words to help clarify the directions. Ask: **¿Cómo podemos corregir las direcciones para que sean más claras? ¿Cuáles palabras puedo usar para mostrar exactamente dónde doblar?** (*Dobla a la derecha en la calle Smith. Sigue el río hasta el final. Camina recto 3 millas. Dobla a la izquierda cuando llegas a las dunas de arena.*) Make appropriate changes.
- Ask: **¿Qué pasaría si olvidaras un paso de las direcciones?** (*No podría encontrar el desierto.*)
- Have children read the directions aloud and then copy it on their papers.

On Your Own

Have children write four steps in a set of directions telling others how to get from the front door of the school to their classroom.

AFTER

Spelling Lesson
page 379I

Connect Spelling and Phonics

RETEACH diminutivos. Tell children to number their papers 1–8. Write *autocito* on the board, and tell children that in the words you will say have diminutives like the word *autocito.* Dictate the following words, and have children write them. After each word is written, write it on the board so children can proofread their work. They should draw a line through a misspelled word and write the correct spelling below it.

1. ratoncitos*	**2. anillito**	**3. abuelita**	**4. arbolito**
5. casita	**6. carrito**	**7. payasito**	**8. deditos**

*** Word appears in *Zelda se muda al desierto.***

Dictate the following sentence and have children write it: *Mi abuelita estaba sentada debajo de un arbolito cerca de su casita.*

Build and Read Longer Words

Remind children that they have learned how to decode words with diminutives. Explain that now they will use what they have learned to help them read some longer words.

INTERVENTION ASSESSMENT BOOK

Write the word *camioncito* on the board. Remind children that they can often figure out longer words by looking for small words or word parts in them. Cover the word *camión,* and have children read the small word part that is left. Follow a similar procedure to have them read the word *camión.* Model how to blend the two smaller words to read aloud the longer word *camioncito.* Do the same to have children blend word parts to read these longer words: *carrito, deditos* and *payasito.*

FLUENCY BUILDER Have children choose a passage from *Zelda se muda al desierto* to read aloud to a partner. You may have children choose passages that they found particularly interesting, or have them choose one of the following options:

- Read pages 230–231. (*Todas las noches*... through ...*de su acogedora cueva.* Total 69 words.)
- Read pages 231–232. (From *Cuando llegó la noche,*... through ...*segura y seca.* Total 96 words.)

Children should read the selected passage aloud to their partners three times. Have the child rate each reading on a scale from 1 to 4.

SCALE	
1	Not so good
2	Pretty good
3	Good
4	Great!

BEFORE
Weekly Assessments

Review Vocabulary

To revisit vocabulary words prior to the weekly assessment, use these descriptions of words. Have volunteers take turns reading aloud the sentence stems and choices. Students identify the correct choice and explain why that choice makes sense in the sentence.

1. Cuando ellos **navegaban** el barco,
   a. estaba parado **b.** viajaba en el agua
2. Si una persona se **escabulló** por la puerta, se metió dentro
   a. silenciosamente **b.** ruidosamente
3. La casa era **acogedora** y todos estuvieron
   a. cómodos **b.** incómodos
4. Cuando ves una **flota** de barcos, ves
   a. un barquito pequeño **b.** muchos barcos
5. Si un barco se fue a la **deriva**, fue
   a. arrastrado por el agua **b.** parado en la tierra
6. Cuando una casa está **inundada**, está
   a. llena de agua **b.** muy seca

Correct responses: 1.b, 2.b, 3.a, 4.a, 5.b, 6.a.

You may want to display the vocabulary words and definitions on page 289 and have children copy them to use when they study for the vocabulary test.

Días maravillosos
page 383

INTERVENTION PRACTICE BOOK
page 118

Focus Skill Review Homophones

To review Homophones before the weekly assessment, distribute *Intervention Practice Book* page 118. Have volunteers read aloud the direction line and the story. Guide children to think about all the reasons authors write stories.

INTERVENTION ASSESSMENT BOOK

Review Test Prep

Ask children to turn to page 383 of the *Pupil Edition.* Call attention to the Tips for answering the test questions. Tell children that paying attention to these tips can help them answer not only the test questions but also other test questions like these.

Have children follow along as you read each test question and the tip that goes with it. Tell children to read each choice twice before making a decision.

Self-Selected Reading

Have children select their own books to read independently. They might choose books from the classroom library shelf, or you may wish to offer a group of appropriate books from which children can choose.

- *La casa en el árbol.* See page 383O of the *Teacher's Edition* for an Independent Reading Plan.
- *Cambrios* por Anthony Brown. Cutiura Económica, 1993.
- *Sapo y el forestero* por Max Velthuijs. Ekaré-Banco del Libro, 1994.

After children have chosen their books, give each child a copy of *Mi diario de lectura,* which can be found on page R35 in the back of the *Teacher's Edition.* Have children fill in the information at the top of the form. Then have them use the log to keep track of their reading and to record their responses to the literature.

Conduct student-teacher conferences. Arrange time for each child to conference with you individually about his or her self-selected reading. Have children bring their Reading Logs to share with you at the conference. Children might also like to choose a favorite passage to read aloud to you. Ask questions about the book designed to stimulate discussion. For example, you might ask if children have ever moved to a new home and how it felt, or how they think it might feel.

FLUENCY PERFORMANCE Have children read aloud to you the passage from *Zelda se muda al desierto* that they selected and practiced with their partners. Keep track of the number of words the child reads correctly. Ask the child to rate his or her own performance on the 1–4 scale. If children are not happy with their oral reading, give them an opportunity to continue practicing and then to reread the passage to you again.

See *Oral Reading Fluency Assessment* for monitoring progress.

LESSON 30

BEFORE

Building Background and Vocabulary

Use with

"Ruth Law asombra al país"

Review Phonics: *g débil, g fuerte*

Identify the sound. Have children repeat the following sentence three times: *Guillermo le regaló un geranio a su amigo el gorila.* Ask children to identify the words that have the hard *g* sound. (*Guillermo, regaló, amigo, gorila*). Now ask them to identify the words that have the soft *g* sound (*geranio*)

Associate letters to sound. On the board, write: *Guillermo le regaló un geranio a su amigo el gorila.* Circle the words *Guillermo, regaló, amigo, gorila and geranio.* Ask children to tell how the words are alike. (*Todos tiene un g. Las primeras cuatro son g fuerte, la ultima es g débil.*)

Word blending. Model how to blend and read the word *geranio.* Slide your hand under the letters as you slowly elongate the sounds /geeraa-neeo/. Then read *geranio* naturally. Follow a similar procedure for *Guillermo, regaló, amigo* and *gorila.*

INTERVENTION PRACTICE BOOK page 120

Apply the skill. *Consonant Substitution* Write the following words on the board, and have children read them aloud. Make the changes necessary to form the words in parentheses. Have children read each new word.

nota (gota)	**sordo** (*gordo*)	**pato** (*gato*)
miro (*giro*)	**resto** (*gesto*)	**casa** (*gasa*)

Introduce Vocabulary

PRETEACH lesson vocabulary. Tell children that they are going to learn six new words that they will see again when they read a story called *Ruth Law asombra al país.* Teach every vocabulary word using the following process.

Write the word.
Say the word.
Track the word and have students repeat it.
Give the meaning or context.

Use the following suggestions or similar ideas to give the meaning or context:

INTERVENTION PRACTICE BOOK page 119

proeza Remind children of the synonym *hazaña.*

heroína Relate by discussing heroines children are familiar with and the accomplishments of each woman.

hospitalidad Relate to the way you are treated when close family and friends meet.

negado Demonstrate by role-playing refusing to do or accept something.

espectadores Related words: spectator, spectacle, speculate

aterrizaje Demonstrate by showing how someone lands in a plane.

For vocabulary activities, see Vocabulary Games on pages 2–7.

Vocabulary Words

proeza acción valerosa o heroica

heroína una mujer que ha hecho algo valiente o útil

hospitalidad tratamiento amistoso de invitados o desconocidos

negado no concedido

espectadores gente que asiste a un espectáculo

aterrizaje tocar tierra

AFTER
Building Background and Vocabulary

Apply Vocabulary Strategies

Use familiar patterns. Write the word *heroína* on chart paper and underline the letters *h-e-r-o*. Tell children that they can sometimes figure out the meaning of the word by looking for letter patterns that they know.

MODEL **Reconozco las letras *h-e-r-o* porque empiezan la palabra *héroe*. Sé que un *héroe* héroe es alguien con mucho coraje o que hizo algo importante, como en un deporte. A lo mejor una heroína tiene algo que ver con un héroe.**

RETEACH **lesson vocabulary.** Have children listen to each of the following groups of words. Tell them to hold up the word card that goes with each group. Reread the groups aloud with the correct answer. Then discuss how children made their choices.

1. parar	hacer escalas	tocar tierra (*aterrizaje*).
2. amistad	huéspedes	bienvenido (*hospitalidad*).
3. asombrosa	difícil	valerosa (*proeza*).
4. mujer	con coraje	da ayuda (*heroína*).
5. personas	mirando	gritando (*espectadores*).
6. no	no quiere	no aceptado (*negado*).

FLUENCY BUILDER Using *Intervention Practice Book* page 119, read aloud each word in the first column and have children repeat it. Then have children work in pairs to read the words in the first column aloud to each other. Follow the same procedure with each of the remaining columns. After partners have practiced reading aloud the words in each column separately, have them practice the entire list. Save *Intervention Practice Book* page 119 for use on pages 301 and 303.

BEFORE

Reading ***Ruth Law asombra al país pages 386–403***

Focus Skill Predict Outcomes

PRETEACH the skill. Point out to children that readers use what they know from real life and clues from the story to make guesses about what might happen in the story. Explain that people make predictions or guesses about things every day. Give examples of predicting an outcome, such as looking at the sky to see what the weather will be. Discuss why it is important to be able to predict outcomes in real life and why predicting outcomes can help readers better understand and enjoy a story.

USE SKILL CARD 30A

Have children look at **at side A** of **Skill Card 30: Predict Outcomes.** Read the definition of *predict outcomes.* Next read the story and then have children reread it with you.

Now call attention to the chart and have volunteers take turns reading the information in the boxes aloud. Ask:

- **¿Qué sabes de la gente que trabaja duro?** (Possible response: Usualmente logra lo que quiere.)
- **Además de las pistas en el cuento, ¿qué más te puede ayudar a predecir lo que va a pasar?** (Possible response: mis experiencias personales.)

Prepare to Read *Ruth Law asombra al país*

Días maravillosos
pages 386–403

Preview. Tell children that they are going to read a selection entitled *Ruth Law asombra al país.* Explain that this is a nonfiction biography that tells about something that really happened. Tell children that *Ruth Law asombra al país* is about a woman who flies a plane many years ago. Then preview the selection.

- **Pages 386–387:** Veo el título, *Ruth Law asombra al país,* y el nombre del autor en las páginas 386–387. Veo el dibujo de una mujer volando un avión antiguo. Creo que esa mujer debe ser Ruth Law.
- **Pages 388–389:** En estas páginas, leo sobre algo que ocurrió hace muchos años. Veo dibujos de Chicago y un dibujo de Ruth Law en su carpa encima de un edificio. Pienso que Ruth debe ser una mujer con mucho coraje.
- **Pages 390–391:** En estas páginas, leo cómo se Ruth preparó para su viaje. Veo que ella trabajó en su avión. Pienso que a Ruth le encantaba volar.

Set purpose. Model setting a purpose for reading *Ruth Law asombra al país.*

MODEL **Por lo que he visto en estas páginas, creo que voy a leer más sobre el vuelo de Ruth de Chicago a Nueva York. Voy a leer para ver si ella pudo hacer lo que nadie había podido hacer.**

AFTER

Reading *Ruth Law asombra al país* pages 386–403

Reread and Summarize

Have children reread and summarize *Ruth Law asombra al país* in sections, as described below.

Pages 388–391 **Leamos las páginas 388–391 para recordar quién es Ruth Law, qué estaba tratando de hacer y cómo lo hizo.**

Summary: Ruth Law fue una piloto que vivió hace muchos años. Ella estaba tratando de volar de Chicago a Nueva York en un solo día. Durmió en una carpa encima de un edificio para acostumbrarse al frío. Se abrigó bien en preparación para su viaje.

Pages 392–394 **Leamos las páginas 392–394 para recordar qué ocurrió al principio del viaje.**

Summary: Fue difícil prender el motor por la temperatura glacial. Después de una hora, recorrió el terreno con dificultad y después se elevó. Ruth se esforzaba por estabilizar el avión mientras éste subía y bajaba contra el viento. El viento disminuyó y la gasolina impulsaba al avión.

Pages 395–397 **Leamos las páginas 395–397 para recordar qué ocurrió cuando Ruth se acercó a Hornell, Nueva York.**

Summary: El motor se detuvo porque el tanque de gasolina estaba vació. Ruth aterrizó con sin problemas. Había volado 590 millas sin escalas.

Pages 398–402 **Leamos las páginas 398–402 para recordar qué ocurrió durante el resto del viaje.**

Summary: Ruth se puso de nuevo en camino hacia la ciudad de Nueva York. Cuando quedaban todavía dos horas de distancia, decidió aterrizar porque estaba muy oscuro para ver los instrumentos en la oscuridad. A la mañana siguiente, Ruth voló a la ciudad de Nueva York y todos dijeron que ella era una heroína.

FLUENCY BUILDER Use *Intervention Practice Book* page 119. Call attention to the sentences on the bottom half of the page. The slashes break the sentences into phrases to allow you to work on natural phrasing. Tell children that their goal is to read each phrase or sentence smoothly. Model appropriate pace, expression and phrasing as you read each sentence and have children read it after you. Then have children practice by reading the sentences aloud three times to a partner.

BEFORE

Making Connections *pages 406–407*

Directed Reading of *Una hazaña asombrosa*

Sonidos alegres pages 238–245

Pages 238–239

Help children read the title of the story aloud. Ask children what amazing feats they or people they know have accomplished. Explain that this selection is about the amazing feats of a woman named Amelia Earhart. Then have children read pages 238–239 to find out about Amelia Earhart. Ask: **¿Quién fue Amelia Earhart?** (*Possible response: una heroína estadounidense, una mujer piloto.*) **NOTE DETAILS** Ask: **¿Piensas que Amelia va a lograr una hazaña asombrosa? ¿Por qué?** (*Possible response: El título del cuento es Una hazaña asombrosa. Amelia Earhart es una heroína.*) Focus Skill **PREDICT OUTCOMES**

Page 240

Have children read page 240. Ask: **¿Qué hizo Amelia después de la guerra?** (*Possible response: Tomaba lecciones de pilotaje y compró su propio avión.*) **SEQUENCE**

Page 241

Have children read page 241. Model how to use the Read Ahead strategy in order to understand the meaning of the word *especatadores.*

> MODEL **Si leo una palabra o frase que no entiendo, puedo leer más adelante. No sé qué significa *espectadores.* Si leo más adelante, leo que "vinieron a vitorearla". Ahora puedo entender que *espectadores* son las personas que vienen a vitorear.** Focus Strategy **READ AHEAD**

Page 242

Read aloud the first sentence of page 242. Ask children what they think Amelia's dream was. Then have them read page 242 to find out. Ask: **¿Cuál fue el sueño de Amelia? NOTE DETAILS** Ask: **¿Por qué sería una hazaña asombrosa?** (*Las respuestas pueden variar.*) **SPECULATE** Ask: **¿Por qué quería Amelia llevar a Fred Noonan?** (*Possible response: Necesitaba ayuda para un viaje tan largo.*) **UNDERSTAND CHARACTERS' MOTIVES**

Page 243

Have children read page 243. Ask: **¿Qué hicieron Amelia y Fred antes de irse?** *(Possible response: Llenaron de gasolina los tanques y comprobaron el motor.*) **SEQUENCE** Ask: **¿Qué le pasó al avión?** (*Possible response: Se le acabó el combustible y desapareció.*) **NOTE DETAILS**

Page 244

Read aloud page 244. Then ask children what they think Amelia Earhart meant when she said, "Los sueños de años se han hecho realidad". (*Possible response: Las respuestas pueden variar.*) **INTERPRET STORY EVENTS**

Summarize the selection. Ask children to think about what they learned about the beginning, middle, and the end of Amelia Earhart's life. Then help them summarize the selection in three or four sentences.

Answers to *Piénsalo* Questions

1. Porque llegó a ser un as de la aviación cuando volar todavía era algo nuevo. Además, voló más alto que ninguna otra mujer hasta entonces. ¡También, en 1937, le dio la vuelta al mundo volando! **SUMMARY**

2. Porque puede existir algún incidente y otra persona puede ayudar si eso ocurre y el piloto no se encontraría solo. **INTERPRETATION**
3. Las respuestas pueden variar. **WRITE A JOURNAL REPORT**

AFTER

Skill Review
pages 407I

USE SKILL CARD 30B

Focus Skill PREDICT OUTCOMES

RETEACH the skill. Have children look at **side B** of **Skill Card 30: Predict Outcomes.** Read the skill reminder with them, and have a volunteer read the story aloud.

Read aloud the set of directions. Explain that children will work with partners to create their own charts. Encourage them to ask or write down questions they have about what will happen next in the story as they read.

After children have completed their Predict Outcomes charts, have them display and explain their work. Point out that they can predict outcomes for the selection *Ruth Law asombra al país.* Ask volunteers to predict some outcomes for *Ruth Law asombra al país.*

Review the Phonics Skill from *Ruth Law asombra al país*

RETEACH *g débil, g fuerte.* Read aloud the following sentence: *Algunas guerras son grandes y otras son pequeñas, pero todas afectan a la gente.* Have children listen for the hard and soft *g* sounds. Then read this list aloud and have children raise their hands when they hear the hard *g* sound: *gorila, grado, generar, granja, gracia, gota, generación, gramo, grande.* Now repeat the process with children listening for the soft *g* sound: *generar, generación, gigante, girar, gato, gesto, genio, generoso, gloria.*

FLUENCY BUILDER Use *Intervention Practice Book* page 119. Explain that today children will practice the sentences on the bottom half of the page by reading them aloud on tape. Assign new partners. Have children take turns reading the sentences aloud to each other and then reading them on tape.

INTERVENTION PRACTICE BOOK
page 119

BEFORE

Drafting Timed Writing
page 407A

Daily Writing: Timed Writing

Build on prior knowledge. Tell children that they are going to talk and write about timed writing. Explain that sometimes people need to write quickly in order to complete their work in a certain amount of time. Even though they are writing fast, they still need to pay attention to punctuation, spelling, and grammar. Guide children to see that timed writing works best if they choose a topic about which they know a great deal and if they keep their writing simple and clear.

Vestirse
Desayunar
Empacar la mochila
Montar el autobús
Ir a la escuela

Construct the text. "Share the pen" with children. Tell them that the list shows information about someone's day. Guide them in using the list to do timed writing. Help them to use the activities on the list to write a paragraph in a set amount of time. For example:

> *Mi día*
> *Hoy me vestí. Luego, desayuné. Luego, empaqué mi mochila. Luego, monté el autobús. Entonces fui a la escuela.*

Revisit the text. Go back and read the timed-writing paragraph together. Ask: **¿Sería fácil escribir un cuento en poco tiempo sobre tu día? ¿Por qué?** (Sé mucho de mi día.)

- Guide children to make the paragraph read more smoothly by combining sentences. Ask: **¿Cómo podemos unir frases para que suenen más fluidas?** (*Hoy me vestí y desayuné. Luego empaqué mi mochila. Después, monté en el autobús para la escuela.*) Make appropriate changes.
- Ask: **¿Qué más podemos añadir al párrafo?** (Lo que pasó en la escuela.)
- Have children read the timed-writing paragraph aloud and then copy it on their papers.

On Your Own

Have children list three topics that they know a great deal about and could use for a timed-writing paragraph.

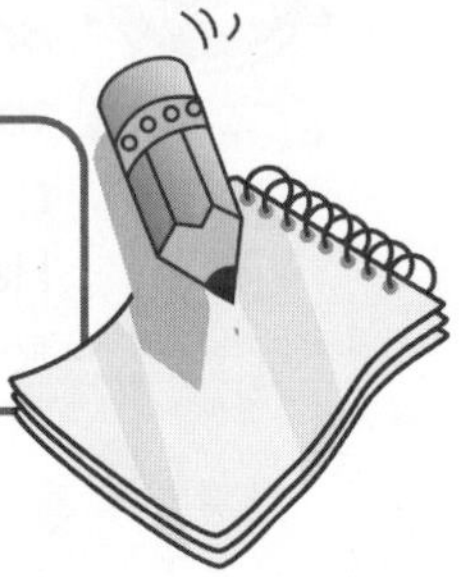

AFTER

Spelling Lesson
page 403I

Connect Spelling and Phonics

RETEACH phonics. Tell children to number their papers 1–8. Tell them that in the words you say, they will hear a hard *g* and a soft *g*. Dictate the following words and have children write them. After each word is written, write it on the board so children can proofread their work. They should draw a line through a misspelled word and write the correct spelling below it.

1. guerra*	**2. rugir***	**3. ninguna***	**4. llegó***
5. agradecía*	**6. gente***	**7. gran***	**8. amigo***

*** Word appears in *Una hazaña asombrosa.***

Dictate the following sentence and have children write it: *Mis amigos llegaron al gran bosque para buscar a los gemelos perdidos.*

Build and Read Longer Words

Remind children that they have learned how to decode words with the hard and soft *g* sound. Explain that now they will use what they have learned to help them read some longer words.

Write the word *gemelos* on the board. Remind children that they can often figure out longer words by looking for word parts they know in them. Ask children which part of the word says *ge*, which part says *me*, and which part says *los*. Then ask what *ge*, *me*, and *los* all together say. (*gemelos*) Do the same to have children blend word parts to read these longer words: *gasolina*, *despegaron*, *grandeza*, and *orgullo.*

FLUENCY BUILDER Have children choose a passage from *Una hazaña asombrosa* to read aloud to a partner. You may have children choose passages that they found particularly interesting, or have them choose one of the following options:

- Read pages 238–239. (From *Amelia Earhart es,...* through *...también quería volar.* Total: 122 words.)
- Read pages 240–241. (From *Amelia tenía un poco...* through *...a la gente de la ciudad.* Total: 116 words.)

Children should read the selected passage aloud to their partners three times. Have the child rate each reading on a scale from 1 to 4.

BEFORE
Weekly Assessments

Review Vocabulary

To revisit Vocabulary Words prior to the weekly assessment, use these sentence frames. Have volunteers take turns reading aloud the sentence stems and choices. Children identify the correct choice and explain why that choice makes sense in the sentence.

1. La **proeza**, es una acción
   a. heroica **b.** perezosa
2. Los **espectadores**
   a. juegan al fútbol **b.** miran el partido
3. La **heroína**
   a. rescató el niño **b.** robó un banco
4. Si el dinero que pidió le fue **negado**,
   a. se lo dieron **b.** no se lo dieron
5. Durante el **aterrizaje**, tocamos
   a. tierra **b.** el mar
6. La **hospitalidad** es un tratamiento
   a. antipático **b.** amistoso

Correct Responses: 1.a, 2.b, 3.a, 4.b, 5.a, 6.b.

You may want to display the vocabulary words and definitions on page 299 and have children copy them to use when they study for the vocabulary test.

INTERVENTION PRACTICE BOOK
page 122

Focus Skill Review Predict Outcomes

To review Predict Outcomes before the weekly assessment, distribute *Intervention Practice Book* page 122. Have volunteers read aloud the direction line and the story. Guide children to think about what might or might not happen in the story as they read it.

Días maravillosos
page 409

Review Test Prep

INTERVENTION ASSESSMENT BOOK

Ask children to turn to page 409 of the *Pupil Edition.* Call attention to the Tips for answering the test questions. Tell children that paying attention to these tips can help them answer not only the test questions but also other test questions like these.

Have children follow along as you read each test question and the tip that goes with it. Tell children not to rush as they think about their answers.

AFTER

Weekly Assessments

Self-Selected Reading

Have children select their own books to read independently. They might choose books from the classroom library shelf, or you may wish to offer a group of appropriate books from which children can choose.

- *Trabajar en el aeropuerto.* See page 409M of the *Teacher's Edition* for an Independent Reading Plan.
- *El viaje de Jenny* por Sheila White Samton. Viking Penguin, 1993.
- *Mi primer vuelo* por David MacPaul. Montena, 1988.

After children have chosen their books, give each child a copy of *Mi diario de lectura*, which can be found on page R35 in the back of the *Teacher's Edition.* Have children fill in the information at the top of the form. Then have them use the log to keep track of their reading and to record their responses to the literature.

Conduct student-teacher conferences. Arrange time for each child to conference with you individually about his or her self-selected reading. Have children bring their Reading Logs to share with you at the conference. Children might also like to choose a favorite passage to read aloud to you. Ask questions about the book designed to stimulate discussion. For example, you might ask if children would want to try to break a record, and why they would want to.

FLUENCY PERFORMANCE Have children read aloud to you the passage from *Una hazaña asombrosa* that they selected and practiced with their partners. Keep track of the number of words the child reads correctly. Ask the child to rate his or her own performance on the 1–4 scale. If children are not happy with their oral reading, give them an opportunity to continue practicing and then to read the passage to you again.

See *Oral Reading Fluency Assessment* for monitoring progress.